**Threats
to Security
in East Asia-
Pacific**

The Pacific Forum was founded in 1975 to promote an international dialogue among thoughtful leaders in the fields of business, government, and scholarship. It is an independent nonprofit international institution whose principal purposes are to conduct policy-focused discussions and studies, to produce analytical reports, and to contribute constructive ideas on issues of national and international policy. The Pacific Forum actively promotes mutual understanding of such vital regional policy issues as economic development; investment; trade; the intelligent use of resources and technology; and threats to security posed by political, economic, and military tensions.

Pacific Forum
190 South King Street, Suite 1376
Honolulu, Hawaii 96813

Threats to Security in East Asia-Pacific

National and Regional Perspectives

Edited by
Charles E. Morrison

A Pacific Forum Book

LexingtonBooks
D.C. Heath and Company
Lexington, Massachusetts
Toronto

UA
830
.T48
1983

Library of Congress Cataloging in Publication Data

Main entry under title:
   Threats to security in East Asia-Pacific.

"Originally written as conference papers for the Pacific Forum's symposium in Waikoloa, Hawaii"—

1. East Asia—Strategic aspects—Congresses. 2. Pacific Ocean Region—Strategic aspects—Congresses. I. Morrison, Charles Edward, 1944- II. Pacific Forum.
UA830.T48   1983   355'.03305   82-48632
ISBN 0-669-06369-x

Copyright © 1983 by D.C. Heath and Company

All rights reserved. No part of this publication may be reproduced or transmitted in any form or by any means, electronic or mechanical, including photocopy, recording, or any information storage or retrieval system, without permission in writing from the publisher. Rights to Japanese-language editions are retained by Pacific Forum.

Published simultaneously in Canada

Printed in the United States of America

International Standard Book Number: 0-669-06369-x

Library of Congress Catalog Card Number: 82-48632

Contents

	Foreword *Lloyd R. Vasey*	vii
	Introduction	ix
Part I	*Regional Perspectives*	1
Chapter 1	**The Uncertain Future: Asian-Pacific Relations in Trouble** *Robert A. Scalapino*	3
Chapter 2	**National Threat Perceptions in East Asia-Pacific** *Thanat Khoman*	19
Chapter 3	**Soviet Strategy in Asia: A U.S. Perspective** *Jacquelyn K. Davis*	23
Chapter 4	**Security in East Asia-Pacific** *Bernard K. Gordon* with *Lloyd R. Vasey*	33
Part II	*National Perspectives*	51
Chapter 5	**Japanese Perceptions of National Threats** *Shinkichi Eto*	53
Chapter 6	**The Roots of South Korean Anxiety about National Security** *Sang-Woo Rhee*	65
Chapter 7	**Indonesia's Security and Threat Perceptions** *Jusuf Wanandi* and *M. Hadisoesastro*	83
Chapter 8	**Malaysian Threat Perceptions and Regional Security** *Zainal Abidin B. Abdul Wahid*	103
Chapter 9	**National Threat Perceptions of Singapore** *Lau Teik Soon*	113
Chapter 10	**National Threat Perceptions in the Philippines** *Carlos F. Nivera*	125
Chapter 11	**National Threat Perceptions: Explaining the Thai Case** *Sarasin Viraphol*	145

v

Chapter 12	Thai Security Perceptions in Historical Perspective *Somsakdi Xuto*	155
Chapter 13	The Indigenization of ASEAN Communist Parties *Donald E. Weatherbee*	161
Chapter 14	Australians' Perceptions of Threats to Their Security *Robert J. O'Neill*	185
Chapter 15	Wanted: A U.S. Policy for Asia in the 1980s *Bernard K. Gordon*	195
	Participants at the Waikoloa Conference	215
	About the Contributors	219
	About the Editor	223

Foreword

During the past year the Pacific Forum has been actively pursuing a detailed examination of different national perceptions of threats to security among the countries of East Asia and the Pacific. This project is designed to improve mutual understanding of divergent perceptions, analyze the implications of these differences for regional cooperation, and recommend new policy directions to strengthen the prospects for peace and security.

The project was initiated in mid-1981, when Professor Bernard K. Gordon of the University of New Hampshire and I visited eight East Asian and Pacific countries and conducted more than three hundred private interviews and discussions with political and academic leaders on threat perceptions and security issues. Our trip report constitutes chapter 4 of this book. The findings confirmed the existence of widely divergent perceptions of security threats around the region and the need for more systematic study and analysis by a multinational group.

Accordingly, the Pacific Forum commissioned a number of area experts and policy analysts to write the papers that form the chapters of this book and, in February 1982, convened a symposium at Waikoloa, Hawaii, on "National Threat Perceptions in East Asia-Pacific—Policies and Future Directions." More than forty East Asian and Pacific and U.S. scholars, private-sector leaders, and government officials participated in the meeting. It was cosponsored by a number of other research institutions from around the region: the Centre for Strategic and International Studies (Jakarta); the Institute of East Asian Studies (University of California at Berkeley); the Institute for Foreign Policy Analysis, Inc. (Cambridge, Massachusetts); the Institute for Sino-Soviet Studies (George Washington University); the Institute of International Studies (University of South Carolina); the Research Institute for Peace and Security (Tokyo); and the Center for Asian and Pacific Studies (University of Hawaii). Major funding for the entire project was provided by the Carthage Foundation.

The study of national threat perceptions and their policy implications will be a continuing activity of the Pacific Forum. At the Waikoloa conference, a steering committee consisting of former U.S. Undersecretary of State Philip C. Habib; Asian Development Bank Executive Director Alejandro B. Melchor, Jr.; and former Japanese ambassador to the United States Takeshi Yasukawa drew up a list of priority issues that need more analysis by governments and private institutions. These topics include U.S. security commitments in the region, the Sino-Soviet dispute and its implications for the balance of power, Japan's changing security role, economic factors in Asian security, China and its relations with its neighbors, Vietnamese expansion in Indochina, tensions on the Korean peninsula, the threats posed by indigenous communist parties, and international terrorism. The Pacific Forum and its collaborating institutions have formed a Core Study Group that will meet periodically to promote increased understanding of these and other issues in the belief that better understanding can lead to more effective action to improve the well-being of the peoples of East Asia and the Pacific.

Sincere appreciation is due to Charles E. Morrison for his editing of this book and for his advice and professional assistance throughout the project. Thanks also go to Richard R. Vuylsteke for his editorial assistance and to JoAnn K. Tufford for her administrative preparation of the manuscript.

Lloyd R. Vasey
President, Pacific Forum

Introduction

East Asia and the Pacific is a vast region of great and small powers, of continental countries and island countries, of nations with rich natural resources and nations with virtually no natural resources, of some of the most technologically advanced economies in the world and countries struggling to overcome tremendous problems of poverty, of ethnically homogeneous societies and societies with incredible ethnic diversity, of countries with long-established political traditions and institutions and countries that live with the constant threat of revolution or coup d'etat. In such a large and diverse region, it is no surprise that there are major differences in perceptions of national priorities and of threats to national security and well-being. There is also tremendous scope for mutually beneficial cooperation in all spheres of activity.

The chapters of this book explore some of the divergencies and their policy implications and suggest means of improving cooperation. As explained in the Foreword, these chapters were originally written as conference papers for the Pacific Forum's symposium in Waikoloa, Hawaii, on national threat perceptions. Although some of the authors were asked to provide overviews or comparative perspectives, the majority presented country perspectives. Since they were not asked to follow any rigid outline, their manner of presentation varies considerably. Some summarize different views within their countries; others take an entirely personal perspective; still others do both. Because the Waikoloa symposium brought additional views from participants who did not write papers and added the richness of interaction, this introduction will refer from time to time to oral comments of the participants as well as to the subsequent chapters.

The Asian and Pacific Security Environment

In chapter 1, Professor Robert A. Scalapino of the University of California-Berkeley provides a thoughtful analysis of overall trends in the security environment. Scalapino believes a major power war unlikely, but the overall tone of his chapter is hardly optimistic for either the region or the world in general. We are witnessing, writes Scalapino, "an erosion of that complex network of positive relationships—economic, political, and in some cases strategic—that earlier seemed to promise a steadily developing regional-international structure of procedure, custom, and law conducive to greater harmony." Some global factors affecting the region include the simultaneous growth of interdependence and (in part as a reaction to this) of nationalism, disparities in economic fortunes, the decline of secular ideologies (leaving a vacuum that is in some instances being filled by fundamentalist religions), the weak political institutionalization of many societies and the lack of political structures on the international level, the growth of terrorism and use of coercion among smaller states, and the loosening of alliance structures in both East and West.

Looking at the strategic triangular relationship among the United States, the USSR, and China in East Asia, Scalapino remarks on the concurrent strengthening of Soviet military power and weakening of its political influence. Politically, he writes, "the Soviet Union is far weaker in the Pacific-Asian region today than it was thirty years ago, and the prospects for rapid improvement . . . are not good." The United States has sought to try to further "limit" Soviet power in Asia, a posture that has moved it toward alignment with China. Scalapino, however, expresses reservations about the longer-term wisdom of U.S.-China policy (as did many of the other Waikoloa participants). He asks a series of important questions: Is China internally stable? Is Sino-Soviet hostility sufficiently durable to warrant strategic commitments? What is the impact on the U.S.-China relationship on the interests of other East Asian countries? What will be its effect on longer term U.S.-Soviet relations?

Scalapino stresses the importance of a healthy domestic U.S. economy for any effective foreign policy. He urges a strategy toward the USSR that combines rewards and punishments and suggests that in relations with allies, "some very painful alternatives must be faced, even the possibility of contracting our global strategic commitments substantially in the event that allied-aligned nations opt for different policies."

In chapter 2, originally the keynote address for the Waikoloa conference, Thanat Khoman also sees a much more complex security threat:

> On the one hand, predators endowed with powerful military means behave like old-fashioned imperialistic powers seeking aggrandizement of their physical domain by de facto annexations of adjacent territories after a war or limited conflict. On the other, they seek to establish an ideological overlordship by setting up satellite regimes with nominal or fictitious independence—regimes that in fact are completely subservient to the central imperial power. This is the pattern created in Eastern Europe and now being emulated in Africa, Southeast Asia, and Latin America.

Thanat points to a number of factors that aggravate the threat in the Asian-Pacific region.

Other Waikoloa participants were more optimistic about overall trends. Robert J. O'Neill of the Australian National University, commenting on the Scalapino chapter, noted a number of important positive aspects in the overall environment—the recognition in the West of the need to rectify the military imbalance with the USSR, less hostile public opinion toward the

Introduction

discussion of security issues, the development of political cohesion and economic strength in noncommunist Asia, and serious Soviet weaknesses on the political and economic fronts as well as some weaknesses in the Soviet military position. O'Neill also cited some concerns: he shares Scalapino's reservations about U.S. China policy; he expresses fear that too much U.S. pressure on Japan could politically backfire in that country; and he believes that the conventional force imbalance is not receiving sufficient attention.

Many of these issues continued to be discussed throughout the three-day symposium. In assessing the Soviet threat, for example, how much weight should be given to military strengths and how much to political weaknesses? Will the change in top Soviet leadership in the 1980s greatly affect Soviet policy, as some participants believed, or have little effect? Can the noncommunist countries devise more effective means of burden sharing in meeting the Soviet threat, or do present trends toward looser alignments portend the end of the Western security relationships that have characterized the postwar world? Virtually all the chapters—both U.S. and Asian— refer to the Soviet role in East Asia as a destructive and threatening one, but the salience given to this threat varied. In chapter 3, Jacquelyn Davis of the Institute of Foreign Policy Analysis, Inc., sees a concerted Soviet effort to detach Asian countries from their relationship with the United States. She gives considerable weight to the political and psychological value of Soviet military power.

In contrast, many Asian participants seem to consider the Soviet threat as one of a variety of threats and not necessarily the most pressing. In chapter 4, Professor Bernard K. Gordon of the University of New Hampshire and Rear Admiral Lloyd R. Vasey, USN (Ret.), of the Pacific Forum, reporting the results of their many interviews in East Asia and the Pacific in mid-1981, note that although "Americans approach East Asia with security issues foremost in their thinking, it is also evident that Asians themselves do not." Regarding the Soviet threat specifically, they remark on the tendency of the interviewees, especially in Japan and Southeast Asia, to emphasize Soviet weaknesses. The Asian chapters in this book also point to other important threats or emphasize that external threat lies in the *interaction* of large power policies. For example, in chapter 7, Jusuf Wanandi and M. Hadisoesastro of Indonesia write that Indonesia considers the PRC as potentially the main threat in the future because it is the only great power in Southeast Asia. In chapter 8, Professor Zainal Abidin B. Abdul Wahid of Kebangsaan University in Malaysia places both the Soviet and Chinese threats in the context of the spread into Malaysia of the Sino-Soviet conflict. Gordon and Vasey refer to South Korean concern about the interaction of U.S. and Soviet policies: the fear the United States will go too far, with disastrous consequences for South Korea.

The question of comparative threats raises another central issue—the future role of China. Thai participants generally found China a valuable ally in containing Vietnam in the post-1975 period, but other Asians tended to regard the Chinese with considerable fear. In chapter 9, for example, Professor Lau Teik Soon of the National University of Singapore, who is a member of parliament in his country, notes that China continues to provide some support for the Communist Party of Malaya (CPM) (the main subversive threat to both Malaysia and Singapore) and writes that Singaporean leaders have "always pointed out that unless the Chinese government and party break off all ties with the CPM, China will continue to constitute a long-term threat to the national security of Singapore as well as that of other ASEAN states." At Waikoloa, Koreans expressed discomfort with China's role as an ally of North Korea with respect to the local Korean situation, but simultaneously sharing strategic interests with the United States vis-à-vis the USSR on the regional and global levels. It was asked whether this would affect U.S. commitments toward South Korea. In general, although the Waikoloa participants seemed to agree that a Soviet threat exists but disagree on its salience and strength, in the case of China there was disagreement about whether a security threat to the rest of the region exists at all, and if so, what its nature is. The assessments varied from country to country, leading us more specifically toward the subject of national threat perceptions.

National Threat Perceptions: Northeast Asia

Despite great differences in their respective situations, South Korea and Japan have a number of characteristics in common. Both are densely populated, resource-poor countries that have experienced high rates of growth in recent years. Hence both are deeply concerned about the security of their access to raw materials as well as secure access to markets needed to purchase the foreign exchange to buy those raw materials and maintain growth. Both countries have relied heavily on bilateral security treaties with the United States, and both are being asked to contribute more toward their own security. In the South Korean case, however, external military-security problems are much more obvious, although in chapter 6 Professor Sang-Woo Rhee of Sogang University writes that South Koreans are less concerned than they should be. In the Japanese case, according to Professor Shinkichi Eto of the University of Tokyo in chapter 5, awareness of issues of military security is still nascent, although it has grown because of recent events like the 1976 landing of a Soviet MIG-25 in Hokkaido and the Soviet invasion of Afghanistan.

Eto's chapter includes a number of tables illustrating changes in Japanese public attitudes toward security issues, the existence of the Self-Defense

Introduction

Forces (SDF), and the reliability of other countries. Although these polls do show rising acceptance of the SDF, Eto points out that there are still strong constraints on a major Japanese military buildup. He refers to three overriding Japanese national goals—a peaceful international order, the maintenance of a system of free trade, and continuing domestic and social efficiency. He notes that in relation to the first goal, Japan fears Soviet military intentions and capabilities. In his oral remarks at Waikoloa, he emphasized that although the Soviet military is one threat, the poor economic performance of the United States is another major threat. This echoes one of Scalapino's concerns.

Rhee also is deeply troubled about U.S. performance, but more in the security field. In the 1950s and 1960s, he believes, South Koreans had few fears about the reliability of the U.S. commitment. In the 1970s, however, a series of developments including the Sino-American entente, the relative military decline of the United States, the Vietnam withdrawal, and the partial South Korean withdrawal made Koreans much more apprehensive about the reliability of their larger supporter. According to Rhee, "South Koreans now realize that the United States is no longer an almighty guarantor of their security, but only a helpful ally that can provide limited military and diplomatic support." This change in perceptions, the continuing military buildup by North Korea despite its economic weaknesses, and a heightened sense of vulnerability to international economic forces are what the South Koreans fear.

Southeast Asian and Australian National Threat Perceptions

Perhaps the most striking feature of all the Southeast Asian chapters, except those on Thailand, is that they deal primarily with internal threats and regard the international environment largely as a source of dangers that affect domestic stability.

Chapter 7 by Wanandi and Hadisoesastro provides an excellent summary of the kinds of challenges Southeast Asian governments face. The two Indonesian authors write that the general view in Jakarta is that for the next decade or more, "the challenge to Indonesia's security stems from internal problems that will have to be solved by Indonesia's national forces and leadership themselves." They describe the major problem facing Indonesia as "dealing with the many societal changes arising out of the process of development." Even successes in developmental efforts, they note, create more social changes, giving rise to new kinds of issues. Indonesia has a continuing task of building a sense of national unity in a country of diverse ethnic and religious groups; of developing a national political system that is compatible with traditional values and new, Western-influenced values; of maintaining an appropriate pace of economic development while providing a more equitable distribution of income; and of institutionalizing firmly a mode of leadership succession.

Other Southeast Asian chapters echo similar themes. Abidin, for example, notes the importance in Malaysia of communal issues, which the government has been tackling through a program of economic development that relies on real growth as a means of equalizing the economic strength of Malaysia's ethnic communities. Failure to sustain such a program could lead to serious communal tensions that the Malayan Communist party would be sure to exploit. The potential dangers of religious extremism are referred to by both Abidin and Wanandi-Hadisoesastro. Abidin notes that raising religious consciousness can be very constructive but that Islam can potentially be abused. Chapter 10 on the Philippines by Carlos F. Nivera also devotes considerable emphasis to religious or religious cum ethnic threats, including "the Christian left" as well as the separatist Moro National Liberation Front (MNLF).

Nivera gives considerable attention to two active insurgencies in the Philippines: the MNLF insurgency in the south and the activities of the communist New People's Army. He believes that strong political leadership and a good economic performance are crucial to the Philippine government's efforts to contain such threats.

The communist insurgencies are also dealt with in the other Southeast Asian-authored chapters, as well as in the chapter 13 overview of the insurgencies in Malaysia, Thailand, and the Philippines by Professor Donald Weatherbee of the University of South Carolina. The general view of both Weatherbee, the Asian chapter writers, and other Asian symposium participants was that the Malaysian and Thai Communist parties had lost potency in recent years as a result of a number of factors, such as their identification with ethnic Chinese, the effectiveness of counterinsurgency operations by the governments, economic growth that has made communist doctrine less appealing, and confusion caused by realignments and splits among communist countries. As Sarasin Viraphol of the Thai foreign ministry notes of the Thai Communist party in chapter 11, however, the insurgencies cannot yet be safely discounted as a continuing source of threat to ASEAN societies. Indeed, Weatherbee's research suggests that frustration and crisis have stimulated a new effort in the Thai and Malayan parties to find new, more effective indigenous doctrines and strategies of revolution to replace the classical Maoist dogma that has lost its appeal. Pointing to the importance of social and economic conditions in the ASEAN countries, he notes the possibility of alliance between the urban left and the Communist parties as a potential internal threat of the 1980s if economies weaken and existing tensions increase.

Introduction

In meeting challenges, Southeast Asians placed considerable emphasis on domestic factors such as strong national leadership, continuing economic development, and the maintenance of national cohesion—to use an Indonesian term now adopted by ASEAN as a whole, *national resilience*. As Somsakdi Xuto notes in chapter 12, there is a complex relationship between internal and external security. In Thailand's case, he writes, "There has been a growing appreciation that unless internal-security threats are reduced and removed, overall national security is weakened."

On the other hand, external factors have an important impact on the domestic environment, heightening or ameliorating social and political problems. All the Southeast Asian chapters give some attention to the continuing conflict in Kampuchea as an external source of instability, and the Thai paricipants regard Kampuchean developments as a direct threat. Sarasin describes the multiple dimensions of this threat—domination of Kampuchea by 200,000 Vietnamese troops, a spillover of fighting into the border areas of Thailand, the aggravation of domestic social problems in these areas as hundreds of thousands of Kampuchean refugees fled across the border, and the growth of Vietnamese dependence on the USSR. Sarasin reflects that Thai security will be affected as long as the fighting in Kampuchea persists—probably for a long time.

Although the Southeast Asian chapters suggest differences in emphasis on the underlying implications of the Kampuchean problem and how it should be addressed in the future, the participants from ASEAN at Waikoloa expressed strong agreement on certain basic principles: that the presence of Vietnamese troops in massive numbers in Kampuchea represents a threat to Thailand; that the invasion was a violation of principles of desirable regional and international order; that continuing disorder in Kampuchea has serious regional implications including the intensification of Sino-Soviet conflict centering around Indochina; that a political solution will require Vietnamese flexibility and concessions that Vietnam has so far showed no willingness to make; and that a lasting political solution would also depend in part on continuing ASEAN solidarity.

A final country perspective comes in chapter 14 from Robert J. O'Neill, who was head of the Strategic and Defence Studies Centre of the Australian National University at the time he wrote his chapter. O'Neill describes a variety of historical changes in Australian threat perceptions as Russia, Japan, China, and Indonesia were in turn regarded as major threats to Australian security. At the beginning of the 1980s, O'Neill writes, "Australians are not consciously aware of imminent direct or major threats to their security. . . . Since the Soviet invasion of Afghanistan, Australian mistrust of the USSR has deepened; but the Soviets are regarded as a problem of the alliance as a whole." The Australian government, however, regards the USSR as a very dangerous threat and subscribes substantially to the window-of-opportunity theory. O'Neill provides considerable detail on what Australia is doing to help share the burdens of meeting security threats, a subject to which this introduction now turns.

A Better Division of Labor in Meeting Security Threats

Despite the divergences in threat perceptions, participants at Waikoloa seemed to believe that increased cooperation on security issues, broadly defined, is useful and desirable. The beginnings of a more effective division of labor among countries in meeting security challenges could be only tentatively sketched out, however. It was agreed that a more concrete definition would require continuing and intensified dialogue. Indeed, a major conclusion of the conference was that the sponsoring organizations should continue an effort to develop a better framework for security cooperation. Before turning to some of the issues that require more analysis, let us review some of the Waikoloa discussion of the roles of various regions and countries.

The Japanese Role

There was considerable discussion of the possible security role of Japan. Ambassador Yasukawa challenged the participants, especially those from other Asian countries, to state what kind of role they desired of Japan. A number of participants took up this challenge.

No Asian participant advocated a military role for Japan in Southeast Asia, but there was no objection to Japan expanding its self-defense role in its immediate neighborhood. As one leading Southeast Asian government official put it: "It is our feeling generally in Southeast Asia that Japan should do more in terms of safeguarding its own security as well as the area surrounding Japan. . . . I think it's about time that Japan should play a certain role in increasing its own defense in order to tie down part of the Soviet force in East Asia and in North Asia in order to prevent them from spilling over in Southeast Asia."

Another Southeast Asian agreed, but added that when it comes to defending sea-lanes in Southeast Asia itself, ASEAN has "a lot of apprehension," and more dialogue is needed by all parties.

Southeast Asians emphasized that there were many other ways in which Japan is already contributing and can contribute further to security in Southeast Asia. One suggestion was that Japan can provide funds to help Southeast Asians finance their own defense needs directly or indirectly.

Introduction

Another prominent Southeast Asian pointed out that financial support for projects like the building of a large dry-docking facility adjacent to the U.S. naval base at Subic Bay was a direct contribution to security, both by accommodating U.S. naval vessels and by contributing to employment in the Philippines. This participant noted that when it comes to the developmental dimension of security, Japan today is "the dominant factor in the region," in terms of both official aid and investment capital.

U.S. views of the Japanese role were somewhat divided. Some clearly felt that Japan should be pressed into assuming a much larger military role. Others thought that Japan's role should be more economic in nature with respect to the rest of the region and that pressure could be counterproductive. One former U.S. military official noted that Japan has already made substantial progress on military aspects that are not very visible when defense spending as a percentage of GNP is examined, but are nonetheless significant. According to this participant, bilateral military planning, joint exercises, and the overall openness of cooperative relationships that now exist between Japan and the United States would have been inconceivable a few years ago. He thought there was much more Japan could do to contribute to its own self-defense, but that if the Japanese continue to "make the progress they are now making, most of us will hopefully be satisfied."

The Southeast Asian Role

Discussion of positive contributions that Southeast Asians could make to the security burden was even more tentative. Some Southeast Asians felt that their countries were not given enough credit for the burden they have already assumed in meeting common threats. For example, a Thai participant pointed out that since 1975 Thailand and other Southeast Asian countries have stood virtually alone in meeting the challenges to security arising from Indochina. The Philippine bases were acknowledged to be an important contribution by all participants. Efforts by Southeast Asian countries to develop a regional order—whether based on a Zone of Peace, Freedom, and Neutrality (ZOPFAN) concept or on some other concept—were referred to. Nearly all Southeast Asian participants vigorously expressed the importance of the ASEAN framework for cooperation in overcoming potential intraregional tensions and developing stronger political and economic cohesion with the five-nation grouping.

Although developing countries may have their hands full in maintaining the momentum of their nation-building efforts, O'Neill's chapter suggests that Australia, though a small country, can make an important contribution to overall regional security in several important ways. These include providing facilities for U.S. forces; strengthening conventional forces; providing facilities for monitoring arms-control agreements; assisting developing countries, and providing intelligence, surveillance, and ready-reaction forces for dealing with threats by terrorists or guerrillas.

The Role of the United States

What, then, should be the U.S. role? In chapter 15, Professor Gordon provides recommendations designed to provoke consideration of new directions in U.S. policy. He urges four changes in U.S. policy, beginning with a conceptual change—that the U.S. "adopt a much more relaxed posture in the Pacific than it has for a generation." Gordon argues that powerful forces of Asian nationalism, buttressed by economic prosperity, guarantee the most fundamental U.S. interests in preventing the domination of the region by a hostile power. Gordon's other recommendations are that the United States correct a policy that "leans too far in China's direction," that it have a more flexible policy toward Vietnam, and that U.S. policy toward Japan's defense role be directed more toward having Japan help underwrite Southeast Asian defense efforts.

When discussed at the Waikoloa conference, these recommendations provoked considerable debate—particularly on Vietnam policy, where a large proportion of the participants saw little value in a new approach toward Vietnam at a time when Vietnam itself showed virtually no flexibility. ASEAN participants generally put their agenda for U.S. policy in different terms.

First, there was general support for a strong U.S. defense role to balance Soviet presence in the region.

Second, a number of Asian participants urged that there be better consultation between the United States and its East Asian friends and allies on such matters as China policy, Japan policy, Vietnam policy, and the Kampuchean situation. It was noted that although consultation is frequently cited as an objective, an effective and satisfying means of consulting and registering regional concerns to top U.S. policymakers has not been fully achieved. Some participants supported a Pacific Community organization to achieve this goal.

Third, there was considerable urging that the United States not neglect the economic side of the security equation. Some Southeast Asian participants believed that Japan has a more effective economic-cooperation policy, one that promotes private-sector investment in projects that can be beneficial in maintaining political and social stability, and urged the United States to look more closely at the Japanese model.

Fourth, some Asian participants emphasized the importance of consistent and effective U.S. leadership. The U.S. image suffered in the 1970s, they felt, because of the lack of a clear direction in U.S. policy. A number of participants believed that this sense of direction had not yet been provided by the new administration, a feeling that was shared by some U.S. participants.

Conclusion

Obviously, differences in perceptions of threat exist not only between countries, but also within the political elites of individual countries. This makes generalization hazardous. Nevertheless, it is clear that dominant perceptions in individual countries in the region show considerable differences. The failure of policymakers on either side of the Pacific to appreciate these differences and devise programs of cooperation that take them into account can compound misunderstandings and prevent or delay needed or desirable forms of collaboration. Bridging these concerns and differences in perception will be a major challenge to both U.S. and Asian policymakers.

**Part I
Regional Perspectives**

1

The Uncertain Future: Asian-Pacific Relations in Trouble

Robert A. Scalapino

Relations among the major Asian-Pacific states range from delicate to hostile at present, with fluidity greater, hazards more pronounced, and predictions more difficult to advance than at any time since the 1930s. The primary risk today is not that of a major power war. The costs of such a conflagration deter all leaders. What we are currently witnessing, however, is an erosion of that complex network of positive relationships—economic, political, and in some cases strategic—that earlier seemed to promise a steadily developing regional-international structure of procedure, custom, and law conducive to greater harmony. The erosion, moreover, affects not only the United States and the USSR, but also the old alliances or alignments of each of the so-called superpowers and those of the lesser states as well.

Our task here is to set forth the dimensions of the problem, its fundamental causes, and possible remedial measures. Initially, however, certain general conditions or trends underlying international politics today must be outlined. Seven interrelated global developments underlie regional trends everywhere, and one must understand these factors before advancing meaningful hypotheses about the Asian-Pacific area.

First, ours is an age of increasing interdependence—economic, political, and strategic. Yet because of the problems induced by this interdependence, nationalism is also rising—not merely in the so-called Third World, where it has represented a natural postcolonial force (albeit largely elitist in nature), but also among the advanced industrial societies, where it is picking up mass support.

Second, we are confronted with a rising economic imbalance not only between North and South, but also within both categories of states. The economic malaise characterizing Western Europe and the United States, for example, in juxtaposition to the thriving Japanese economy, is responsible for some of the tensions afflicting mutual relations among those nations. In the near term, at least, this situation will show no dramatic improvement, nor will North-South problems decrease. On the contrary, the massive debts now owed to the rich nations by the poor are but one sign of the crises ahead.

Third, there has been a significant decline in secular ideology. One result has been a vacuum with respect to political values, a vacuum filled in certain instances by the largely unexpected resurgence of religion in politics—

fundamental Islam, fundamental Christianity, fundamental Judaism. All these play a heightened role today. Yet the ideological confusion surrounding almost all states—communist or liberal—continues.

Fourth, political institutionalization remains weak in many societies, with the result that the role of personal leadership is crucial. In the economic realm, also, current systems—socialist or capitalist—are under challenge. Hence the quest for effective political and economic models is widespread, with no answers yet forthcoming.

Fifth, political structures above the nation-state level are weak, with limited law and custom prevailing. Neither the United Nations nor the key regional organizations have acquired great legitimacy or power in peacekeeping or the management of political disputes.

Sixth, although the chance of avoiding major nuclear war is reasonably good, violence will be endemic in coming years. Terrorism, undeclared wars (many combining civil and international elements), and small-state wars will all be important phenomena in the decades immediately ahead. The task is to contain these as much as possible, since they cannot be eliminated.

Finally, ours is an age in which the broad movement is from alliance to alignment. Relations that were once relatively tight and all-encompassing, with fixed obligations for the parties concerned, have become looser and more porous, permitting much greater independence and even fairly high levels of discord. For the United States as for the USSR, the management of alignments will be a crucial test of diplomacy and a central determinant of power.

In this context, U.S.-Soviet relations will continue to be the predominant factor in measuring global tension. These are the only two states that can intervene in any continent and that have the capacity to influence the broadest economic, political, and military trends in societies with which they choose to interact. Today, the U.S.-Soviet relations in the Asian-Pacific region are a product more of global than of regional considerations. The existing confrontation stems less from crises within the area (although some exist), than from graver tensions with respect to other regions of the world, and from issues of a global nature.

In strategic terms the crucial issue between the United States and the USSR is that over the past decade the USSR came abreast of the United States in military capacities and thus became for the first time in its history a global power. This took place, moreover, under the aegis of detente and during a period in which the United States was essentially marking time with respect to its own military program. It also occurred under global conditions rife with the potential for local upheavals affecting the regional or global balance of power. The economic, political, and social circumstances of many societies—especially for the developing states—remain complex and fragile. Thus the rising Soviet capacity for global involvement, whether directly or indirectly through aligned states, coincides with the presence of multiple targets of opportunity. Here lies the nexus of the problem as perceived by the United States. The USSR is highly nationalistic and prepared to rationalize expansionism with the rhetoric of liberation and socialist obligation. It is largely untempered by experience (including misadventures) and now has the capacity as well as the opportunity to shift the global balance of power.

For its part, the USSR sees itself as the underprivileged global power, lacking equal access to—or involvement in—crucial regions previously established and still strongly influenced by the United States. Engaged in the game of catch-up, it demands recognition as an equal to the United States, with full participation in global and regional decision making. Further, it seeks to apply the formula "once in the socialist bloc, always in that bloc"—with changes possible only if they add to socialist strength. In reality, however, the USSR faces the same problems of slippage that worry the United States. Not only has it lost its influence in China, at least for this era, but it also sees a worrisome degree of independence developing much more widely within its bloc and among the nonsocialist states aligned with it.

The USSR is especially frustrated with respect to Asia. Its military power in this region has grown appreciably and will continue to increase, especially since the USSR is committed to the development of Siberia, its great Asian possession. Yet its political influence in Asia is at a low ebb, notwithstanding the alliance with Vietnam and the alignment with India. Indeed, in political terms, the USSR is far weaker in the Asian-Pacific region today than it was thirty years ago. The prospects for rapid improvement, as we shall note, are not good.

As a Eurasian empire, furthermore, the USSR cannot avoid a feeling of great apprehension about the advent of powerful developing societies on continental Asia, whatever their political-ideological coloration, since it has not—and cannot—fully assimilate its own Central Asian peoples. The weaknesses of empire thus help to shape the character of Soviet foreign policy in Asia—a policy that continues to have strong elements of defensiveness, resting on deeply entrenched feelings of insecurity.

The United States, confronted with this situation, has steadily gravitated toward a commitment to tie down Soviet power in Asia in order to weaken Soviet capacities elsewhere. It is a classic gambit, one with which the USSR was confronted earlier, when the principal Soviet adversaries were Europeans and Japanese. Thus, from an initial position of seeking to treat the USSR and China evenhandedly and aspiring to occupy the strategically important centrist position—being able to talk effectively to both large communist nations when they could not talk to each other—the United States has moved progressively toward alignment with China against the USSR and toward encouragement of a U.S.-Japanese-Chinese entente that would in some degree match the NATO alliance in Europe (albeit with significant differences), thereby causing Soviet resources and energies to be as widely dispersed as possible.

It can certainly be shown that Soviet actions were themselves primarily responsible for the basic shift in U.S. policy. Although there were always advocates of the two-front strategic policy, they were in a minority until Afghanistan. Nor is the issue fully and finally resolved.

The new thrust faces problems, quite apart from the question of whether it can serve U.S. national interests in the long term. As will be indicated, U.S. relations with both China and Japan have recently been in a delicate phase, with the future clouded. Nevertheless, if one is to speak of the broadest trend characterizing U.S.-Soviet relations in Asia recently, it has been the movement toward confrontation. The USSR has relied primarily on its heightened military power to assert itself to the east. In response, the United States has increasingly espoused an Asian united front against Soviet expansionism, in the process seeking to make the Asian-Pacific region an enhanced factor in the global balance.

Meanwhile, recent U.S. relations with the other major communist state of the Asian-Pacific region, the People's Republic of China (PRC), have revealed the complex problems involved in working with the Beijing government. By the end of 1981, U.S.-PRC relations had reached a very delicate stage, with the immediate issue at stake the familiar one of Taiwan. At the time of the normalization agreement, in December 1979, PRC officials had clearly understood that the United States intended to continue to sell so-called defensive weapons to Taiwan. An agreement to disagree was reached, since Beijing realized that normalization would be acceptable neither to the U.S. public nor to the Congress under any other conditions. The Taiwan Relations Act subsequently passed by Congress and accepted by the Carter administration, moreover, reiterated this position in firmer language. Although the PRC government protested this resolution, under its provisions the Carter administration sold Taiwan arms in 1980 with minimal PRC protest.

When the Reagan administration came to office, however, PRC leaders began to take a harder line on the Taiwan question, seeking in effect to change the rules. They argued that since the United States had "recognized" the fact that there was only one China and Taiwan was a province of China, arms sales to Taipei in any form represented an interference in China's internal affairs and was therefore unacceptable. The PRC threatened to downgrade relations with the United States should arms sales proceed, with some vagueness concerning what would constitute absolutely unacceptable sales and what steps would be pursued should a downgrading take place. The action taken against the Netherlands was presumably a signal. A Dutch agreement to sell submarines to Taiwan was followed by a reduction of diplomatic relations to the chargé level.

There has been much speculation about why the PRC suddenly pushed the Taiwan issue to the fore, threatening to make it a litmus test of future U.S.-Chinese relations. It has been argued that Reagan's campaign speeches suggesting that his administration might restore diplomatic relations with the Republic of China (ROC) alarmed Beijing authorities, inducing the new counteroffensive. Some also have suggested that Deng's earlier concessions on the Taiwan issue created internal fissures in the PRC, necessitating a tougher position. These factors may have been salient, but it seems unlikely that they were the central considerations. The PRC is undoubtedly increasingly concerned over developments in Taiwan itself. Within less than a decade a new generation of leaders will emerge on the island; with them, the nature of the issue is likely to change. The rise to power of a mix of mainland refugee children and Taiwanese will accelerate the process of Taiwanization. The central issue will no longer be, "Who is China?" but rather, "Does Taiwan have the right to a separate existence?" For the PRC this will greatly complicate the issue of returning Taiwan to province status.

Thus, on the one hand, PRC authorities proffered a series of concessions to Taiwan involving promises of extensive autonomy (but insisting on an abandonment of any claim to sovereignty). On the other hand, the PRC not only refused to outlaw the possible use of force should its soft policies produce no results, but also accused the United States of stiffening Taiwan's resistance to any peaceful settlement by continuing arms sales, and privately insisted that a terminal date for such sales must be fixed.

In concert with these demands, PRC media began to voice increased criticism of a widening range of U.S. policies in the latter part of 1981. There had never been any agreement on such issues as Korea or the Middle East, for example; and Beijing had not hesitated to criticize Washington on these and other matters throughout the process of normalization (in contrast to the United States, which was extremely careful to avoid any official attacks on PRC policies). The central Chinese objective has always been a strategic—but *not* political—alignment with the United States. Beijing has seen its own national interest served by political alignment with the Third World. In the course of 1981, however, the scope and intensity of criticism against the United States was increased, with references to U.S. imperialism (albeit treated as a weakening force in comparison to Soviet social imperialism) and the dangers of superpower indifference to the plight of Third World nations, as well as a sharpening of the thrusts against U.S. policies on specific regional questions.

The immediate issue came to a head in early 1982, when Washington announced on 11 January that it would continue to authorize sales of F5E planes as well as spare-part replacements (authorized slightly earlier), but would not sell advanced FX fighters. At the time, a U.S. delegation headed by Assistant Secretary John Holdridge was in Beijing to continue discussions on security matters. Beijing authorities announced that they would vigorously protest this U.S. action taken during ongoing discussions. It appeared, however, that Beijing would avoid going further, while making the basic point that it expected to be consulted on all future arms sales to "its province, Taiwan," and thus to have a voice in this matter, looking toward the earliest possible termination of such sales.

It seems unlikely that the Taiwan issue will disappear. As indicated earlier, the process of Taiwanization is certain to accelerate, barring external interference or heavy internal suppression. From all the evidence, moreover, the current ROC government is largely reconciled to this development, with the only issues being those of timing and procedure. There is no evidence that these leaders—or the population whom they govern—are interested in union with the PRC, given the huge economic and political disparities now existing. Autonomy cannot be attractive, since sovereignty is lost and a province cannot engage in future negotiations with the nation of which it is a part with any hope of equality. Unquestionably, Beijing's offers have placed Taipei on the defensive, especially with respect to economic, cultural, and other exchanges; indeed, such exchanges are taking place unofficially. The chances of peaceful reunification in the foreseeable future are very slim, however, at least until major improvements in PRC economic standards and political stability occur. Thus the issue will not go away.

The large issues confronting U.S.-PRC relations from a U.S. perspective are found in both the security and the economic-cultural-political realms. Should the modernization of China's armed forces—currently a relatively low priority—be encouraged and supported? Can China be expected to be more than a defensively oriented, relatively backward nation, able in concert with other factors to keep approximately one-quarter of Soviet military power on guard on its eastern front, but not likely to assist actively should any major confrontation threaten? Looking to the future, are internal conditions sufficiently stable? Is Sino-Soviet hostility sufficiently assured to warrant strategic commitments? What will be the impact of such a policy decision by the United States on its major allies—both Japan and Western Europe—as well as on other Asian nations? On the economic, cultural, and political fronts, can and should the United States effectively assist in China's four modernizations; and to what degree should reciprocity—together with supportive treatment in official pronouncements and media treatment—be emphasized? When there is evidence that a retreat from political liberalization is occurring, as in the recent past, should the United States respond, either publicly or privately?

There are no easy answers to these questions. Before attempting some assessment related to U.S. policy alternatives, however, let me turn to central trends in other bilateral ties, commencing with U.S.-Japanese relations. It scarcely needs to be emphasized that in two areas—economic and security relations—significant problems have existed. With the U.S.-Japan trade deficit in the neighborhood of $18 billion in 1981 and scheduled to go higher in 1982, and with the rise of numerous issues relating to nontariff barriers and other matters, the immediate future seems likely to be one of heightened tension. In the defense realm, also, the Japanese response has been far less than that requested by the United States, although recent Japanese pledges in this field have been gratefully received.

Japan's governing elite and its allies in the business community regard the Japan-U.S. economic imbalance as essentially a product of U.S. mismanagement of its own economy, not of Japanese barriers or unfair competition. Consequently, they are reluctant to make major concessions but, on the contrary, have been increasingly assertive in defense of their own position. In the defense arena, as long as the issue is posed in terms of a Soviet threat to Japan, the sense of risk is low. Using the U.S.-imposed constitution as their shield and Japanese public opinion as their primary weapon, successive Japanese governments have exhibited a strong reluctance to move away from a mimimal-risk/maximal-gain foreign policy.

Thus the usual criteria of highest importance for Japan have related to the minimum that must be done to propitiate the U.S. administration, Congress, and people. Recently there has been a growing recognition in Japan among policymakers that measures taken to date have been too little and too late for optimal benefit to Japan. Consequently, new Japanese pledges, especially on the security front, have been more forthcoming. Yet the central differences remain; and there are reasonable prospects that for the next several years, U.S.-Japanese relations will be faced with higher levels of tension—at least sporadically—than characterized the halcyon days.

In surveying the current status of U.S. relations with the major Asian-Pacific states, some consolation can be taken from a comparative analysis. As noted earlier, Soviet relations with both China and Japan are at a low ebb. As for USSR-PRC relations, the events of recent years have added to rather than subtracted from the levels of tension and hostility. The Soviet involvements in Indochina and Afghanistan have increased Chinese apprehensions and made rapprochement far more difficult. The Chinese do not fear a Soviet invasion. They are confident that their very size precludes such a development, and Soviet difficulties in Afghanistan have intensified this belief. Their concern stems from the knowledge that the Soviet encirclement—particularly the use of surrogates like Vietnam and Afghanistan—furthers the likelihood of long-term Soviet pressures that can inhibit and restrict Chinese foreign policy, as well as adding greatly to the costs of border defense.

The possibilities of abrupt changes in the bilateral relations of two countries can never be wholly ruled out, but the prospects for a meaningful Sino-Soviet rapprochement in the near term are extremely slight. Chinese spokesmen have indicated privately that even if U.S.-Chinese relations were to deteriorate, the shift, at least immediately, would not be toward the USSR. The more likely swing would involve some return to self-reliance and greater emphasis on the Third World, even though such policies could not possibly serve China's interests with respect to either modernization or security.

Soviet relations with Japan may offer greater hope for improvement. Here the USSR has long counted on the lure of Siberia, combined with a growing crisis in Japan's economic relations with the West, to draw Japan into a more cooperative framework without any Soviet need to make significant concessions on territorial or security issues. Soviet-West German economic relations have been seen as a model, further encouraging Moscow in this hope. There have also been signs that Japan's interest in omnidirectional diplomacy—voiced strongly a few years ago—is not dead. Ideally, Japan would like to do business wherever possible, serving both as the engine spearheading China's industrial revolution and as the foremost source of Siberian development. Thus Japan is not likely to fall behind Western Europe in seeking access to the Soviet market.

Unfortunately for the USSR, however, Soviet policies toward Japan have been uniquely inept, creating a huge reservoir of ill will among the Japanese people. Specific issues like that of the four northern islands, moreover, cannot be dismissed. There are few cultural links or possibilities of political identification to smooth the path of rapprochement. All hinges on the claims of the marketplace; even here, the USSR has not always made an interchange sufficiently attractive to the Japanese in economic terms. Thus, although there is a possibility for a growing economic tie between two nations that could easily complement each other in terms of needs, progress is likely to be slow and uneven given the security, political, and psychological barriers.

One turns finally to Sino-Japanese relations, which on the surface at least are the most promising among the bilateral relations under discussion. Contrary to general trends, these relations are improving—after some rocky times a short while ago when the Chinese decided on an economic retrenchment and canceled a number of contracts, many of them with Japan, involving the importation of industrial products. Japanese loans to China have been advanced and certain construction projects reopened. Sino-Japanese trade is again on the rise. Cultural relations are expanding, and kind words flow when the elites of the two nations meet. The Chinese generally support Japanese foreign policies, and criticism of Japan is seldom voiced. Neither Taiwan nor Korea constitutes a thorny issue, despite the massive Japanese presence in both settings. On the Japanese side, those policy differences with China that do exist—and there are clearly a number of such differences—are not allowed to interfere with the pledge to improve bilateral relations.

Confronted with this evidence, some observers see a trend toward a new Pan-Asianism, with a Sino-Japanese alignment gradually occupying center stage, serving as a countervailing force to both the United States and the USSR, and aiding in the stabilization of East Asia with the possibility of a later global impact.

I consider such a view misplaced. Although there are some points of common interest between China and Japan, and a capacity exists for expanding a meaningfully complementary relationship at present, there are also clear limitations to that relationship. Privately, those Japanese who matter do not relish a strong China. In the words of one perceptive observer, "We would like to see a weak China that aims at strength"—a very sage observation. Japan realizes that a strong China might have hegemonistic ambitions for Asia, despite solemn pledges to the contrary, and might also be a formidable economic competitor with Japan. For its part, China wants to see an aroused Japan vis-à-vis the USSR but is at least ambivalent toward policies that would enable Japan to become a major political-military force in Asia or the world. These two societies have grown apart from each other culturally and politically for many decades, as their stages of economic development became more widely separated. Pan-Asianism may still have a romantic, even racial appeal in some circles; but it is not viable in hard economic, political, or strategic terms.

Under the prevailing circumstances, what should U.S. perspectives and policies in the Asian-Pacific region be? The main arena for U.S.-Soviet relations is not in this area; nevertheless, recent Soviet actions and U.S. reactions in Asia have potentially far-reaching consequences. On the one hand, as noted earlier, the USSR via its policies in Indochina and Afghanistan has deepened its conflict with China and at the same time provided the momentum for the substantial U.S. tilt toward the PRC that has ensued.

Is there any basis on which U.S.-Soviet relations can be stabilized or even improved? The key test lies outside this region, in the strategic arms negotiations now getting under way. Given the costs and risks of an open-ended arms race, both the United States and the USSR should have strong reasons to desire an equitable agreement. The arms issue, moreover, is being played before a global audience, especially a European audience, making the political stakes equal to the economic and strategic ones.

In its recent policies toward the USSR, the United States has sought to mobilize the U.S. people to make the sacrifices involved in rebuilding U.S. military strength—at the same time summoning its major allies to support varied sanctions against the USSR. Yet there is now considerable doubt that a fully unified policy can be achieved. Consultation has been inadequate. Beyond this, the Reagan administration's policies have raised doubts—doubts quickly exploited by Soviet spokesmen. The mounting of a two-track approach—military strength *and* negotiations—came too late to achieve optimal political benefits. Even moderate U.S. sanctions face an uphill battle, especially since the lifting of the grain embargo, and since the effectiveness of sanctions subsequently proposed has been widely challenged within the allied camp.

The task now confronting the United States is a dual one. On the one hand, the economic health of the nation must be restored. Our serious economic problems, together with those of Europe—and the resulting gap between the West and Japan—lie at the root of many of the problems plaguing the old alliance structure. The United States and Europe have a sizable element of political instability today; few governments have a long life expectancy, largely because the remedies for the economic malaise affecting these societies are not easily forthcoming. This is scarcely a position of strength from which to defend Western values and policies. Thus the priority must be on fundamental economic reform. It now appears that the military-strengthening program must be stretched out if the Reagan administration is to reach an economically sound and politically viable set of policies.

At the same time, the United States must help to rebuild the alliance-alignment structure that has served the cause of open societies reasonably well in recent decades. The emphasis is on the word *help* because the responsibility is by no means unilateral. Indeed, whatever errors of omission or commission may have been made by Washington in matters pertaining to nations aligned to it, the attitudes and actions of the latter nations generally bear at least an equal responsibility for the current disarray.

It is conceivable that a majority of Western Europeans are not prepared to risk opposing a militarily ascendant USSR but, rather, will accommodate to this condition, avoiding confrontation by accepting de facto Soviet dominance in terms of power and seeking eventually to moderate Soviet behavior through economic and political interaction. If this is the case, the United States should be prepared to contemplate a radical shift in its current foreign policies.

It is also conceivable that Japan—equally concerned about the costs and risks of a policy of challenging Soviet expansionism—will swing back even more firmly to the idea of omnidirectional foreign policy, hoping to refurbish its maximum access to resources and markets in the process. Once again the United States may have to accommodate to a situation dramatically different from that contemplated under current policies. It is conceivable, finally, that China—for reasons best known to itself—will stake everything on a U.S. abandonment of Taiwan, demanding this as the price for the continuance of its strategic alignment with the United States. If this is the course of events, then the United States will again confront a set of decisions having far-reaching repercussions, no matter which course of action it takes.

These brief remarks should indicate that there are grave problems within the alignment structure and that the United States cannot assume that long-

Asian-Pacific Relations in Trouble

range policies can be established at this time. For now, however, efforts should be made to strengthen the wavering, amorphous, interconnected set of relations that serves to balance somewhat the newly achieved global military power of the USSR and, in the process, to deter what might otherwise be a much greater military role within Soviet society and much greater risk taking in Soviet foreign policy.

Specifically, how can the United States aid in this task? First, consultation must be thorough and genuine so that responsibility for decisions will be as collective as possible. Each successive U.S. administration has paid lip service to this principle. Each in turn, however, including the current one, has proceeded to advance on a largely unilateral basis, seeking approval in the aftermath of decisions taken in camera. One excuse is that other governments sometimes wish not to be consulted, thereby maintaining a greater degree of noninvolvement or flexibility. From the standpoint of U.S. national interest, however, this is all the more reason for a thorough consultation process.

Second, the Washington administration should forego bold or extreme rhetoric that on the one hand cannot be matched by action and, on the other hand, frightens allies, suggesting the possible willingness of the United States to take drastic measures. The political contest in which we are engaged is no less serious than the military competition; and we have been doing badly in part because of the amateurism that again prevails in too many quarters among those recently come to power.

Third, the United States should formulate carefully what it expects of itself and of allied or aligned states, both in general terms and in specific settings, and then be prepared to negotiate quietly and at length if necessary, with a willingness to listen carefully to other views and to compromise the initial position where logic dictates. In this process, however, several rules must be observed. The United States must not accept a defensive, retreating position taken under threat. While seeking to understand the political realities within the societies with which the United States seeks to cooperate, it must clearly explicate the political realities within U.S. society, especially the fact that the U.S. people are no longer prepared to accept what they regard as an undue share of the burdens—economic, political, and military—for the maintenance of world order. In this connection, moreover, we should make it clear that policy alternatives—even drastic ones—are available to the United States, should meaningful cooperation prove impossible to achieve. This should be advanced not as a threat but as an expression of fact, a fact of increasing political salience in the United States.

Finally, specifically with respect to U.S.-Soviet relations, the United States should pursue a complex, sophisticated policy that is finely tuned to the existing situation. On the one hand, it should maintain a firm stand with respect to Indochina, refusing any diplomatic relations with Vietnam as long as Hanoi pursues its present policies. The naive thesis that the United States can compete with the USSR for Hanoi's affections ignores the serious repercussions that U.S. recognition of the Democratic Republic of Vietnam (DRV) would have on U.S. relations with the Association of Southeast Asian Nations (ASEAN) and China. Moreover, such assistance should be given to the Afghan rebels as they can usefully absorb. On the other hand, strategic arms discussions should be continued with the USSR and cultural contacts maintained with Soviet intellectuals—an ever more necessary source of communication in times of crisis.

Against this background, let us now turn to U.S.-Japanese relations. As has been indicated, the primary problems fall into two politically interrelated categories—namely, mutual defense and economic interaction. With respect to defense, there is one basic need at present. The issue for Japan must be rephrased from, "What must we do to keep the United States minimally satisfied?" to, "What commitments should Japan make to economic and political stability and to a broad military equilibrium in a region—and a globe—on which it is extensively dependent?"

This latter question permits Japanese defense policies, as well as those in the economic and political arenas, to be formulated in terms of Japanese national interests. Of course, there will be important differences of opinion. In the final analysis, however, no nation has a greater stake in a stable, open Asian-Pacific region than Japan. Thus it is time to stop posing the issue either in terms of what will keep the United States happy, or on the narrow basis of whether the USSR will or will not attack Japan proper. Nor can satisfactory answers be found in the comfortable thesis that Japan will tackle its economic problems, leaving to others the more costly, risky problems in the political and security arenas. Any analysis based on a concept of Japanese national interests must deal with the fact that Japan is now a global power economically, with global interests and a far greater stake than most societies in a stable, peaceful, open world.

The key problem today thus lies less in current trends in Japanese security policies and more in the premises on which they appear to rest. Japan will probably increase its defense expenditures some 4-5 percent in real terms in fiscal 1982. It is engaged in a ten-year program scheduled for completion in 1987, emphasizing a highly modern but small conventional force. Joint planning and military exercises with the United States have been advanced, including some agreements about responsibilities in the event of an emergency. Moreover, Japan has agreed to expand its surveillance to several hundreds of miles by air and more than a thousand miles by sea to the east and south—the first step toward some regional commitment. These actions are not negligible, although they fall far short of the Western European contribution to mutual security.

Economically, Japan is in trouble not merely with the United States but also, for similar reasons, with Western Europe and various newly industrial and developing states, especially in Asia. The problems derive in part from the striking success of the Japanese economy in contrast to the weak performances of other advanced industrial states, with structural differences underlying the varying results. There is merit in Japan's complaint that it is being penalized or threatened because of its success resulting from effective policies: a disciplined, energetic managerial and work force, and priorities based on economic development over all other considerations. There is, however, also merit in the complaint of others that whereas Japan has been able to build on technical advances first scored elsewhere and then to saturate relatively open foreign markets with extraordinary speed, its own markets are largely closed—less because of tariffs than because of the unique, tightly interwoven nature of Japanese society.

This situation is likely to worsen before it improves. All projections indicate that the Japanese economy will continue to perform with better productivity, lower inflation, and higher quality on balance than the economies of either the United States or Western Europe in the immediate future. Trade imbalances are likely to grow unless greater restrictions are imposed. Of even more significance, Japan is now investing at considerably higher levels in industrial research and development compared with other industrial states, including the United States. It intends to move rapidly into the highest technology industries, heightening U.S.-Japanese competition.

Japan's pledges to take drastic steps to open its economy—removing or reducing administrative controls that inhibit foreign access, lowering remaining tariff barriers, and sharing technology—are greeted with a mixture of hope and skepticism abroad.

In the long run, of course, certain Japanese vulnerabilities can be foreseen—resource costs and scarcities, and an aging labor market, among others. The next few years are likely to be ones of considerable tension, however, with the pressures for protectionism high and Japan on the defensive until structural and policy alterations in both that nation and its major economic partners—including the United States—permit more equitable relations. Again the situation demands effective U.S. economic policies at home, including bold new initiatives designed to make the United States more competitive internationally. In addition to its other pledges, moreover, Japan must act to emphasize its domestic market more strongly.

In sum, although the U.S.-Japanese relationship remains vital, even under the best of conditions the next few years will be hazardous ones. On both sides, it can no longer be business as usual.

The issues arising in U.S.-Chinese relations are very different, but no less serious. Whether the United States was wise in seeking a strategic alignment with China, as indicated earlier, remains debatable. Although there is no doubt that the USSR must bear the responsibility for this policy, many still have grave doubts about current U.S. commitments. The central argument advanced in favor of present policies is that since the United States is not sufficiently powerful to contain the USSR alone, the largest united front must be created—one that encompasses both Europe and Asia. It is further argued that given the limitations imposed on Japan and the major antagonisms built up over the years between the USSR and China, China can provide stable and ultimately substantial assistance to the strategic containment of the USSR.

Yet powerful counterarguments exist. A strategic alignment with China has had only limited support from other U.S. allies, including Japan, and has created apprehensions elsewhere in Asia. Is a militarily strong, economically weak China desirable? China has its own goals for Asia, which are not necessarily U.S. or Japanese goals, as has been made manifest with respect to such issues as Taiwan, Korea, and even Southeast Asia, not to mention other regions of the world.

The immediate issue, however, is not that of a militarily strong China, since that is not on the horizon. At least vis-à-vis the USSR, China will be militarily weak for the foreseeable future. Therefore, the question is whether China can do much more than it is now doing to tie down Soviet power. What it is doing at present, it was doing before the United States proffered military assistance, for reasons connected with its own perceived national interests. Presumably, as China sees its national interests served by seeking to counter Soviet encirclement with sizable forces on its frontiers, it will continue such policies. Could China under any conceivable circumstances be expected to shift from its defensive position vis-à-vis the USSR? Would any move offensively be directed only at an Asian state?

Another troublesome fact remains. By using the so-called China card is the United States locked into an uncomfortable dilemma? Although military assistance has been advanced very cautiously so far, with pledges of consideration on a case-by-case basis, the normal progression of such a relationship is toward more extensive assistance. If such a development occurs, it is likely to complicate U.S.-Soviet relations for the indefinite future, including the issue of strategic arms limitations. If, on the other hand, future Soviet good behavior should appear to warrant a freeze on military aid to China, the PRC understandably would be resentful, not wishing to be a pawn in the U.S.-Soviet contest. This could have been avoided by confining arms sales to China to Western European sources, particularly since it is clear that at least for now such transfers will be requested on a highly selective basis only.

In any case, for now the issue in U.S.-Chinese relations has been posed in different terms. Whereas Washington had hoped to propitiate Beijing by offering military assistance while continuing its pledge to furnish Taiwan with defensive arms until the reunification issue could be peacefully resolved, the PRC has chosen this time to raise the issue of Taiwan to one of top priority.

Thus U.S.-Chinese relations currently have a sweet-sour quality, with sourness increasingly coming to the fore. On the one hand, some six thousand Chinese citizens are now in the United States, attached to colleges, universities, and institutes, the overwhelming majority studying science and technology. A vastly smaller number of Americans are in China, mostly in the humanities and social sciences, both as students and researchers. Trade has developed rapidly, largely because of heavy Chinese purchases of grain. It reached $4.6 billion in 1981 and may come to $6 billion in 1982, with a strong imbalance favoring the United States. Tourism also has boomed, with prospects of further increases when facilities permit.

On the other hand, most U.S. banks and companies seeking to do business in China have been disappointed and frustrated. Many are reducing their staffs; some are leaving. Researchers have also encountered difficulties with a tightening of restrictions that has paralleled that imposed on the Chinese intellectual community. The most graphic evidence of the souring of Sino-American relations lies in the positions taken by the PRC media and by certain Chinese leaders on a wide range of subjects. China has reverted at times to an earlier stance wherein so-called American imperialism was coupled with Soviet social imperialism as a global problem. The USSR, to be sure, still is defined as *the* most serious threat. NATO is supported, as is Japanese rearmament. Signs of U.S. sternness against the Soviets are applauded. At the personal level, individual Chinese and Americans are communicating on an ever broader basis, and with remarkable good will.

Yet the signs are disconcerting, and the dilemma for the United States is severe despite some indications that Beijing is now pulling back from any immediate precipitous action. In effect, the United States is being asked to aid in the reunification of Taiwan with China by cutting off defense support for Taiwan and thereby persuading it to enter negotiations with the PRC, accepting the terms currently offered. These terms, though very generous from a PRC perspective, rest with pledges of autonomy for a province—pledges that undoubtedly would be reexamined and reinterpreted by future Beijing authorities, as has been the case with other autonomous provinces.

Quite apart from any moral concerns, for the United States to adopt such policies would reopen major issues of U.S. credibility—issues not fully settled since Vietnam. Yet for the United States to hold firm or even to make the concessions recently proffered by the Reagan administration appears unacceptable to the present Beijing government, and the PRC warnings about the future continue.

What is to be done? There comes a time when the United States must stand by certain principles—principles that in the long run serve U.S. national interests. These interests do lie in an economically developing, politically stable China, and there are many ways in which the United States can assist in this development, if permitted to do so. It can and should help in training managers, scientists, social scientists, and technicians—both in China and in the United States—and this has begun. Both countries have a stake in a peaceful, stable Asia and in containing Soviet expansionism. Often, however, they can perform their tasks best in their own respective ways, although certain areas of cooperation are desirable.

With respect to Taiwan, the Reagan administration should have reiterated the Carter administration's position that the United States would continue the sale of defense weaponry, but that since the military threat was low, there was no need to upgrade the equipment at this time. The United States must make it clear to the PRC that it cannot be blackmailed, thereby ending the highly defensive position that has marked the Haig approach. If the PRC chooses to make this the litmus test of U.S.-Chinese relations, this would be regrettable and foolish from the standpoint of Chinese national interests. The sooner the United States makes it clear that it is not going to abandon Taiwan and that it continues to hold to the principle that reunification must be peaceful—with future relations between China and Taiwan determined by the peoples involved—the better.

One must hope that a viable, progressively developing relationship among the United States, Japan, China, South Korea, and the ASEAN community will eventuate despite the current uncertainties. One must also hope that the problems of Afghanistan and Indochina, combined with a structure of punishments and rewards, will induce changes in Soviet international behavior and a trend toward international stabilization that will abet a new strategic-arms limitation treaty. Yet it would be unwise to assume that these desires are certain to be fulfilled and hence to base all U.S. policies on them. Indeed, some painful alternatives must be faced, even the possibility of contracting U.S. global strategic commitments substantially in the event that allied-aligned nations choose different policies.

Under any circumstances, an effective U.S. foreign policy now begins at home. The supreme priority must be to create and maintain a healthy domestic economy. Without this, no meaningful foreign policies can long be sustained. With this, various alternatives are possible.

2 National Threat Perceptions in East Asia-Pacific

Thanat Khoman

The question of how nations perceive threats to their security, their well-being, indeed their very existence is a universal one that faces governments and peoples the world over. Such perceptions are neither static nor permanent. Rather, they are fluid, and varying with developments occurring at certain places and time in the world at large. The diverse national outlooks and surrounding circumstances also greatly influence the perceptions of threat confronting each of the countries belonging to the same group or the same organization. All this is well known and represents the most worrisome preoccupation of many government leaders.

In East Asia and the Pacific in particular, the threat has evolved from the expansion of imperial power to an ideological threat, then back to more or less the old form, although under a new banner, that of colonial expansion. The new terminology uses the so-called liberation movement as a camouflage for political or military conquest, but the result is hardly different. It implies a loss of freedom or independence for the liberated and dominance and control for the liberators.

In the past Thailand has shown a particular acumen in perceiving threats from one major source—namely, colonial expansion from Western countries, especially the Western Europeans, who sought to conquer territories for markets to absorb their manufactured products, for sources of raw materials, for fuel and provisions for their ships that plied the seas between Europe and Asia. In fact, colonial expansion was so widespread that all the territories surrounding Thailand, then called Siam, fell under the domination of Western European countries. Only Thailand continued to enjoy its independence and sovereignty, along with Japan farther to the East. Thus in the case of Thailand the important problem was not so much to perceive the threat as to how to cope with it.

Lacking adequate military means to match the nations of the west, Thailand thought it best to avoid the type of head-on collisions that were fatal to some other Asian countries. Instead it resorted to diplomacy and particularly to the strategem of balancing one European country against another. Although this diplomatic expediency cost Thailand large tracts of territory, it did save the country from colonial subjection.

After the colonial era the threat shifted to ideological expansion, which combines old-style imperialistic designs of dominance with ideological allegiance and subservience. The victims of such ideological conquests may have the appearance of independence, but it is only nominal. In most cases they are bound by more or less visible chains to political, economic, and ideological obligations imposed by the leader, with no possibility of rejection. Czechoslovakia, Hungary, and now Afghanistan and Poland are flagrant illustrations.

Nowadays the threats have taken an even more complex form. On the one hand, predators endowed with powerful military means behave like old-fashioned imperialistic powers seeking aggrandizement of their physical domain by de facto annexations of adjacent territories after a war or limited conflict. On the other, they seek to establish an ideological overlordship by setting up satellite regimes with nominal or fictitious independence—regimes that in fact are completely subservient to the central imperial power. This is the pattern created in Eastern Europe and now is being emulated in Africa, Southeast Asia, and Latin America. In the Asia-Pacific region the threat has developed and become aggravated by miscalculations and mishandlings of a number of situations.

First it may be recalled that for years governments and people in this region have been brainwashed into believing that the main threat lay with the People's Republic of China (PRC), whence derived all evils menacing the Free World. That shallow deduction flowed from certain facts, such as the eviction of the Chinese nationalist regime from the mainland; the Korean War, which saw the intervention of the Chinese People's Liberation Army (PLA); and the Vietnam War, in which large amounts of materials were supplied by or through China to North Vietnam to sustain its struggle in the south. These events blinded many people to the reality that a victorious North Vietnam supported by a powerful modern protector and sponsor could become a more menacing threat than the populous but underdeveloped Chinese colossus.

It must be noted that for decades the USSR and its allies have been receiving enormous involuntary assistance in the realm of high technology, precision equipment, and private financial support, which helped to launch them into the ranks of the top producers of missiles and other sophisticated weapons.

Also, during the past decade or so, whereas the United States is lagging in its armament development, the USSR, after its humiliation in the Cuban missile crisis, has vowed to become an equal to the former militarily so that it will not have to back down in any future confrontation.

That explains why, in the Asia-Pacific region, there is now a latent challenge to the naval and air power of the United States stemming from the Asian provinces of the USSR as well as from the northern islands seized from the Japanese at the end of World War II. Likewise, the strong Soviet position casts a long shadow over Japan. That powerful display of military might serves many purposes, such as the assertion of Soviet presence in the area stretching from Northeast Asia down the China Sea to Southeast Asia, and possibly beyond to the Indian Ocean and the Middle East. It can also be used to apply pressure on the PRC both along the coastline and on land in Laos, Kampuchea, and Vietnam when increased activities are taking place. It undoubtedly holds a strategic command over the sea-lane installations at Cam Ranh Bay and Danang. Could anyone fail to perceive this as a threat to the security of many individual nations, as well as a threat to the stability of the entire region?

With respect to the USSR, there is no divergence of perception among ASEAN members. They all recognize that the USSR represents a potential threat by itself as well as by its rivalry with other competing powers, such as the PRC or the United States. They also deduce from that conclusion, that the root cause is the inconsistency of U.S. policy, which at one time threw its full weight into the Vietnam War, then abruptly decided at Guam to proclaim opposite policy, the Nixon doctrine of disengagement. That encouraged the USSR to step in to fill the power vacuum in Southeast Asia, where it has built its position in Vietnam, Laos, and Kampuchea ever since.

The concern of Southeast Asian governments lies rather with the rivalry between the USSR and the PRC because of the possible destabilizing effects for the entire region. Once the USSR had stepped into Indochina, it hastened to consolidate its position and promptly saw the advantage of using Indochina as a point of pressure on China's southern flank. The local forces of those countries have been strengthened with modern Soviet equipment and trained by Soviet cadres and instructors. Electronic monitoring has been directed toward neighbors to the east and west. Other activities are also conducted from the main naval and air bases in Vietnam that relate to the operations of the United States. Such rivalries, actual or potential, can constitute threats to the peace and tranquility of the region that no one can neglect. In addition, although assertions that the USSR will not export revolution have often been heard, they cannot lull anyone into complacency because this pledge does not exclude Soviet willingness to support by various means the transformation of the present-day societies into socialist or Marxist ones.

There is still no consensus on which represents the most urgent threat, Vietnam or the PRC. To some countries the latter appears more ominous, possibly because of its size and its past proclivity to get involved in the internal affairs of others, especially in political and ideological matters. The fact that Vietnam has sent troops outside its borders and has installed by force of arms a government of its choice in place of another one, however, obviously gives rise to fears that if Vietnam can intervene militarily in Kampuchea, it may also try to interfere elsewhere. This kind of threat is not merely an imagined one.

So far the countries of the region and ASEAN in particular have faced the threat with equanimity. Although they are not willing to yield to the threat and remain firm in their legitimate and reasonable position, they have kept the door open for dialogue. If no compromise or solution has yet been reached, it is probably because certain larger powers have no immediate interest in helping to reach an agreement. They may even find an advantage in prolonging the conflict.

The question arises whether problems like that of Kampuchea do or do not constitute a threat to the peace and stability of the region. The answer can only be in the affirmative. The lack of solution or agreement on questions such as the one mentioned here is undoubtedly a destabilizing factor that should be removed by reasonable considerations, not by yielding to force.

A close look at the situation will reveal a few important elements that we can ill afford to neglect. First, the Kampuchean problem, with its threat to Southeast Asia, will persist as long as Vietnamese troops are camping in that country. Second, those alien troops will occupy Kampuchea, fighting there and threatening to spill over into neighboring lands, as long as they are sustained financially and militarily by a major power—in this case the USSR. That power is conducting a two-pronged policy. On the one hand, it seeks to foster a socialist or Marxist society everywhere by various means, open or concealed, economic, political, or military; on the other, it wants to gain recognition, goodwill, and respect as a superpower from noncommunist nations. So far this double-barreled policy has succeeded with certain Asian nations eager to receive aid and sustenance in their development; but it has not made many inroads into Southeast Asia, where the USSR has been told in no certain terms that it will have to choose between the two. If the USSR continues to support Marxist states that undermine Asian societies and peristently destabilize the region, it will not win goodwill and approval there. On the contrary, it will be looked on with suspicion. Our efforts should be concentrated on making the USSR realize that good relations with noncommunist ASEAN countries represent, notably in terms of trade, economic, and political benefits, a greater value than the military facilities in Vietnam. This undoubtedly represents an uphill task as long as the U.S.-Soviet rivalry and the PRC-USSR feuding remain intense. However difficult that task may be, the security and welfare of the nations in this region are too important to ignore.

3

Soviet Strategy in Asia: A U.S. Perspective

Jacquelyn K. Davis

Soviet politicoeconomic and military policies toward the Asian-Pacific basin states form part of a global strategy characterized by several broad objectives: (1) to enhance the security of the USSR by developing a network of buffer states along its borders; (2) to decouple, politically and militarily, the United States from its allies and friends in the region; and (3) to extend Soviet influence over strategically important Third World states. Relying heavily on economic incentives—primarily in the form of aid agreements, offers of friendships, and even security guarantees—the USSR has sought to increase its political influence in Africa, the Middle East, and Asia.

By virtue of its geostrategic setting, the USSR has always had interests in the Asian-Pacific area and specifically in East Asia. In the aftermath of the U.S. debacle in Vietnam and the subsequent drawdown of U.S. forces and logistical infrastructure in the region, the USSR has been expanding and modernizing its Asian-Pacific forces. Whereas Soviet involvement in the Asian-Pacific region could, in the two decades following World War II, be explained in terms of the defensive strategic-military requirements of the USSR, over the last decade this defensive strategy seemingly has given way to an offensive one designed not just to contain the People's Republic of China (PRC), but also to extend Soviet influence far into the Asian-Pacific basin region. In seeking to contain what is perceived in Moscow to be the Chinese threat to the USSR itself, and at the same time to erode Chinese attempts to enhance Beijing's influence in regional affairs, the USSR has adopted a two-pronged strategy designed to encircle the PRC by establishing a network of hostile buffer states around its periphery. This includes attempts to increase Soviet influence in Mongolia and in Vietnam, Laos, and Cambodia, as well as in India and Afghanistan. A second aspect of this strategy concerns the modernization and expansion of Soviet military power as the basis for a carrot-stick diplomacy in the region. As has been suggested elsewhere, "[i]t can be correctly asserted that in some instances, and particularly in northeast Asia, the Soviet Union is substituting (military) power for political weakness."[1]

A major element of Soviet strategy in Asia has been the progressive erosion of China's relationship with its southern neighbor, Vietnam. In the wake of the U.S. withdrawal from South Vietnam and the subsequent consolidation of Vietnam by North Vietnamese forces, the USSR was in a position to offer economic aid for postwar reconstruction and development of the country. Probably because the Vietnamese perceived Moscow—on the basis of a combination of geographical, cultural, and historical factors—to be less of a threat to their security interests than China, the government in Hanoi was quick to accept the Soviet offer in return for diplomatic support of Moscow's political initiatives on a wide range of issues. The Soviet-Vietnamese relationship entered a new, more intimate phase afer the armed confrontation between Vietnam and Kampuchea, which resulted in a de facto alliance between the Chinese and the Pol Pot regime. With the termination of all Chinese economic assistance to Vietnam and renewed support from the USSR, including an offer of full membership for Hanoi in the Council for Mutual Economic Assistance (CMEA) in June 1978, Vietnamese policies were designed to support Soviet interests in the region. The institutionalization of the Soviet-Vietnamese relationship in Council for Mutual Economic Assistance (COMECOM) carries with it long-term implications for the future relationship of these two nations beyond the apparent trade and aid benefits. Together with the People's Republic of Mongolia, which was also drawn by the Soviets into COMECOM, Vietnam is guaranteed of a long-term economic relationship with the USSR and its Eastern European allies, providing the basis for a regional economic unit that could subordinate nationalist tendencies to the higher, institutionalized loyalty owed to the USSR.

Confirmation of the development of a new stage in Soviet-Vietnamese relations came on 3 November 1978 with the signing of a Treaty of Friendship and Cooperation. Whether this pact was a Soviet response to the Sino-Japanese Peace Treaty of August 1978, or whether Moscow or Hanoi—for reasons having to do with Vietnam's relationship with Moscow—had pressed for such an arrangement prior to that time, is uncertain. It is clear, however, that both countries had been decisive in terms of their respective strategies and objectives in the region. The overt challenge to the PRC was evident, as was the implicit understanding that military power could be used in support of Soviet and/or Vietnamese regional objectives. In this context, two considerations may have dominated Soviet thinking with respect to the formalization of a security tie to Vietnam. The first related to a calculated risk that Moscow's credibility as an ally could be demonstrated with relatively little cost to the USSR (that is, support for Vietnamese military action against the Chinese-backed regime in Kampuchea). The second—and probably the quid pro quo in negotiations—concerned Soviet access to Vietnam's naval and airbase facilities, which was finally realized in February 1979, after the Chinese intervention in Vietnam. Yet, even as the end of the decade of the 1970s saw the buildup of Soviet military force in the region, Moscow's use of Vietnamese facilities was intitially limited to small naval deployments off Vietnam, aerial reconnaissance of the Gulf of Tonkin, and small-arms resupply. It may have been that negotiations with the United

States on strategic-arms limitations (SALT II), which were entering a crucial stage, prompted Soviet restraint in support of its Asian ally. More likely, however, was Moscow's perception of the potential impact on the noncommunist states in the region of what was seen as Chinese aggression. That Vietnam's Danang and Cam Ranh Bay bases and Kampuchea's Kampong Som base have not yet come under Soviet control is less important than the fact that these facilities are available to the USSR. More recently, in 1981, it was reported that the USSR has constructed a communications station at Danang and an electronic intercept station in Cam Ranh Bay.[2] Reportedly this latter facility has the capability to intercept both Chinese internal communications and U.S. naval signals traffic. Thus it has been suggested by some Western analysts that the cost to the USSR of supporting its Vietnamese ally—estimated at an average of $3 million a day—may be of less significance than the potential politicostrategic benefits that Moscow has derived from this relationship.

In cementing its relationship with the Vietnamese, however, the USSR has had to endure the evident increase in suspicion and distrust among many of the states in the Asian-Pacific region. It appears that at this stage the USSR regards as less important the potential for alienation by nations in Northeast and Southeast Asia than the strategic advantage wrought by cooperation with Vietnam. Through its Vietnamese proxy, the USSR has been able to extend its influence into Laos and Kampuchea in Southeast Asia, and thus to extend its presence on China's southern border.[3] Perhaps even more important from its perspective as a global power, access to—and perhaps control of—the region's important sea-lines of communication promises to yield greater benefits in its adversary relationship with the United States.

From a geostrategic perspective, the forward development of Soviet maritime power in the Asian-Pacific basin holds several attractions for the USSR in its pursuit of a changing global correlation of forces. With the signing of the SALT I Anti-Ballistic Missile (ABM) Treaty and Interim Agreement on Offensive Weapons Launchers, the codification of Soviet strategic-nuclear parity with the United States was confirmed. The perceived U.S. loss of strategic superiority over the USSR increased the importance to the West of regional-force balances in the principal theaters of potential conflict around the world. In contrast, from the Soviet perspective, the codification of strategic parity—together with the deployment of quantitatively and qualitatively superior forces in important global regions—could strengthen its position by contributing to doubts in third countries about the willingness of the United States to sustain overseas security commitments.

The politicopsychological dimension of the projection of power through the deployment of superior military forces is an important element of Soviet global strategy and tactics. Located almost at the center of the Eurasian continent, the USSR regarded a buildup of military forces in the Pacific Far East military districts as necessary following the escalation of the Sino-Soviet dispute and the rapprochement between the United States and China, on the one hand, and Japan and the PRC on the other. Accordingly, the Soviet Pacific fleet has been reinforced with additional warships, whose total tonnage was estimated in 1980 at 140,000 tons.[4] Noteworthy in this regard was the delivery in July 1979 of the Minsk VSTOL aircraft carrier, the *Petropavlovsk*, a Kara-class cruiser, and the *Ivan Rogov*, the first of a new class of amphibious-assault transport docks. Soviet naval aviation and long-range air forces in the Pacific Far East Command have been modernized with the deployment of the nuclear-capable *Backfire* bomber; ground forces have been augmented with changes in the divisional structure that include the deployment of T-72 tanks and modernized armored fighting vehicles. The Japanese Defense Agency's 1981 White Paper estimates the ground-troop strength of the USSR to be 184 divisions, with 51 of them deployed along the Sino-Soviet border and 39 of the 51 divisions in the Far Eastern military districts (the Far East Zabaikal and Mongolian).[5]

In terms of the East-West relationship, however, probably the most significant development has been the deployment in the Far Eastern portions of the USSR of the SS-20 intermediate-range ballistic missile. Reportedly a highly accurate missile system, which carries three independently targeted reentry vehicles, the SS-20 is said to be targeted against important counterforce aim points in Japan, China, and presumably South Korea. The alleged capacity of the SS-20 to strike U.S. allies and friends in Northeast Asia preemptively, with little warning, has contributed to perceptions in the region of a changed strategic environment in which the growth of Soviet conventional and maritime forces is perceived as even more alarming by states in the region whose leaders have also viewed with alarm the progressive drawdown of U.S. forces and basing facilities in the Asian-Pacific basin. This is in sharp contrast to the qualitative and quantitative growth of Soviet forces, as well as to the search by the USSR for a forward-basing structure in the region. In Northeast Asia, Soviet forces have established a presence in Kunashiri, Etorofu, and Shikotan, the northern so-called lost territories of Japan.[6] Basing facilities have been constructed on Kunashiri and Etorofu and construction is now underway on Shikotan island.[7] In addition, the USSR reportedly has access to Najin on the North Korean coast. Beyond the presumed objective of intimidating Japan and the Republic of South Korea, the augmentation of Soviet forces in the Far East serves to threaten nascent Chinese military capabilities and, at the same time, provide greater protection for the developing economic-industrial infrastructure of the Siberian portions of the USSR.

It is clear from the military-political literature of the USSR that in recent years its Pacific-Far Eastern regions are regarded as of greater importance because of the abundance of mineral resources, including natural-gas fields, but also because of its potential for population dispersal away from the densely populated European regions of the USSR. For a nation that adheres to a strategy of deterrence emphasizing the synergism of offensive and defensive measures, the capacity to disperse population away from areas that are seen as the likely targets of an enemy attack rates as a significant, if only secondary, rationale in the development and defense of this region.[8]

Viewed in the context of Soviet attempts to expand Moscow's influence in Southeast Asia, the deployments of the USSR in Northeast Asia take on an ominous character. Together with the three major naval bases of Vladivostok, Nakhodka, and Sovetskaya Gavan', on the western seaboard of the Sea of Japan; with Moscow's access to the North Korean bases of Wonsan and Najin; and with the establishment of a military presence on the Kuril Islands, the Sea of Okhotsk has become virtually a protected sea, giving Soviet shipping assured access to the Pacific Ocean. The southward deployment of Soviet forces can be explained in the context of the relationship between the Far East and Indian Ocean theaters. Using basing facilities in Vietnam, the USSR has demonstrated that it can sustain a presence simultaneously in the western Pacific and the Indian Oceans. With a capacity to operate in these two interrelated areas, the USSR has attained a capability to menace the important shipping lanes from the Straits of Malacca to the Sea of Japan and to challenge the maritime approaches to Australia and New Zealand. By its ability to threaten those vital sea routes and choke points (such as the Straits of Malacca), the USSR holds the potential to exert influence over nations whose survival depends on access to those sea-lanes.[9]

Presumably the use of military power to close sea-lanes of communication in the Asian-Pacific region is the least preferred option of the USSR. More likely, Moscow seeks control over the sea-lanes of the Pacific and Northeast and Southeast Asia by means of its influence over the states in the region. Toward that end, the USSR has sought to exert influence over the ASEAN states, in particular—because of the important geostrategic location of these countries astride the supply routes for resource-dependent Japan—and in that way to pressure Asian nations to support Moscow's politicodiplomatic initiatives. Thus the USSR has had to adjust its attitude toward ASEAN, which was initially condemned by Moscow as an anticommunist military alliance and "a union for rallying the Vietnam war participants."[10] From the Soviet perspective, Moscow has long sought to protect the ASEAN nations against the expansionist designs of the PRC and its U.S. and Japanese partners. In seeking to improve relations with the ASEAN nations, moreover, Moscow has voiced support for ASEAN's role in contributing to the peace and stability of the region. Yet the USSR remains cool to the ASEAN proposal for a Zone of Peace, Freedom, and Neutrality (ZOPFAN) in the region. Instead, it has endeavored to attract ASEAN support for its proposal for a collective-security system in Asia. In its latest manifestation, this proposal includes the use by Soviet vessels of port facilities in ASEAN states.[11]

Although membership in Moscow's proposed system is ostensibly open to all countries in the region, those singled out for mention in the original proposal provide clues to Soviet intentions. With India, Pakistan, Afghanistan, Burma, Singapore, and Cambodia as important members of the proposed system, the focus on strategic access to the Indian Ocean and subcontinent was evident. In a subsequent Radio Moscow broadcast in August 1969, it was declared that "India, Pakistan and Afghanistan would form the nucleus of the [collective security] system, which would eventually embrace all countries from the Middle East to Japan."[12] Subsequently, so-called Soviet friendship treaties with India (1971), Iraq (1972), Afghanistan (1978), and Vietnam (1978) provided the basis for the extension of Moscow's influence in the region, but also a foundation for the realization of its Asian security system.[13] The invasions of Afghanistan by the USSR and of Kampuchea by Moscow's Vietnamese proxy can be assessed in terms of the Soviet interest in controlling access to the Persian Gulf and the Straits of Malacca, the key arteries for transport of Middle Eastern oil to Western Europe and Japan, in addition to the major trade routes for the Asian nations. Moreover, two of the world's greatest ports—Singapore and Hong Kong—are located close to the southern and northern approaches to the South China Sea. The straits afford access to the South China Sea, which, in addition to its strategic military significance, is believed to contain rich mineral deposits (especially oil). For this reason and because of conflicting claims over possession of the island groups in the South China Sea (notably the Paracel and Spratly Islands),[14] the area seems ripe for Soviet meddling, the ultimate objective being domination of the region by Soviet-sponsored forces or so-called neutralist nations as a means of linking the Indian Ocean and Pacific Far East subregions. Naval and air supremacy in the South China Sea would also enhance the position of the USSR in its attempts to exert political pressure against the Philippines, presumably with the objective of removing the U.S. military presence from that island chain.[15] Such a strategy—whether or not it succeeds in its ultimate objective of decoupling the United States from its friends and allies in the region—would effectively sever the links among the members of ASEAN by isolating Thailand and western Malaysia from the rest of the group. In recent months, the late Soviet President Leonid Brezhnev has expressed a "readiness to establish and strengthen relations of friendship and cooperation with Indonesia, Malaysia, and all peaceloving countries."[16] Playing on Asian fears of China's long-term foreign-policy objectives in the region, Moscow and

Hanoi have muted their criticisms of Singapore and Thailand and have, at the same time, sought to increase informal contacts with the ASEAN nations. According to one analyst, the signal from Moscow seems to be "that patient diplomacy and discreet contacts rather than military pressure should be used to soften up Asian opposition" to Soviet and Soviet-sponsored moves in the region.[17]

In contradistinction, however, the Soviet intervention in Afghanistan and the Vietnamese incursion into Kampuchea clearly represent not isolated, regional incidents, but rather aspects of a Soviet global strategy that increasingly involves the projection and use of military power in regions beyond Soviet shores in the pursuit of specific foreign-policy objecives.[18] Just as the timing and tactics of Moscow's invasion of Afghanistan were doubtless dictated by domestic developments in that country, so the overt employment of Soviet military power suggests that Moscow will no longer tolerate foreign- or domestic-policy independence in nations perceived as essential to the security of the USSR itself. The statements by President Brezhnev in February 1980 justifying the Soviet military intervention in Afghanistan provided an extension outside of Europe of the Brezhnev Doctrine, which legitimized (from the Soviet perspective) Moscow's use of armed forces in a fraternal nation (first Czechoslovakia) to protect the socialist cause. Consequently, it is reasonable to assume that the Soviet presence in Afghanistan and Southeast Asia will be a protracted one and, when possible, at the expense of the PRC and the noncommunist nations of the region. Armed confrontation by the USSR on a major scale in the region is unlikely, but it is likely that Moscow's support of proxy warfare (through its Vietnamese ally and also through the support of so-called progressive revolutionary elements in noncommunist nations) will persist. The Soviet pursuit of such indirect tactics will be enlarged by the overt extension and buildup of Soviet military power in the region, supplemented by a range of economic and diplomatic initiatives aimed at detaching the nations of that diverse region from their respective ties to the West and the United States.

Notes

1. Robert A. Scalapino, "Containment and Countercontainment: The Current Stage of Sino-Soviet Relations," in *China, the Soviet Union and the West*, ed. Douglas T. Stuart and William T. Tow (Boulder, Colo.: Westview Press, 1982), p. 166.

2. See Takashi Tajima, *China and South-east Asia: Strategic Interests and Policy Prospects*, Adelphi Paper 172, (London: International Institute for Strategic Studies, 1982), pp. 15, 31.

3. Reportedly, on 11 July 1981 the USSR signed a treaty on economic and trade cooperation with Kampuchea. See "USSR Signs Agreement Establishing Trade System," *Foreign Broadcast Information Service* (FBIS), East Asia and the Pacific, 14 July 1981, p. H1.

4. *Defense of Japan 1980 White Paper*, p. 50. The Defense Agency's 1981 White Paper estimates the strength of the Soviet Pacific Fleet at 800 ships, including subsidiary ones.

5. The U.S. Department of Defense estimates Soviet ground troop strength at more than 180 divisions, with 45 divisions assigned to the Asian regions of the USSR.

6. Reportedly, the USSR has established a new Air Force Command on the island of Sakhalin. Establishment of this command follows a reported buildup of Soviet aircraft, particularly MIG-23 and MIG-27 *Floggers*, on the northern islands. See "Japan Claims New U.S.S.R. Command," *Strategy Week*, 26 October-1 November 1981, p. 6.

7. Whereas the precise size of Soviet units deployed on the Japanese northern islands is unknown, estimates of up to a divisional level have been projected by U.S. and Japanese defense officials. In addition to guns (130-mm cannons), antiaircraft guns, and armored personnel carriers deployed on the islands, Western intelligence sources have observed troop exercises that have included the use of MI-24 attack helicopters and, more recently, the *Ivan Rogov* assault landing craft.

8. Particularly noteworthy in this regard is the development of the Baikal-Amur Mainline (BAM) railway system, which will facilitate the transfer of troops from the east to the western fronts of the USSR. The double tracking of the Siberian Railway and the expansion of Siberian (and Sakhalin-Kuril) military facilities further support this supposition.

9. It is interesting to note in this regard that two squadrons of swing-wing MIG-23 interceptors have apparently been deployed at Kep airbase, north of Hanoi, and at the former U.S. base of Kontum in the central highlands of Vietnam. These deployments coincide "with the return from the Soviet Union of 24 Vietnamese pilots after 18 months special training. While the squadron at Kep is expected to act as a deterrent against further Chinese invasions, the Kontum-based aircraft could provide air cover for Soviet ships and aircraft in Cam Ranh Bay and Da Nang, and parts of Laos and Cambodia." "Hanoi Rules the Skies," *Far Eastern Economic Review* (Intelligence), 11 December 1981, p. 7. In early 1981 Australian intelligence sources reported that the USSR's deployment of the TU-22M *Backfire* bomber at Cam Ranh Bay, Vietnam, was imminent. William T. Tow, "ANZUS and American Security," *Survival* 23, no. 6 (November-December 1981):262.

10. Tajima, *China and South-east Asia*, p. 31.

11. The original proposal for an Asian collective-security system was first floated in the Soviet press (*Izvestiya*, 28 May 1969) by political com-

mentator Vikenty Matveyev. Since then proposals for Asian collective-security systems have intermittently been put forth by the USSR. In February 1981, at the Twenty-sixth Congress of the Communist Party of the Soviet Union, Secretary Brezhnev himself alluded to the development of an Asian collective-security system. More recently, in the Communist-party-controlled newspaper *Izvestiya*, an article reviewing the international situation in the Far East again referred to the Soviet proposal for an Asian collective-security system, calling it an initiative "aimed at safeguarding security both in Asia as a whole and the Far East." See S. Agaforov and V. Gansha, "The Far East: Two Courses, Two Objectives," *Izvestiya*, 10 May 1982 (Reprinted in *Foreign Broadcast Information Service (FBIS)*, Soviet Union, 14 May 1982, pp. CC 3-6.)

12. See Marian K. Leighton, "Soviets in Asia: Evolution of a Blueprint," *The Wall Street Journal*, 12 February 1981.

13. It should be noted that in February 1978 the USSR endeavored to get Japan to accede to a similar document, in all probability to counter Japan's impending rapprochement with the PRC. Failing in this diplomatic initiative, the USSR turned to another diplomatic instrument—the projection of its military power in the seas off of Japan, including the establishment of a presence on the northern territories (of Japan) in an apparent effort to intimidate or influence Japanese foreign policy and diplomacy.

14. An excellent assessment of the conflicting claims over these island groupings may be found in David Jenkins, "Trouble over Oil and Waters," *Far Eastern Economic Review*, 7 August 1981, pp. 24-26.

15. The USSR has proposed, to the Philippine government the development of joint fishing and shipping ventures. Such overtures have so far been rejected by the Philippine government, which has warned that such a deal could result in "possible interference with our communications network, monitoring of the movement of the United States naval vessels in and out of Subic [Bay] and possible contacts with subversive areas of the country." See "Philippines Wary of USSR Venture," *Strategy Week*, 28 September-4 October 1981, p. 5.

16. Nayan Chanda, "Summit Discretion," *Far Eastern Economic Review*, 18 September 1981, p. 13.

17. Ibid., p. 13.

18. In this respect, it is important to note that Soviet efforts to extend Moscow's influence into the Asian/Pacific region have extended to the South Pacific as well. So far, however, incipient Soviet (and Chinese) penetrations into Tonga, Western Samoa, and the Cook Islands have been checked by "timely military and economic assistance to these states" by Australia and New Zealand in particular, as well as "by their extensive training of South Pacific political and military elites, and by their support for intra-regional peace-keeping activities in *Vanriatu* and in other locales." Tow, "ANZUS," p. 268.

4 Security in East Asia-Pacific

Bernard K. Gordon with *Lloyd R. Vasey*

This chapter presents the results of a study tour of eight East Asian and Pacific countries undertaken in mid-1981 by Rear Admiral (Ret.) L.R. Vasey, executive director of the Pacific Forum and by Professor Bernard K. Gordon of the University of New Hampshire.[1] Drawing on their combined backgrounds in all the nations of the Asia-Pacific region, the authors met in each capital (as well as in Sydney and Hong Kong) with the foreign ministers and other cabinet ministers; senior military officers; foreign-ministry and defense-ministry senior staff; university specialists and those in related research institutes; bankers; businessmen; prominent journalists; and certain opposition-party and other informed persons. In addition, meetings were held with the U.S. ambassadors and other embassy officials in Tokyo, Manila, Bangkok, Singapore, Kuala Lumpur, Jakarta, and Canberra. More than a hundred such meetings took place from 13 July through 18 August 1981. In some cases, in order to bring together an especially wide range of views, group seminars and discussions were convened. All told, we met with several hundred people with relevant expertise and responsibilities.

It quickly became clear during those meetings that there are indeed important cross-national differences in perceptions of security threats. In some cases these differences suggest significant public-policy issues that deserve wide attention, and the purpose of this chapter is to identify briefly some of the major concerns that emerged in mid-1981.

Security in the East Asian Context

Before focusing on problems that any of the East Asian states may face, it is important to remember that compared with any other part of the world—and certainly with any other developing region—East Asia is largely a success story. It is a region of successes already accomplished—as in the case of Japan and increasingly that of Singapore—and of successes that are within reach.[2] In terms of overall economic performance, even the worst achiever in the group, the Philippines, has an annual growth of approximately 6.5 percent that in any other part of the world would be regarded as an undreamed-of accomplishment.

Among the other ASEAN nations, annual increases in gross national product (GNP) are normally higher than 7.5 percent and sometimes exceed 8 percent. South Korea in recent years has experienced even higher figures—10 percent and more—and its entrepreneurs and builders are now active in other developing regions as exporters of heavy equipment, ships, and infrastructure-related construction. Indeed, in several capitals we visited during July-August, the bloom was still on in connection with an impressive tour that President Chun had recently undertaken to the ASEAN nations. South Korea would like to supplant Japan as a supplier of ASEAN's industrial needs, and the prospects for an important North-South economic complementarity are very promising, not least because South Korea has the motivation and wherewithal and because ASEAN's great size and prosperity add to the logic of the connection.

Two points must be made about the rapidity of East Asia's economic growth. First, it reflects a general shift in the center of world affairs to the Pacific region. Americans will have to get used to the idea that in trade, for example, more U.S. commerce now moves across the Pacific than the Atlantic. Beyond that, the dynamism of contemporary East Asia poses a separate intellectual problem when security issues are considered; Americans may find it especially difficult to make the conceptual adjustment. This is because there has been no period since 1945, and particularly since the attack on South Korea in 1950, in which the United States has not been concerned heavily and often passionately with issues of security in East Asia.

It was, after all, the outbreak of the Korean War that hastened the signing of bilateral U.S. security treaties with Japan, the Philippines, Australia, and New Zealand—and of course Taiwan. The same period saw the series of events beginning with U.S. financing of the French effort in the first Indochina War that led to the establishment of the South East Asia Treaty Organization (SEATO). Ultimately, that U.S. inolvement in Indochina led to the highest postwar level of U.S. involvement in East Asia: the war in Vietnam. That war required a significant U.S. military role for almost fifteen years and sensitized an entire generation of Americans to Asia as a place of relevant security problems and dangers.

Against that generation-long background, it is hardly surprising that when Americans in this era think of East Asia, they see principally a scene of troubles and a field for great-power conflict. That perception is underscored by some of the events that have characterized the region even since the end of the Vietnam War. There has been increasing attention to Japan's defense debate and a growing belief in the United States that the Soviet presence in the Pacific calls for increases in Japan's defense spending. There has also been Vietnam's invasion of Cambodia and the resulting so-called punishment of Vietnam by China. Those events were pictured in the United States principally in terms of a Sino-Soviet proxy war. They served as a vivid reminder that although the Vietnam War may have come to an end in 1975, Indochina remains in conflict.

Although it may therefore be understandable that Americans approach East Asia with security issues foremost in their thinking, it is also evident that Asians themselves do not. One of the most striking findings of the study tour is that security issues do not have high salience among Asian leaders. This is noteworthy, given that almost all the discussions were with people for whom military and foreign affairs are in one way or another a professional responsibility. Had we met with officials involved in more clearly domestic areas of public policy, security threats would certainly have been even more remote from their perspectives.

Asian Perceptions: Reduced and Different Threats

The point can be well illustrated by a reference to Thailand, now often termed the front-line state in the Indochina conflict. Despite the fact that this is now Asia's most intense conflict and has been given considerable attention in the United States and elsewhere, the attitude in Thailand itself would have to be described as relaxed. Indeed, leading Thai believe that in terms of a perception of serious threats to national security, it is not so much in the present as in the 1975-1976 period—particularly the first few months after the fall of Saigon—that Thailand has experienced a challenge. Both a senior official in the Thai government and one recent cabinet minister put it to us in the same way: 1975 was a watershed year, and Bangkok was indeed apprehensive in those days.

As several Thai said, however, Thailand survived that time of shock and looks at its environment today with equanimity and even optimism. For example, the issue of Vietnamese ambitions regarding Thailand is not taken seriously at Thai leadership levels, nor are those ambitions given credence by experienced independent observers and diplomats stationed in Bangkok. Moreover, whatever Thailand's tough posture may have been up to now in connection with the continued Vietnamese occupation of Kampuchea, it is also likely that there is no consensus, even among the Thai military, about the continued viability of that posture. Indeed, in mid-1981 publicity was being given to recent discussions in Paris between former Thai Foreign Minister Bhichai and current Vietnamese Foreign Minister Nguyen Co Thach. Through that venue, the prospect of a softer Thai approach has been given currency; and the point should be made that this represents a respectable alternative to the present and still-official hard-line public posture toward Vietnam.

Variations on the same theme were encountered in Northeast Asia, both in Korea and in Japan. In Japan, for example, one of the clearest impressions of our meetings is a widespread tendency to deemphasize the capacity for troublemaking on the part of both the USSR and China. In connection with China, in particular, its capacities for initiatives of any kind have been greatly downgraded by the Japanese. This probably reflects the close contact with the Chinese economy to which so many Japanese have been exposed in the three years since full normalization of ties in 1978. Major attention has been given in Japan to China's cancellation and deferment of many contracts with Japanese firms, and this has had its impact. Although Japan expects to continue a broad-gauged economic relationship with the Chinese, the view is prevalent now in Tokyo that China is an essentially backward state with enormous problems of organization and infrastructure.

Japanese attitudes toward the USSR in this period are much more complex and are heavily overshadowed by the high attention to what is seen as Soviet intransigence on the issue of the so-called northern territories (the four main islands and associated islets north of Hokkaido). Moreover, the Japanese have followed—possibly even more closely than the Americans—the growth of Soviet naval power in the Pacific. At informed levels, all are aware of the Soviet pattern of calling in to the facilities made available to them in Vietnam (at Cam Ranh Bay and at Danang). Nevertheless, almost all the Japanese with whom we met were concerned to put Soviet power into perspective.

In this perspective, the major problem addressed by the Japanese is a concern that the Soviet threat (to Japan and to Pacific stability generally) not be overemphasized. There is special awareness in Japan of the relative weakness of the Soviet economy, probably reflecting the fact that Moscow so strenuously seeks to attract Japan's heavy-construction expertise, finance, and other assistance in connection with its Siberian development needs. This is closely connected to the question of Soviet ability to project significant forces in the Pacific region, for the Japanese are familiar with the long and tenuous supply line on which Vladivostok and other Soviet Pacific ports depend. The BAM (Baikal-Amur Mainline railway) is still not completed, and Soviet forces therefore remain tied to a single-track rail link from the Urals to the Pacific that comes perilously close to the Chinese border.

The Japanese emphasize, moreover, the extent to which—in their view—the USSR has given other regions higher priority. Europe and the Persian Gulf, with the added complications of the Polish problem and the Afghanistan involvement, are seen as the major foci of Soviet attention and the principal drains on Soviet capacities.[3] Japan's low assessment of China's potential threat to Soviet interests further persuades Tokyo that the Soviets too must have downgraded this worry. In this connection, one of

Japan's leading strategic specialists pointed to recent conversations he has had in China, where he met with, among others, the PLA vice-chief of staff. He stated that China's decision to reduce its military expenditures was powerful added evidence of the reduced estimate of a Soviet threat.

In this and other conversations in Tokyo, there was a related emphasis on the USSR's internal problems. Among the issues identified were those of political succession, economic mismanagement, and the challenge implicit in Soviet demographic trends: the relatively much higher birthrates among the USSR's non-Russian nationalities. This is likely both to dilute Russian control of the Soviet state and to reduce overall industrial and military capacity in the midrange future. Japanese who monitor Soviet developments closely are acutely aware of these trends and are reinforced in their increasingly low estimate of Soviet capabilities by a separate but related sentiment now evident in Japan.

There is a certain smugness in Japan about the failure of all foreigners to cope effectively with modern industrial challenges. This affects Japan's assessment of the USSR, among others. The Japanese, having pulled themselves up by the bootstraps over the past thirty-five years, and enjoying a prosperity that allows their opinion makers to travel everywhere and see firsthand the best that Europe and the United States can boast, feel increasingly confident that the rest of the world has little to teach Japan. The USSR, which so starkly trails behind the West in so much, tends in this perspective to be even further discounted in Japanese eyes.

This is not the place to attempt a full-scale analysis of the contradictions and ambivalence of Japanese views on these issues. The point is that although traditionally the Japanese are exceedingly insecure and share a long-standing and general dislike of Russians and the USSR in particular, we found strong evidence of a tendency in Japan to discount the salience of any realistic foreign threat. This development deserves careful examination; and any analysis must assess carefully both the reasons that are given and those that may be unstated for deemphasizing Japan's concerns about a possible Soviet threat.

It may be, for example, that Japan's very success in avoiding a buildup of its defense capacities has led to a false sense of security. For many years Japanese opinion has been exposed to arguments designed to resist pressures for too sharp an increase in defense capacity. One result is that those who now warn that the environment warrants a change can expect to encounter much doubt. Especially in the light of the well-known Japanese belief that the United States has been demanding too quick a pace for Japan's rearmament, Americans in particular will be told—as we were—that Washington exaggerates the Soviet threat.

There are, of course, internal reasons as well for downplaying concerns about the USSR and for seeking to avoid the growth of what is called defense consciousness in Japanese public thinking. Many oppose a perspective that they believe will unleash strong pressures for increased defense spending and, they fear, will lead to a much more active role in world politics than, in their view, Japan can or should sustain. Others, fearful of the consequences for *domestic* politics that accompanied Japan's last experiment with a high posture in foreign and military affairs—an era in which civil and political liberties were severely restrained—have different reasons to resist. Still others believe that Japan simply has too many unmet internal needs to allocate significant sums for defense at this time.

Outside Japan many observers discount all these factors. They prefer, to explain Japan's deemphasis on the Soviet problem with a narrow economic argument. In that view, Japan now understates the potential threat from Moscow largely because Tokyo seeks to maintain good business ties there. Yet there is good reason to believe that many Japanese genuinely do fear what is seen as the growing polarization in world politics. In this light, a Japanese posture that deemphasizes the Soviet threat stems from a desire to avoid provoking the USSR needlessly.

One straw in the wind is the leadership's evident discomfort with the word *alliance* to describe Japan's relationship with the United States (however precisely accurate that term may be). Another is the clear apprehension in Tokyo of a too close U.S. connection with China. Many Japanese are concerned, in other words, about the dangers of seeming to pose to the USSR an environment of too much constraint—and their reasons stem less from a belief in Soviet strength than from a concern about a deep and foreboding weakness in the USSR. The Japanese are in the forefront of those who are concerned about what can be called the cornered-dog syndrome in dealing with Moscow—a belief that the long-term prospects for the USSR are not bright and, for that reason, a fear that the next several years may be the most demanding of all in dealing with Moscow.

For example, professors Coral Bell of the Australian National University and Robert Tucker in the United States are among a growing number who take a position strongly consistent with important Japanese thinking about the USSR. In this view, it is Moscow itself that is most acutely aware of its long-term difficulties and for that reason may see itself entering a now-or-never window of opportunities that will soon shut. Professor Bell wrote recently that this window may exist only until the mid- or late 1980s. Tucker regards the period, which he warns can be extremely dangerous, as somewhat longer, perhaps through the end of the century.[4] Those Japanese who share this conceptual estimate of Moscow's situation are concerned not to see their government or its close friends undertake policies that will either bring us close to the period of greatest danger or add to its tensions as we enter the window.

Accordingly, it is common now to encounter Japanese cautions against adopting foreign or defense policies toward the USSR that might be regarded as too harsh—for fear that U.S. firmness will be seen as provocation and thereby become a self-fulfilling prophecy. Such an approach can lead Japan to adopt a threat assessment of the USSR sharply at variance with that held in the United States. It will probably lead increasingly to Japanese coolness about specific aspects of United States policy toward Moscow. For example, the Japanese are known to feel that Washington again failed to consult properly when it ended the Afghanistan-related grain embargo directed against the USSR. Although up to now it has been possible to paper over such specific irritants, that task will become more difficult against a background of increasingly divergent U.S.-Japanese views of the nature of the Soviet threat. Because an intimate Japanese-U.S. relationship is fundamental to global stability (and certainly to the goals of U.S. foreign policy), such a divergence in views can cause profound problems for both Tokyo and Washington.

Even in South Korea, which might be expected most closely to share U.S. perceptions of security threats, certain important divergences are now evident. North Korea is, of course, recognized as the principal adversary by Seoul's leaders; but they question how widely their perception is shared. There is a growing concern that to the present generation—those under 30—the North Korean attack in 1950 (and the resulting Korean War) represent, as it was put to us, "only a legend." Moreover, the very success of the South Korean economy, along with the obvious dispute between the USSR and China, has helped to mute the North Korean threat to which the leadership regularly points. Even among the leadership there are areas of disagreement in terms of both the severity of the threat and the circumstances that might cause it to come alive again.

As in Japan, for example, in Korea there was a barely hidden concern that U.S. policy toward the USSR might become too sharp. This must be expressed carefully, since Koreans generally welcome the change in U.S. policy adopted by the Reagan administration. It should be recalled that President Carter's announcement that he would withdraw U.S. ground forces from Korea struck considerable fear there. It was known also to be destabilizing in Japanese circles. Although the Carter administration ultimately dropped that approach, the damage was done. Accordingly, the Reagan administration's assurances that this will not be done in the near future, and the generally firmer posture that the president and former Secretary Haig adopted toward the USSR, have been appreciated in Seoul.

Nevertheless, a strong and potentially troublesome ambivalence in Korean thinking should be noted. On the one hand, many Koreans—not forgetting the Carter approach—believe the U.S. guarantee to be uncertain and seek reaffirmation. They suspect that in the event of an emergency from the north, the U.S. media (and many U.S. public figures) would argue powerfully against maintaining the U.S. guarantees to South Korea.[5] On the other hand, Koreans simultaneously worry that in its tough posture toward the USSR, the United States might go too far, with disastrous consequences for South Korea.

The thinking behind this view stems from the Korean assessment of U.S.-Soviet relations. As expressed to us at high official levels and among independent specialists, there is a growing belief that as a result of the changing nature of U.S.-Soviet relations, the main threat to South Korea emanates not so much from North Korea directly as from the USSR. The fear, in other words, is that the USSR may be tempted to repeat (though under circumstances very different from those of thirty years ago) the events of 1950.

On that occasion it was almost certainly the USSR that was principally responsible for the outbreak of the Korean War. In today's environment, Koreans believe that under certain circumstances the USSR might again perceive an essentially no-loss scenario that would lead Moscow again to promote a North Korean attack. In this view, the USSR would be prompted to take action in this era partly in order to put great pressure on China. The Chinese would be torn between coming to the support of Pyongyang, on the one hand, and risking continued friendly relations with both Japan and the United States, on the other. Indeed, a Chinese posture of support for North Korea in such circumstances would greatly undermine China's relations with the United States.

The important point about this scenario is that leading Koreans discount almost entirely the possibility that North Korea would unilaterally provoke such a conflict. Seoul estimates that Pyongyang's likely activities on its own would be limited to various kinds of harassment, probably increasingly by sea. Moreover, and especially in the light of recent Beijing-Pyongyang relations, the South Koreans do not expect China to encourage the North to undertake significant military operations. The USSR is seen as the principal source of worry, and the question now being addressed in Seoul is this: Under what circumstances might Moscow take such a rash and possibly profoundly dangerous action?

The answer in Seoul—which represents essentially what South Korea regards as its principal external security threat—is based fundamentally on the nature of U.S.-Soviet relations. Although Seoul welcomes the firmer posture toward Moscow that now characterizes U.S. policy, South Korea simultaneously hopes that this firmness will not lead to an escalation of tension. There is a fear that if Washington adopts too provocative a posture toward the USSR (for example, through the sale of significant armaments to China), then the USSR will find less and less reason to continue the restraint that has until now maintained an uneasy peace on the Korean peninsula.

The Reagan administration's posture toward detente, in other words, is seen by Korean observers as having an immediate impact on Korean security. If the USSR concludes that there is nothing of value left of detente, and sees little to gain by restraint in its dealings with the United States, then it will again seek to foment the sort of troubles for which it was responsible in an earlier era.

Much the same attitude was encountered at the highest levels in several of the ASEAN capitals. Leaders who look to the United States for security reveal a profound ambivalence about U.S. policy: a desire on the one hand to have the United States maintain a firm posture, and simultaneously a worry that U.S. missteps will escalate Asia's tensions and even bring on war. The issue is not simply the reservation, widespread in East Asia, that the United States is becoming too close to China (although that is now being said everywhere). It is instead that certain dangerous inferences are being drawn from current trends in U.S. policy. Both in Northeast Asia and in the ASEAN region, the ultimate logic we encountered—to put a fine point on it—is that to the extent that there are threats to national security discernible in the current environment, *those threats can be traced to elements in U.S. foreign policy.*

In one ASEAN capital, where we had a conversation of several hours with an official with many years of intimate responsibility for security and foreign affairs at the highest level, a variation on the same theme was encountered. Here, too, welcome and appreciation were expressed at the more realistic posture adopted by the new U.S. administration toward the USSR. Yet grave caution was expressed that this posture not go too far or be applied too crudely. This goes beyond the well-known concern among Southeast Asian leaders that the United States may have embarked on intrinsically too warm a connection with China. That prospect *is* feared because it tends implicitly to endorse China'a role in the region and to add to the legitimacy of Beijing's policies—for example, in connection with Kampuchea and Vietnam. Beyond that, Southeast Asians worry about the type of military equipment that Washington may ultimately sell or provide to the PLA. As one leader said, "We hardly care if you sell them tanks, or strategic weapons for that matter—what worries us is that you will provide them with M-16s and other small equipment that will find its way down here in the hands of local insurgents."

In a manner reminiscent of what we heard in Japan and especially in Korea, some in the ASEAN region caution that the major danger of current U.S. policy in the region, and especially in connection with China, is that it will lead Moscow to conclude that detente has been abandoned altogether. This might occasion a return to former patterns of Soviet behavior that would seek to put more pressure on Western-associated governments in ways reminiscent of the Cold War period. In Southeast Asia, some of the manifestations of such a Soviet approach would be higher levels of covert and overt assistance to disaffected elements in the rural indigenous population (for example, in Indonesia and Malaysia); to radical labor-union leaders; and among agricultural workers (for example, in the Philippines).

What is especially noteworthy about these views is the widespread tendency—especially in Japan and the ASEAN countries, much less in Korea and Australia—to regard the USSR as essentially defensive and reactive. The most common view is that the Soviet presence in East Asia and the Pacific is mainly a function of Soviet concerns with China. Some argue that it is either equally or secondarily a result of Soviet concerns with China or the United States. With some notable exceptions, however, few leaders take the position that Soviet roles in the region derive largely from independent Soviet (or for that matter, Russian) goals. Prime Minister Fraser in Australia and Deputy Prime Minister Goh Keng Swee in Singapore have long held views that approach that position, but their assessment of Soviet motivations seems a minority position among Asian leaders.

The issue is not new, and goes to the heart of one's analysis of the origins of the postwar great-power conflict. In contemporary East Asia the debate finds many manifestations, one of the sharpest at present pertaining to the meaning of the Soviet naval presence—in the Pacific generally, and in terms of Moscow's utilization of facilities at Cam Ranh Bay and Danang in particular. This issue, which of course is not easily separated from the question of Vietnam's continued occupation of Kampuchea, was one explored in scores of meetings throughout East Asia, and is worth separate identification.

The USSR, Kampuchea, and Vietnam

Our overall finding on the question of the Soviet presence in Vietnam is that East Asians are hardly concerned about it. As a U.S. ambassador in one of the ASEAN nations remarked, "The view here is that if something does not affect daily events, visibly, then it doesn't exist. The people here are not very longsighted." A foreign minister in another ASEAN capital said that the Soviet facilities in Vietnam are largely dismissed because they are so vulnerable. He emphasized the long supply lines already involved, which will be further stretched if Moscow hopes to make increasing and more intensive use of those facilities. In another ASEAN capital the foreign minister made the same point: "Cam Ranh Bay is vulnerable to your forces from Subic and Clark, just as your facilities there are vulnerable to Soviet forces based in Vladivostok."

This is the common view throughout Southeast Asia. Even in the Philippines, which has experienced numerous overflights into its air space by Soviet planes flying from Danang (approximately a hundred in the past year), the question is regarded with little concern. Generally, we encountered three explanations for the Soviet presence at the installations in Vietnam: (1) Moscow fell into a good thing and could hardly be expected not to take advantage of these former U.S. facilities; (2) the Soviet interest in the facilities is principally for reconnaissance and perhaps to make its political presence more visible; and (3) the main reason for Soviet interest in these installations is to help put pressure on China.

Each of these explanations may be correct, but what is notably missing is an alternative view: that the Soviet presence in Vietnam is quite independent of more recent Sino-Soviet troubles and stems instead from a more deep-seated and long-standing Russian aim to position forces near the South China Sea. This approach considers that Moscow's growing presence in the Pacific is rooted in the Soviet concern to be regarded as a great power—equal in global presence to any other, and strategically on a par with the United States.

This view attaches importance to the almost-forgotten speech by Chairman Brezhnev in 1969, when he outlined a Soviet aim to establish a collective-security system in Asia. Although that concept has received little attention outside the USSR (and in some cases has been derided), the fact that it has been given repeated attention by Moscow, along with the continuity and constancy of Soviet practices in Asia, suggests that it may be worthwhile to take the Asian collective-security proposal more seriously. The Soviet insistence on consolidating its hold in Afghanistan; its impressive commitment to India's economic and defense needs (including the fact that the USSR is now principally responsible for the equipping, training, and doctrine of the Indian navy); and the compelling fact that Moscow extended COMECON membership to Vietnam all suggest that Asia occupies a higher priority on Moscow's agenda than is widely believed.

Indeed, it was striking to us to hear in each capital, but especially in the ASEAN region, that East Asia (particularly Southeast Asia) is so low on the list of Soviet areas of interest as not to warrant major concern as a threat. Time and again the view was expressed that China represented the real threat, the long-term problem. For the most part, only Australia took major exception to that view, and even then not uniformly, but principally among those Australian specialists (in and out of government) who focus on the central balance. Here we did encounter a perspective on Asian security issues that is broadly familiar to important U.S. thinking.

Unlike the dominant opinion in Japan and the ASEAN region, this view regards the Soviet-Vietnam relationship as so valuable to both Hanoi and Moscow that it will not soon diminish. In this perspective, the USSR is seen as in the region to stay; and the Kampuchean conflict must be understood in that light. Even in Australia, however, those who take this position, although they may be influential at the moment, consider themselves a beleaguered minority. Their view that the Soviet presence in the Pacific is less a reaction to Chinese or U.S. hostility than the result of objective Soviet goals tends to be seen by the most vocal strand of Australian thinking as a crude return to simplistic Cold War posturing.

Much ASEAN opinion shares in that derision. Although the group has until now rallied behind the tough line urged by Singapore and Thailand—that Vietnam's conquest of Kampuchea must not be legitimized—ASEAN's internal differences on how best to reach a settlement are well known. From those differences, a majority opinion is now developing: that the Vietnamese fait accompli will have to be accepted, and that Vietnamese nationalism will aim to eject the USSR as soon as possible. A settlement in Kampuchea, it is believed, will allow the Vietnamese to achieve that ejection and thus is the key to how best to deal with the Soviets in Southeast Asia.

Those in ASEAN who share that view believe as well that what ASEAN seeks in Kampuchea is also acceptable to Vietnam: a Cambodia that, if not altogether neutral, will at least not be fully incorporated into Vietnam's sphere. Equally important, this ASEAN perspective believes (though without demonstrable evidence) that China too will have no choice other than to accept such a settlement—even if it means some form of leading role for Vietnam in all of Indochina.

Because this is the developing consensus in ASEAN, there is considerable apprehension there over aspects of U.S. policy toward China. That apprehension derives mainly from the belief that the United States, in order to achieve a better global relationship with the USSR, has been too willing to overlook East Asian and Southeast Asian fears of China. This was one of the central themes we encountered everywhere, and to it must be added a further, closely related distressing note. This is the view that the United States recognizes its weakness in global politics. That weakness is made all the more apparent to Asians precisely to the extent that Washington has concluded that it must rely on China in order to deal more effectively with the USSR.

Southeast Asians see this tendency in the tacit and even explicit U.S. support for the Chinese position in the Kampuchean conflict. They fear this further stiffens Beijing in its campaign to bleed Vietnam, and they believe this stems in part from a need by the United States to placate China—at their expense, or so they fear.

This also suggests that many East Asian nations look on China with far more suspicion than do most Americans. There are long-standing and understandable reasons for this, and the suspicion is reinforced by China's insistence on giving what it calls political and moral support to antigovernment rebels in Malaysia and elsewhere. Nevertheless, and without digressing too much from the main point, most objective analyses of internal-security problems in the region today—with the possible exception only of the Philippines—would hardly place insurgency high on the list of genuine threats to these nations. Even where internal disaffection is a serious problem—and that is restricted principally to areas of Luzon and South Thailand—the evidence for any significant external support is slim indeed.

More to the point is the fact that the obsession with China found in most of the ASEAN countries, along with the sometimes different reservations about U.S. policy found in Japan and Korea (and to the smallest extent in Australia), are all part of the same cloth. The common element is that there are widely divergent perceptions of threat now evident throughout East Asia; and all too often the United States is seen either as insensitive to these threats or, worse yet, as responsible for actions that heighten them.

The United States in Asian Security: Leader, Guarantor, or Threat?

This is an unsettling thought, especially to Americans. The matter goes well beyond one of pride, however; the nations surveyed in this study are all deeply integrated in the Western international system. All are active in the global international economy; all aspire (although internal practices obviously vary) to the political norms and values of the West; all frankly acknowledge, both at the official leadership level and among nongovernment supporters (and often even opponents of particular regimes) a deep distaste and distrust of communism; and all look to the United States for political leadership and ultimately military security.

At the same time, if the reservations that have been expressed about U.S. policy directions are not soon attended to, they can be seriously corrosive of East Asia's essentially Western stance and its U.S. connections. For example, the foreign minister of one ASEAN nation told us that at the U.N. meetings on Kampuchea in July 1982, the United States had reneged on its obligations to the ASEAN group. That is a strong term; and, whether it is justified or not, the notion can not be taken lightly that in foreign ministries of friendly governments the United States is seen as so tied to China that it does not keep its word.

Although that particular irritant can be resolved, what is more important to recognize is that although these are like-minded governments, for the most part they fashion their foreign policies with little awareness of what motivates those others in East Asia with whom they share most. This is least applicable to ASEAN; since 1967 that grouping has provided for increasingly intense consultations on major issues of Asian politics. It is also true that as a coincidental result of ASEAN, leaders of Australia, New Zealand, Japan, and the United States have in recent years had an opportunity to come together annually.[6] Nevertheless, an honest assessment of the frankness of the exchange that characterizes those gatherings (except for ANZUS and ASEAN) leads to the conclusion that something important is missing.

What is missing is an acknowledgment of the fact that in their separate ways, all look principally to the United States as the overall guarantor of security in the region—and that this major fact of life is not reflected in their exchanges. In this respect, the East Asian environment can usefully be pictured as a wheel with many separate spokes—each of which is discretely connected to the central hub represented by the United States. Simultaneously, however—and on the outer rim of that imaginary wheel—each of these states has a perception of its security environment that is necessarily and uniquely national. As a result, each sees threats and problems of which the United States—and others in the same region—may be only dimly aware.

Important strains are now evident as a result of these different perceptions. Although those strains are certainly not beyond recovery, they can become more troublesome, particularly if—as appears to be the case—the Western-oriented nations of East Asia are inchoate in their approaches to security, whereas the USSR (and perhaps China) do have a set of Pacific-region objectives. Some may exaggerate the significance and capacity of those objectives, but it is clear from this study that many Americans, some Australians, and very few others see Soviet objectives as more threatening to the stability of the region than is the common view in East Asia.

For most Asian leaderships, in fact—and this is not a point of criticism—the principal issues of national security are understood almost entirely in internal terms. One of the clearest findings to emerge from our study is that most leaderships now take a sophisticated approach to problems of internal disaffection and insurgency. In all governments that have this problem, every responsible leader began by emphasizing that ultimately the success of economic development and related programs would determine the future of the nation in question. The United States has relatively little to say or do about such issues. The true question is whether the indigenous governments will exercise the will and retain the stamina to take the necessary steps to reduce the appeals of those who seek radical change and revolution.

It is, however, at the external level that a more serious problem may exist, having to do with a lack of consensus about the nature of threats, not to mention coordination that might better deal with them. Here the anomaly is that the United States is seen by all as the ultimate guarantor of security, although simultaneously it is seen surprisingly often as a source of instability and even of danger. The United States thus may have a special role to play.

It may take a U.S. initiative to facilitate, among leaders of governments throughout East Asia, much franker exchanges about security issues than appear to have been attempted so far. What is probably needed is not simply a reinforcement of the essentially bilateral exchanges that now operate. Possibly the Pacific Forum conference planned for February 1982 can help to begin such a process, but it cannot be a substitute for what now seems needed. That is a pattern of regularized consultation and exchange on security issues among all those governments in the region whose commitment to open societies and economies ties them both to one another and in various ways to the United States.

Conclusion: Time to Rethink the Environment?

Necessarily, we have been concerned in this chapter with issues of threat and instability in the Pacific region. Only a Pollyanna would suggest that the East Asian environment is not threatened: the conflict in Indochina; the interesting development whereby the USSR has offered maritime assistance to the newly independent ministates of the Southwest Pacific (those in the South Pacific Forum group); and the continuing question of what will come of the Soviet-Chinese enmity in Asia—these and others tells us that there are serious problems. Yet the central fact of East Asia and the Pacific today is that in its developing portion it is the most prosperous and attractive of all global regions, and that at its northern and southern extremities it includes some of the main political and economic success stories of all time. It is an Asia starkly different from that which existed in the wreckage of World War II, and in no way akin to what was there in 1941. Indeed, when we recall that war was fought in the Pacific to prevent Japan from becoming the single dominant state in the region, and that the Korean War was fought because the West feared that a Sino-Soviet combination aimed for East Asian dominance, it is possible both to look back with satisfaction at what was achieved, and to look to the future with considerable optimism.

Asia today is no longer susceptible to the threat of single-nation dominance. Whatever else the USSR aims for, the central fact of its adversary relationship with China, along with the enormous power and stability of Japan, provides a profound obstacle to any such goal. Japan, of course, despite those Asian quarters that still look on Tokyo with suspicion, simply cannot again be thought of as an aspirant to Asian hegemony. As one foreign minister said to us, in criticism of the remarks of an adjacent-state prime minister who warned recently about Japanese ambitions in this era, "1941 is not 1981, and that's all there is to it."

Other mythologies abound in the region, and it would be well for all in Asia who are concerned with the issue of security threats to reexamine the assumptions on which certain convictions are based. Some long-standing threats to security may be real, whereas others have not yet received enough attention. Many, however, belong most properly in the realm of myth and fantasy. One of the most obvious candidates for that category is the continued emphasis, still unfortunately current in the Philippines and Indonesia, on the assertion that the overseas Chinese represent a potential fifth column obedient to the Communist leadership in China. Another candidate for the trash heap of mythology is that the United States seeks dominance in East Asia or that its policies cause others to be more threatened than they would be otherwise. A minority continue to express that view in the Philippines and in Australia; but since that attitude has been expressed for so many years with so little impact and success, perhaps it need not be considered a cause of major concern.

At the same time, Americans—possibly even more than all others—need to reexamine their assumptions and practices regarding the Pacific. As indicated at the outset, they may be forgiven for approaching the Asian-Pacific environment with security so much in mind, for there has been hardly any period since 1941 when the region did not seem to call for external—essentially U.S.—defense support. Now, however, the scene is so vastly different that the main problem for Americans may be the difficulty in adjusting to the fact that in the Pacific region today, a generation of effort has succeeded.

It needs to be recalled that the United States entered Asia and the Pacific at the turn of the century largely for trade and commercial reasons. It became involved militarily only much later, when conflicting national interests made war essentially unavoidable. For the following generation, the U.S. presence continued to be manifested principally in its defense and security role. In this era, however, a potential danger for the United States is that it may continue to perceive the region as still so much in need of U.S. defense roles that it overlooks both the successes that have been achieved and the reasons for which Americans became involved in East Asia in the first place.

There may be some in Asia who would welcome that and who indeed talk of a division of labor in which the United States provides for the military security of the Pacific, while others realize its prosperity.[7] That would be tragic and wasteful for all involved, for the United States is a principal exponent of both a vibrant economy and a free society, in the Pacific and everywhere else. This is not to say, of course, that either the United States or others should ignore necessary and continuing requirements for security as it is normally understood. Without question, the United States must maintain the central strategic deterrent and a continuing major naval capacity in the Pacific, on which its own security and that of all others ultimately depends. Nevertheless, for the United States to be seen—or to see itself—as the last martinet of the Pacific does an injustice to the needs of all the peoples in the region.

Notes

1. This chapter, drafted by Professor Gordon, reflects many hours of discussion between the two authors.

2. See, for example, the discussion by E.S. Browning, "East Asia in Search of a Second Economic Miracle," *Foreign Affairs* (Fall 1981). As he concludes, "East Asia is likely to continue as a world center of prosperity and high economic performance" (p. 147).

3. In these respects Japanese views are strikingly close to those of John M. Collins, senior specialist in national defense at the Congressional Research Service in the Library of Congress in Washington, D.C. Collins recently remarked, for example, that in the short- or midterm future it is highly unlikely that the USSR will attack Western Europe, attempt to seize petroleum resources in the Persian Gulf, or mount large-scale Far Eastern military operations. He cites, among a number of other constraining factors, the Soviet difficulty in Poland, where it faces a no-win situation. As a result, "The heat's off Western Europe, the heat's off the Persian Gulf, the heat's off the Far East." *The New York Times,* 10 October 1981.

4. See Robert W. Tucker, "America in Decline: The Foreign Policy of Maturity," in *Foreign Affairs: America and the World, 1979* 58, no. 3, p. 449.

5. In fairness to the South Koreans, they believe that some of the reasons for doubting the U.S. commitment derive from their own clumsiness. There is considerable embarrassment in Seoul associated with the so-called Koreagate scandal and the activities of Tongsun Park. Koreans tend to fear that those episodes have deeply eroded the base of U.S. public support for their plight.

6. Of course, since the 1950s the annual ANZUS council meetings have provided an opportunity for those three states to consult at the highest levels.

7. For a fuller statement of this false dichotomy, see Bernard K. Gordon, "Japan, the United States, and Southeast Asia," *Foreign Affairs* (April 1978).

**Part II
National Perspectives**

5

Japanese Perceptions of National Threats

Shinkichi Eto

Sir Harold Nicolson once distinguished between the diplomacy of the merchant and that of the warrior.[1] The merchant pursues profit and possesses little determination; the warrior possesses much determination and pursues little profit. Prewar Japan was clearly under the direction of the warrior, but postwar Japan exhibits all the style of the merchant. Before examining more recent phenomena, a few historical comments on the prewar diplomatic style of Japan will be useful.

As the international environment became intelligible to Japanese elites and political leaders of the late Tokugawa shogunate era—that is, from the 1840s to the 1860s—there developed the firm conviction that to cope with the Western powers, a military strengthening of the nation was indispensable. Leaders and future leaders learned about the British style of diplomacy in the Opium War, the Arrow War, and the intervention in the Taiping Rebellion. They concluded that might equals right. Such a notion was brought home to ordinary people by such bitter experiences as the visits of U.S. and Russian fleets to Japan in 1853, the British bombardment of Kagoshima in 1863, the reluctant executions of the eleven Tosa samurai who stopped French sailors from illegally landing on Sakai beach in 1868, and the vandalism of the Peiyang sailors in Nagasaki in 1886. In fact, examples are nearly innumerable. Japan craved a militarily strong nation. The Japanese perceived the world to be a jungle where power was law and regarded Japan as the liberator of Asian peoples oppressed by the Western powers. The Sino-Japanese war of 1894-1895 demonstrated a Japanese willingness to cross swords with rivals for desired territory—in this case, Korea. The Russo-Japanese war of 1904-1905 established Japan as a world power. Military strength became the paramount concern, and a confident warrior style of diplomacy was developed.

The loss of confidence brought on by defeat in the Pacific War and the subsequent seven years of allied occupation made the Japanese government and people reluctant to resume any active political role. Rather, Japan preferred to speak softly and take no leadership in international politics. Postwar Japan can be compared to the big boy who wants to sit in the back of the classroom, hoping that obscurity will allow him to escape notice. This posture made it difficult to have a candid discussion of the military and political situation. Even the economic threats were investigated in terms of vulnerability, but few Japanese dared openly to investigate improving military and political capabilities to decrease Japan's economic vulnerability.

As a result of a number of incidents in the 1970s, however, Japanese attitudes toward the external environment gradually began to change.

External Stimuli That Have Affected Perceptions

In the 1950s and 1960s Japan was often said to be a house divided against itself with respect to the defense question. Approximately two-thirds of the Japanese people either positively or reluctantly supported the U.S.-Japan Security Treaty System and an adequately armed Japan, whereas the remaining third tended to advocate an unarmed, neutral Japan. In the 1970s, however, various affairs shocked the Japanese people, and attitudes toward the external environment have gradually changed. The 1973 Middle East War, followed by the first oil crisis, resulted in a decrease in annual GNP in 1974, the first such occurrence in postwar Japan. India, a long-respected model by some Japanese advocates of an unarmed and neutral Japan, conducted its first nuclear weapons' test in the same year. In 1975 a Japanese fishing boat was shot at and detained by North Korea, and two fishermen aboard were killed.

Soviet First Lieutenant Berenko, piloting a MIG-25, landed safely in the Hakodate Airport in 1976, without being intercepted by the Japanese air defense command. The Japanese people were seriously shocked by this incident, which showed the weakness of the Japanese defense system. In its wake a vague uneasiness remained, and the public felt a discomfort vis-à-vis the military. Interested people began to discuss openly whether or not Japan had sufficient military capability. The argument was further provoked by then U.S. President Carter's decision in 1977 to have U.S. ground-based troops withdrawn from South Korea within a few years. About this time many nations unilaterally declared 200-nautical-mile economic zones. In this development the Japanese perceived an economic threat with heavy overtones of a tactical military nature.

The crude-oil trade ban and a sharp decrease in Iranian oil production, preceded by the shah's overthrow and Ayatolla Khomeini's repatriation in 1978, brought heated debates on the vulnerability of sea-lanes and communication between the Middle East and Japan. At the same time, Japanese business people became nervous about this economic threat, and socialists and other progressives became disillusioned by the Vietnamese aggression in Kampuchea, the Chinese self-styled punitive expedition against Vietnam in 1979, the Soviet military intervention in Afghanistan in the same year, and the Soviet intimidation of Poland. Increased Soviet troop levels in East Asia, widely reported by the media in 1979 and 1980, had a remarkable influence on the Japanese people as a whole, leading to an open discussion of the Soviet threat. Several books with detailed scenarios of potential Soviet aggression against Japan were published in these years.

The aforementioned developments, among others, have awakened the heretofore dormant Japanese; and a realistic consideration of national security has begun.

Japanese Attitudes toward the Self-Defense Forces

The existence of the Japanese Self-Defense Forces (SDF) has always been controversial among the Japanese. When the predecessor of the SDF began to be organized in 1950, female employees of the Iwanami Publishing Company, a first-rate publisher in Japan, assembled and publicly concluded a resolution never to be married to a member of the SDF. About twenty years later, when Okinawa reverted to Japan, union leaders, including the teachers' union, tried to stop SDF troops from entering Okinawa. They agitated strongly to refuse school entrace to children of the troops.

But public-opinion polls undertaken by the Japanese government indicate a gradual increase of acceptance of the SDF, as in table 5-1. Jiji Press recently conducted similar polls, and the latest three show the same tendency as the government conducted polls (see table 5-2).

A remarkable increase in the number of those who accepted the SDF in 1980 was obviously a result of the widely reported increase of Soviet troops in East Asia, together with the Soviet military intervention in Afghanistan. Even public-opinion polls conducted by *Asahi Shimbun*, the progressive and anti-military-oriented newspaper, indicate a similar tendency (see table 5-3). The aforementioned statistics demonstrate that approximately 77-86 percent of the people support the SDF, one-fifth support an increase of the SDF, and only 5-5.9 percent advocate its abolition.

Table 5-1
Public-Opinion Polls by the Government

Year	Better to Have the SDF (%)	Better Not to Have the SDF (%)	Do Not Know (%)
1972	73	12	15
1975	79	8	13
1977	83	7	10
1978	86	5	9

Source: Japan, Public Relations Section, Defense Minister's Office, ed., *Public Opinion Polls Concerning the SDF and Defense Problems* (in Japanese), 1979, p. 4.

Table 5-2
Public-Opinion Polls by Jiji Press

Year	Better to Have the SDF (%)	Better Not to Have the SDF (%)	Do Not Know (%)
1979	68.5	8.1	23.5
1980	78.2	5.5	16.3
1981	77.1	5.9	17.0

Source: Figures are based on Jiji Press, *Public Opinion Polls of Jiji* (in Japanese), nos. 167, 11 November 1979, and 242, 11 December 1981.

Ambivalences in Japanese Attitudes toward National Security

The Japanese are ambivalent and confused about national security. Article 9 of the constitution reads, ". . . land, sea, and air forces, as well as other war potentials, will never be maintained." No one doubts that the modern SDF is a complex of land, sea, and air forces; but recent polls, as shown in table 5-4, reveal two points: first, a remarkable change of attitude toward Article 9, and second, is a strong reaffirmation of support for the present constitution. A changed attitude toward the unconstitutionality of "war potential" is easily understandable when the aforementioned incidents are considered. Widespread support for the present constitution is, however, a bit puzzling. Why do so many Japanese accept the SDF but refuse to amend Article 9? The only possible explanation is that the pacifist idealism implied by Article 9 strongly attracts the Japanese heart, whereas the intellect, aware of the objective situation, is left in a dilemma—hence the ambivalent attitude of modern Japan toward defense.

The results of another questionnaire point to a contradiction between support of the SDF and advocacy of an unarmed, neutral Japan. A public-opinion poll undertaken by *Asahi Shimbun* included the question: What is the best way to defend Japanese national security?[2] Forty-eight percent of

Table 5-3
Public-Opinion Polls by *Asahi Shimbun*

Year	Should Strengthen the SDF (%)	Should Maintain the Status Quo (%)	Should Reduce the SDF (%)	Should Abolish the SDF (%)
1978	19	57	11	5
1980	18	61	11	5
1981	22	57	11	5

Source: *Asahi Shimbun*, 1 November 1978, 3 January 1981. (All magazines and newspapers, unless noted otherwise, are in Japanese.)

**Table 5-4
Public-Opinion Polls concerning Article 9 of the Constitution**

	Should Amend It (%)	Should Not (%)	Do Not Know (%)
1978	15	71	14
1981	24	61	15

Source: *Asahi Shimbun*, 1 November 1978, 25 March 1981.

the answers supported the current policy of defending Japan by collaboration between the SDF and U.S. troops. Fourteen percent advocated an independent defense with a dramatic increase of SDF capabilities. Eight percent didn't know; and, strangely, 30 percent advocated unarmed neutrality. How do we reconcile these results with the 77-86 percent acceptance of the SDF? Again, the only answer is a strong ambivalence of Japanese attitudes toward the problem. When Japan observes the cold reality of international relations, the SDF becomes acceptable; but the romantic pacifist vision of unarmed neutrality has an undeniable attraction.

These romantic pacifists are also extremely selfish. Another question the *Asahi* raised in the same poll was whether one would fight or not, should foreign troops invade Japan. Only 34 percent said they would fight; 21 percent would flee from the aggressor, and 16 percent would surrender. Seventeen percent would decide on the spot, and 12 percent did not answer.[3]

Public-Opinion Polls regarding Threats

Jiji Press has conducted polls that asked direct questions about the perception of threats to national security. The results are shown in table 5-5. Those who feel threatened were asked to indicate what country threatens Japan the most. Table 5-6 shows these results.

Yomiuri Shimbun publicized the result of a similar public-opinion poll in September 1981, and the results were almost identical to those of the Jiji

**Table 5-5
Public-Opinion Polls by Jiji Press**

	Threats to National Security: Do You . . .				
	Feel Greatly (%)	Feel to a Certain Extent (%)	Feel a Little (%)	Not Feel at All (%)	Do Not Know (%)
1979	6.0	24.5	41.6	10.2	17.8
1980	7.5	32.4	36.0	5.6	18.6
1981	5.1	24.0	34.3	8.7	27.9

Source: Figures are based on the same materials used for table 5-1 and 5-2.

Table 5-6
What Country Poses the Greatest Threat?

	USSR (%)	United States (%)	North Korea (%)	PRC (%)	South Korea (%)	Others (%)	Do Not Know (%)
1979	77.3	11.2	6.9	6.1	2.5	1.5	9.3
1980	83.6	7.1	1.5	1.6	2.4	1.0	8.4
1981	77.4	12.5	2.5	1.2	0.5	1.6	11.1

Press poll.[4] Those Japanese who live in Hokkaido, however, feel much more threatened by the USSR, according to a public-opinion poll undertaken by *Hokkaido Shimbun*.[5] *Hokkaido Shimbun* raised the question, "Do you feel a 'Northern threat,' i.e., a Soviet willingness to invade Hokkaido?" Of those polled, 55.2 percent answered yes; 36.4 percent, no; and 8.4 percent didn't know. The national response to a similar question was a mere 24-32 percent yes (see table 5-5). Over half of those polled in Hokkaido answered positively, and the difference is certainly attributable to Hokkaido's geographic propinquity to the USSR.

Gallup and the *Yomiuri Shimbun*, which now claims the largest circulation in Japan (over 8 million), have been conducting comparative public-opinion polls between Japanese and Americans since 1978.[6] Table 5-7 shows, first, a steady increase in U.S. trust of Japan: Japan is now the sixth-most-trusted country by Americans in the world—more trusted than France, West Germany, and Mexico. Second, table 5-7 indicates that the Japanese trust of the United States has been consistently first, showing a gradual increase until 1980, with a 4-percent decrease in 1981. The decrease reflected a steep drop from 75 percent in 1980 to 61 percent in 1981 among professionals and managerial personnel. This can be explained by events in 1981. Edwin O. Reischauer, former U.S. ambassador to Japan, revealed that the Japanese government acquiesced to U.S. ships entering Japanese waters with nuclear weapons aboard. A U.S. submarine and a Japanese merchant ship collided at sea; although the merchant ship sunk, the submarine left the scene without any effort to rescue the survivors. Tense debates on trade problems were also constantly in the news. Third, data on countries the Japanese trust indicate that the Japanese are much cooler to Israel than the Americans, and the Americans to South Korea and Brazil than the Japanese, despite the presence of U.S. tripwire troops in South Korea. Fourth, the Japanese regard the People's Republic of China as the most trustworthy next to the United States, whereas the Americans rank mainland China very low.

Table 5-8 illustrates a difference in opinion on how Japan should improve its national security. The Americans believe in a free economic system

Table 5-7
Choose the Five Most Trustworthy Countries out of the Following Thirty Countries

	Answers of the Japanese					Answers of the Americans		
	1981	1980	1979	1978		1981	1980	1979	1978
1. United States	55.9	59.2	45.7	40.8	1. Canada	71.4	76.8	68.6	61.2
2. PRC	34.6	38.1	28.3	24.4	2. United Kingdom	47.6	55.8	43.0	43.3
3. United Kingdom	32.6	34.7	28.4	22.6	3. Australia	41.2	46.3	47.4	43.6
4. Switzerland	26.9	25.3	24.3	21.4	4. Switzerland	32.4	31.3	34.9	35.0
5. West Germany	26.6	24.7	21.5	19.5	5. Sweden	28.8	23.8	29.6	26.8
6. Canada	24.7	27.1	23.0	19.6	6. Japan	26.0	21.8	17.1	12.6
7. France					7. Mexico				
8. Australia					8. West Germany				
9. Brazil					9. France				
10. Holland					10. Norway				
14. South Korea					11. Israel				
17. USSR					12. Holland				
20. North Korea					17. PRC				
29. Israel					18. Brazil				
					21. South Korea				
					27. USSR				
					28. North Korea				
Do not know	25.1	25.3	32.9	40.8	Do not know	11.6	4.5	4.9	14.3

and military alliances much more than do the Japanese, and feel much more strongly than the Japanese that Japan should increase its military capability.

The role of the United Nations and neutrality still attract many more Japanese than Americans. Finally, the high rates of "don't know" groups among the Japanese with respect to judging trustworthiness (table 5-7) or priorities for national security (table 5-8) show that the Japanese hold much vaguer and more ambiguous notions of international affairs than do Americans. Americans have more clear-cut notions, biased or unbiased, than the Japanese.

In an attempt to ascertain more concretely the concerns of those polled, the Gallup-Yomiuri polls asked where a serious military clash would be most likely to take place if and when peace in East Asia were destroyed. Table 5-9 indicates that there is not much difference between Japanese and Americans. They agree that the most probable battle will occur between the PRC and the USSR, followed by Indochina and the Korean peninsula.

Popular Debate

Debates on national security that have appeared in the Japanese media in the 1950s and 1960s centered mainly on the acceptance or rejection of the U.S.-Japan Security Treaty and the SDF. One position advocated an unarmed, neutral Japan. Recently, however, the debate has diversified. Whether or not the SDF should maintain its present nature or increase its

Table 5-8
Choose Two Items from the Following regarding Japan's Effort to Strengthen Its National Security

	Japanese	Americans
Strengthen the free economic system in the West	18.3	32.8
Strengthen military-alliance system in the West	5.5	44.6
Strengthen Japan's defense capability	24.6	46.6
Increase aid to developing countries	18.9	7.4
Strengthen the United Nations	28.8	15.8
Develop a neutral policy	27.8	10.3
Accelerate disarmament negotiation with the USSR	8.4	23.4
Increase economic and cultural intercourse with the East	12.1	8.6
Do not know	24.2	3.1

Table 5-9
Dangerous Spots

	Japanese	Americans
Indochina	22.2	29.5
Taiwan-PRC	2.0	5.5
Korean peninsula	13.8	10.6
PRC-Soviet	27.3	29.6
Japan-Soviet	7.6	5.0
Do not know	27.1	22.4

military capability, what kind of threats Japan faces, and how to cope with them are the current topics of debate.

In 1979 Morishima Michio, Japanese professor of economics at the London School of Economics and Political Science, provoked Seki Yoshihiko, professor emeritus of sociology at Tokyo Metropolitan University, with his firm belief in an unarmed, neutral Japan.[7] In *Bungei Shunju,* Morishima asserted that any military-defense buildup cannot provide the people with happiness, but rather will assure the disaster of war. Moreover, Morishima continued, should the USSR invade Japan, the Japanese government and people should surrender with dignity and order. Then the Soviet occupation troops will respect the occupied and allow Japan to maintain its own political system. Seki immediately opposed Morishima in an article that appeared in the same magazine.[8] Referring to various historical cases, Seki argued that military weakness often invites foreign aggression, and therefore Japan needs some kind of military capacity plus U.S. military support in order to cope with the formidable Soviet military buildup. Seki also asserted that any military occupation would be terrible and that Soviet occupation troops would never allow Japan to preserve its own polity. Many authors participated in the Morishima-Seki debates, the majority of them highly critical of Morishima.

Shimizu Ikutaro recently provoked another debate by his switch in favor of a nuclear-armed Japan. Shimizu, formerly a professor of sociology at Gakushuin University, once vehemently advocated an unarmed, neutral Japan. His influence was so great that many of his students became leaders of left-wing student movements in 1960, when the Kishi Cabinet was implementing a revised U.S.-Japan Security Treaty. Much later he dramatically converted into a realist. The realist Shimizu published an article in 1980 calling for a nuclear-armed Japan to cope with the Soviet threat.[9] This article provoked further arguments among various media commentators, retired military officers, social scientists, and others. Among them was Inoki Masamichi, former rector of the National Defense College. He described Shimizu as "a man converted from utopian pacifism to utopian militarism" and criticized his article as "a gigantic lie inlaid with glittering truths."[10]

Furthermore, Inoki also criticized the assertion that the USSR is a threat. He emphasized Soviet weaknesses in another article and warned that it is dangerous to provoke Soviet antagonism by vocal exaggeration of the Soviet threat.[11] A young associate professor at Tsukuba University was quick to attack Inoki, asserting that the Soviet threat is overt and obvious and that therefore, if Inoki persists in distorting the facts, he is playing the role of a Soviet agent.[12]

The Government Position

The Japanese postwar regime is characterized by the fact that the Conservatives have succeeded in maintaining a majority in the National Diet and in holding the government almost continuously, except for a short period between May 1947 and March 1948. The conservative parties in postwar Japan, including the present ruling Liberal Democratic party (LDP), have been nothing more than a loose alliance of factions whose members have close human and political relations among themselves, regardless of ideology. The only major point of ideological consensus among them during the Cold War era was the need to maintain a strong anticommunist stance. Even the current LDP prime minister and party leader, Zenko Suzuki, was a member of the Japan Socialist party when he first became a National Diet member in 1947.

The defense policy of the postwar Japanese government reflects a consensus among the LDP Diet members, who include both hawks and doves. Consequently, there is a great deal of ambivalence, which affects the policymaking process in the national-security and defense area. The official policy of the Japanese LDP government at the moment can be summarized as follows: (1) Article 9 of the constitution does not deny Japan's self-defense capability; therefore, (2) defensive weapons are not unconstitutional; (3) to send troops abroad or to equip them with offensive weapons is unconstitutional; consequently, (4) a mutual collective-security treaty, if it included reciprocal military cooperation, would be unconstitutional. During the 1960s a theory of national-security capability was developed that stressed various policies to increase capability by nonmilitary means. This theory evolved into the concept of *comprehensive security,* a term adopted by former Prime Minister Masayoshi Ohira as the government's policy on national security and defense.

The Conditions Underlying Japan's Prosperity

A *threat* is that which seeks to destroy a desirable status quo. What is the status quo that at least most of the Japanese enjoy and want to maintain? It is an affluent society with a liberal and democratic political system.

Every day Japan imports over 700,000 tons of crude oil and more than 110,000 tons of iron ore. In 1981 it exported approximately $140 billion in goods and services to the rest of the world. In order to support a population of 116 million—more than half the size of the U.S. population—on a land area of only about 145,000 square miles—only 4 percent of the territory of the United States—95 percent of the raw materials necessary for Japanese industry must be purchased abroad, processed, and then 30 percent reexported as manufactured goods and services. This process represents the structure of Japan's present affluence, as well as the elements that are crucial to its survival. Even if the current economic and social system of production were replaced by a socialist system, these basic structural facts would not change. It is also unalterable that any attempt to raise the standard of living or to support a larger population will necessitate a further increase of these figures.

This is the basic system that the Japanese enjoy and want to maintain. For this purpose, three conditions are necessary: a peaceful international environment, a world system of free trade, and the maintenance of domestic social and economic efficiency. Therefore, Japan's national goals vis-à-vis any threat must adhere to the maintenance of these three conditions.

The first condition, the existence of a peaceful international environment, is essential to ensuring the uninterrupted flow of capital and goods to and from Japan. In an earlier era, when it was possible to ensure that flow by sheer military might, Britain and other mighty powers secured raw-material sources and markets for their goods by subjugating other countries militarily. Japan practiced the same technique, though as a latecomer. Today the use of military power for economic ends not only is of extremely limited efficacy, but is often condemned. Therefore, today only a complex of military and nonmilitary maneuvers can help to maintain the international peace against any disturbances or disruptions. This is the reason that Japan fears Soviet military intentions and capabilities.

The maintenance of a system of free trade is the second crucial element in Japan's continued economic success. As a capitalist economy, the Japanese system is premised on the principle of laissez-faire competition among enterprises. The production of high-quality, inexpensive consumer products has allowed Japan to compete successfully in the international marketplace. Other than this, Japan has no particular leverage in its international dealings. Thus the tendency toward protectionism and other constraints on free trade that have developed in the 1970s have been of concern to Japan, although few people would use the word *threat* vis-à-vis these problems.

The third and final condition to maintain the status quo is to prevent a disruption of domestic social and economic efficiency. To avoid the so-called British disease requires not only a high level of efficiency in private industry, but also a balance between individual rights and social responsibilities. No matter how huge the SDF budget grows, soldiers without a sense of responsibility cannot make a strong military. Creating a balance between respect for individual human rights and the preservation of social efficiency is a serious matter. The aforementioned problem, constituting a threat from within, will become the most serious threat confronting Japan in the years ahead.

Notes

1. Harold Nicolson, *Diplomacy,* 3rd ed. (London: Oxford University Press, 1963), pp. 51 ff.
2. *Asahi Shimbun,* 25 March 1981. (All magazines and newspapers, unless noted otherwise, are in Japanese.)
3. Ibid.
4. *Yomiuri Shimbun,* 14 September 1981.
5. *Hokkaido Shimbun,* 6 August 1981.
6. *Yomiuri Shimbun,* 14 November 1981.
7. Michio Morishima, "A New 'New Defense Plan,'" *Bungei Shunju,* July 1979.
8. Yoshihiko Seki, "No Country Can Maintain Peace without a Military Capability," *Bungei Shunju,* July 1979.
9. Ikutaro Shimizu, "Japan, Be a State!—the Nuclear Option—," *Shokun!* July 1980.
10. Masamichi Inoki, "From Utopian Pacificism to Utopian Militarism," *Chuo Koron,* September 1980.
11. Masamichi Inoki, "Truths and Falsehoods in Defense Polemics," *Chuo Koron,* January 1981.
12. Yahiro Nakagawa, "Outrageous Is a Grand Chorus 'the Soviet Is Not a Threat,'" *Getsuyō Hyōron,* nos. 547, 20 July 1981, and 549, 3 August 1981.

6

The Roots of South Korean Anxiety about National Security

Sang-Woo Rhee

The South Koreans now live in a war situation. Along the 150-mile truce line drawn only 30 miles north of the capital city of Seoul in 1953, more than a million combat-ready armed personnel of two hostile Koreas are facing each other. Both sides are on full alert, and there are sporadic border incidents. On the sea, North Korean gunboats occasionally cross the North Patrol Limit Line (NPLL) that serves as a customary boundary between the adversaries and kidnap South Korean fishing boats. In the air, combat planes patrol twenty-four hours a day on both sides of the 4-km-wide demilitarized zone (DMZ) along the truce line.

Ever since the foundation in 1948 of the two hostile governments—the Republic of Korea (ROK) in Seoul and the Democratic People's Republic of Korea (DPRK) in Pyongyang—there have been no formal contacts between the two governments. Neither recognizes the other as legitimate. No treaty has ever been signed between the two to define mutual relations.[1] Thus there is no institutionalized peace system of any kind between the two Koreas, and the cease-fire is maintained only by sheer balance of military power. No other boundary in the world is more fragile than the inter-Korean demarcation line.

Inter-Korean hostility has characteristics of both an *intra*national and an *inter*national conflict. Neither the South nor the North Koreans regard each other as aliens. In the minds of the Koreans, a sense of ethnic homogeneity prevails. Intra-Korean conflict, then, is a kind of political game between two competing governments for a sole legitimacy over the one Korea. On the other hand, both Koreas are so strongly tied with the outside powers that the conflict between the two Koreas reflects regional as well as global rivalry among the superpowers. For example, the South Korean governmment cannot initiate war without the consent of the U.S. government because the entire Korean armed forces are under the ROK-U.S. Joint Command, whose commander is a U.S. general appointed by the president of the United States. North Korea, too, is not entirely free from its supporting powers, the USSR and the People's Republic of China (PRC). Especially without a supply of sophisticated weapons from the USSR, North Korea cannot sustain a threatening military posture against South Korea.

At present the ultimate concern of the South Koreans is about the possible outbreak of another full-scale military confrontation between the two

65

Koreas. Since the chance of outbreak of an all-out war is affected not only by the local balance between the two Koreas, but also by the regional and global balance of powers among the great powers, the South Koreans' apprehension about their own security is also multitiered. At the lowest level, an uneasy local military balance between the two Koreas is the primary source of the South Koreans' anxiety; at the middle level the unstable regional power balance among the United States, the USSR, Japan, and the PRC makes them nervous; and at the highest level erosion of U.S. military superiority to the USSR undermines their sense of security. For example, the South Koreans worry about any unusual military buildup of North Korea. They are concerned about any move of the USSR. They are also keenly touched by slight policy changes in the PRC. Their sense of security fluctuates from confidence to panic depending on policy changes in the United States.

As in other countries, in South Korea there is no popular consensus about the seriousness of the threat. Those who are directly involved in analyzing the security environment are usually pessimistic and feel that a crisis is at hand. On the other hand, most people do not have complete information about the security situation and generally show groundless optimism. Especially among the unsophisticated general public, there is still a prevalent myth of the almighty United States that can and will save the Koreans from any danger. This myth effectively works as a tranquilizer, easing public anxieties.

This chapter will try to describe South Korean threat perceptions as objectively as possible and analyze the new threats faced by South Korea.

North Korean Belligerence: The Primary Source of Apprehension

The Military Threat and South Korean Responses

For the South Koreans, the primary and most imminent threat comes from Pyongyang. For the last thirty years the South Koreans have lived under direct threat from the north. The South Koreans have never been able to relax because of the belligerent nature and superior military capability of the North Korean regime.

When they established a communist government in Pyongyang in 1948, Kim Il-Song and his associates proclaimed that their highest priority was to liberate South Korea from the so-called U.S. imperialists and their puppet government in Seoul, and to accomplish socialist revolution in the entire Korean peninsula. Since then they have never changed their policy stance or relaxed their efforts to achieve these goals.[2] Kim has already transformed

South Korean Anxiety about National Security

North Korean society into one of the most rigid totalitarian societies in the world as the springboard for the South Korean revolution, and has built formidable military forces sufficient to start an all-out war when they can instigate a pro-Pyongyang revolution in South Korea.

Will Kim Il-Song really attempt to invade South Korea? No one knows for sure, and even in South Korea reactions to this question vary. In a recently conducted survey of Korean elite members, about 40 percent of 74 respondents gave affirmative answers to this question, whereas about 60 percent predicted that it is not likely that Kim Il-Song will start another all-out war.[3] Young intellectuals are slightly more optimistic. In a survey conducted three years ago of 237 college students who majored in political science, only 15.2 percent answered positively, whereas 39.2 percent did not consider a war likely.[4] Including the students who did not anticipate an all-out war but predicted heightened guerrilla warfare (43.5 percent), however, over half of the students believed that North Korea intended to launch some form of military attack against South Korea.

At great sacrifice to the welfare of its people, North Korea has steadily strengthened its military for the past twenty years to maintain superiority over South Korea. More important, in the past few years North Korea accelerated the pace of its military buildup. Table 6-1 gives cumulative military investments since 1949 of both Koreas to show trends in the North and South Korean efforts, and table 6-2 provides several indicative figures to show North Korea's current war capability.[5] Figure 6-1 shows changing

Table 6-1
North and South Korean War Preparations: Trends in Cumulative Military Investment since 1948
(in millions of U.S. dollars)

Year	South Korea	North Korea
1950	1.6	4.1
1953	15.5	20.2
1955	30.8	41.7
1960	66.6	142.7
1965	92.6	806.9
1970	186.4	2,556.9
1975	810.5	5,965.7
1976	1,396.4	7,001.1
1977	2,141.2	8,052.1
1978	3,237.7	9,410.1
1979	4,461.3	10,894.2
1980	5,941.3	12,538.4
1988	31,000	31,400[a]
1990	44,500	37,900[a]

[a]My own projections.

Table 6-2
Military Forces, North and South Korea

	As of the End of 1981	
	South Korea	North Korea
GNP	$74,191 mil.	$15,023 mil.
Defense expenditures	$4,451 mil.	$3,280 mil.
	(6% of GNP)	(22.5% of GNP)
Regular forces	620,000	782,000
Army	520,000	700,000
Navy	67,000	31,000
Air forces	32,000	51,000
Reserved	5,100,000	2,660,000
Infantry division	24	35
Special combat brigade	7	24
Tank division	—	2
Mechanized division	1	3
Tank brigade	2	5
Artillery batallion	36	100
Tanks	1,100	2,800
APC/BMD	600	1,100
Gun/howz	2,700	6,300
SSM	12	39
Combat airplanes	400	716
Support airplanes	230	510
Naval ships	124	600
Submarines	—	20
Destroyers	17	2
Missile boats	11	21

Source: Data are from *Military Balance, 1981-82*, but some of them are modified with recent information.

patterns of the war capabilities of the two Koreas in terms of a composite index of statistical data using factor analysis.[6] Figure 6-1 also suggests that North Korea has enjoyed remarkable military superiority over South Korea and that the margin of superiority has dramatically widened as a result of the sharp upsurge of North Korea's war preparation since 1977. With statistical measures alone we cannot argue that North Korea is stronger than South Korea, but the serious numerical imbalance illustrated here is sufficient to make informed South Koreans anxious.

In such an alarming situation, why are South Koreans still optimistic about their security? Two possible sources of such optimism are discernible: distorted public perception due to government manipulation of the relevant information, and almost blind public trust in U.S. power and willingness to help. In the past the South Korean government has not always been honest in releasing information on North Korea, including its military capabilities. When the government wanted to give the people confidence, it deflated estimates of North Korean capabilities; on other occasions, when the

South Korean Anxiety about National Security

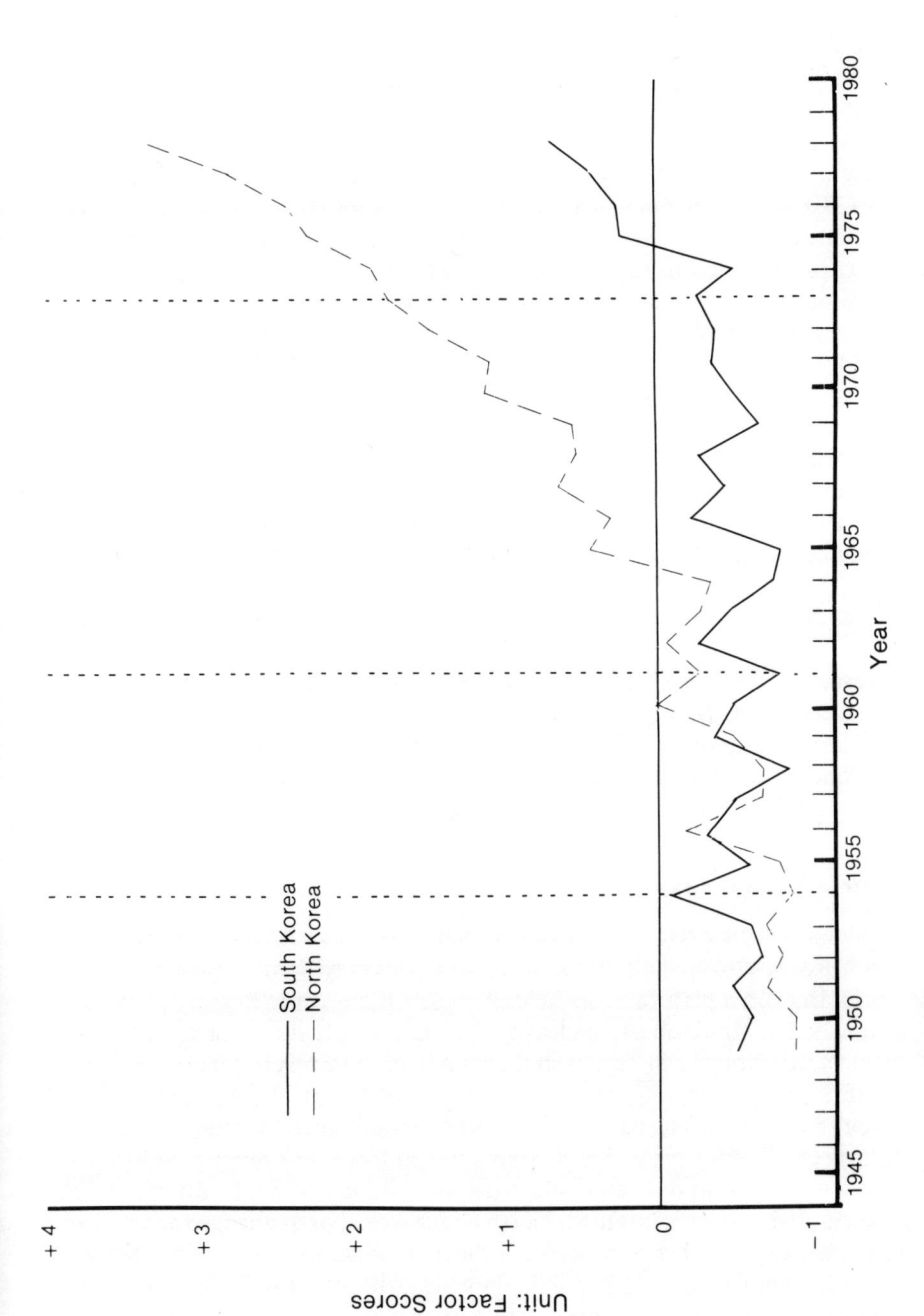

Figure 6-1. Changing Patterns of South and North Korea's War Capabilities

government wanted to stir up concern for domestic reasons, it inflated the estimates. Under these circumstances the Korean public has developed a deep distrust of government information on North Korea, and it is understandable that many people simply do not take the government's honest warnings about the recent North Korean threat seriously.

As for U.S.-Korean relations, many South Koreans are confused because of a lack of correct information. For example, although *The New York Times* or *Time* magazine continuously reported on the deteriorating relations between the two nations, Korean newspapers emphasized improvements in the relationship. In this confused situation some Koreans feared the United States would sever the alliance with Korea, whereas others retained strong confidence in the U.S. commitment to their defense.

Most South Koreans still remember vividly what the United States did during the Korean War of 1950-1953. Thus it is natural that the general public, which has little access to the foreign media, retains a strong belief in U.S. willingness and ability to defend South Korea from any new North Korean aggression. Likewise, it is natural that some sophisticated Koreans who do keenly observe the outside world suspect that the United States would not jump into another Korean War. These fear that the United States no longer sees South Korea as a vital element in the strategic design of the United States in an era of detente. They are also aware that the U.S. public is no longer so friendly to South Korea and would not easily support a government decision to help South Korea, and this greatly undermines their confidence in U.S. support in the event of war.[7] In short, there is great divergence of opinion between those who are well informed about the situation and those who are not, and this gives South Koreans mixed views toward security issues.

North Korea's Political Threat

In addition to its overt military threat, North Korea's subversive activities in South Korea also make the South Koreans nervous. Some time ago North Korea drew up a plan for a so-called People's Democratic Revolution in the south, and it continuously endeavored to implement it.[8] According to the plan, North Korea will first install an underground revolutionary party in South Korea, which will serve as the nucleus of the pro-Pyongyang revolutionary movement. The party is supposed to organize various antigovernment elements of South Korean society into a united front for toppling the incumbent government in the name of the democratization of South Korea. Once the new government is installed, North Korea would persuade it to accept the North Korean formula of peaceful unification under the name of the Koryo Confederated Democratic Republic, in which, theoretically, both North and South Korea are equal members, with current political systems intact.

South Korean Anxiety about National Security 71

North Korea publicly claims that since 1964 an underground revolutionary party called the Tong-Hyok dang has existed, and that this is the time for forming the united front of all the democratic elements in South Korea. At present there are no visible activities of the so-called Tong-Hyok dang, but the fact that North Korea attempts this kind of subversive action alone is sufficient to make South Koreans feel uneasy. So far North Korea's subversive activities have not disrupted the daily life of the South Koreans. The threat has remained dormant. Once domestic political crisis erupts, however, the South Koreans worry that this dormant threat will surface and in the confusion North Korea may find an opportunity for achieving its objectives.

Because the North Korean strategy is a political one, political stability is the most important factor in eliminating this threat. This means that as long as the South Korean government can marshal strong support from its people and prove its own effectiveness, no room will exist for the North Korean penetration. Thus an improvement of the accountability of the government will be an effective countermeasure against such political subversion.

The political attitude of the proletariat in South Korea will be a crucial variable in the success of North Korean subversion and South Korean defense, because the proletariat is theoretically the main target of North Korean agitation. As long as the South Korean government has the firm support of the proletariat, North Korean instigation for a communist revolution will be discouraged. If the living standard of the working class is improved far above subsistence level and their opportunities for political participation are widened, North Korean revolutionary propaganda will not be persuasive. Fortunately, thanks to the determined government effort to enhance the overall status of the have-not class in South Korea, the proportion of the people who regard themselves as members of the middle class is rapidly increasing.[9] When the time comes that most of the people, including low-income people, believe that they are far better off than the North Koreans, the North Koreans should realize that their strategy of staging a pro-Pyongyang revolution in South Korea has no chance of success.

The Changing Regional Power Balance

Unavoidable Foreign Intervention

The geopolitical location of the Korean peninsula makes it difficult to think of the Korean security issue apart from the regional power balance among the PRC, the USSR, the United States, and Japan. Although neither North or South Korea is a weak nation in an absolute sense, they are destined to be influenced by their neighbors because they are surrounded by the four most powerful nations in the world. In terms of Ray Cline's overall national-power index, for example, North Korea ranked thirty-first and South Korea thirteenth in 1978.[10] In terms of his military-capability index, North Korea ranked eleventh and South Korea fourteenth in 1979.[11] Thus neither Korea belongs to the group of weak nations. Surrounded by the giant powers, however, both Koreas are dwarfed in relative terms. In this geopolitical setting, notwithstanding their struggle for independence, both Koreas are doomed to be victims of competitive interventions by their neighbors.

Geographically, the Korean peninsula is an ideal pier into the Pacific Ocean for the USSR; a buffer for the PRC against the ocean powers; a land bridge for Japan to penetrate into continental Asia; and a foothold for the United States to play a balancer's role in East Asia. Especially for the PRC and the USSR, it is crucial not to allow the peninsula to come under the monopolistic control of any competing large power. If the PRC controls it, the USSR will lose its outlet into the Pacific and Southeast Asia; if, on the other hand, it lies under Soviet dominance, the PRC will be surrounded by the USSR and its proxies and will be severed from Japan and the United States. Thus for their own interests, both the PRC and the USSR must fight for the dominant position in the peninsula or at least prevent the other from obtaining a dominant position.

South Koreans generally believe that the United States does not have a territorial interest in the Korean peninsula. It is a small (85,000 square miles) piece of land that has no valuable natural resources. South Koreans understand that U.S. interest in Korea is situational; the United States is interested in Korea only as it relates to other strategically important objectives. For example, a friendly Korea may be needed to protect Japan from the threat of any Asian continental power, or the United States may desire to keep Korea anticommunist to block Soviet expansionism in East Asia. The fact that U.S. interest in Korea is just situational, however, does not imply that the United States will easily concede its dominant position in South Korea to other powers. At present, keeping a strong foothold on the Korean peninsula is important for the United States in terms of its relations with Japan and the PRC. In short, the geopolitical location of the Korean peninsula makes foreign intervention in Korean affairs inevitable, no matter what kind of interest the concerned powers may have at the moment.

Incongruence between the Local and the Regional Balance

During the Cold War era the South Koreans did not worry much about the regional balance because the local power balance in the peninsula and the larger regional power balance coincided. At that time a regional balance was maintained between the U.S.-Japanese alliance and the PRC-Soviet alliance, whereas in the Korean peninsula a local balance was between communist North Korea, supported by the two communist giants, on the one side, and South Korea, backed by the United States and Japan.

The South Koreans have felt threatened since the mid-1970s, when the regional balance shifted toward a new balance between a tripartite pseudo-alliance of the United States, the PRC, and Japan on one side and the USSR on the other, while in the Korean peninsula the old local balance between two Koreas was retained. In this new era the PRC plays a double role: on the regional level it sides with the United States, whereas on the local level it still supports North Korea, along with the USSR. This double role causes South Koreans great concern because it is logical to believe the United States will give more value to the maintenance of the regional stability than to retaining local peace in the Korean peninsula. The United States has a bigger stake in keeping the PRC and Japan in its orbit than in protecting a small ally in the peninsula. Under these circumstances, the South Koreans cannot give as much credit to the U.S. pledge of defending South Korea as they did before. Suppose that another Korean War breaks out and the PRC participates in the war on the North Korean side. Will the United States fight against the PRC? This important question lingers in the minds of the South Koreans and becomes another source of their present apprehension about their security.

U.S. Credibility at Stake

For several years after the end of World War II, the United States maintained an unchallenged position in world politics and had the power to keep political order in the international community with its military might, which exceeded the total for all other nations combined. At that time the United States could have done whatever it wanted. Unfortunately, however, the United States has not maintained a firm stance against the challenges of the USSR, the second-ranking power, and has conceded most of the contended areas to the USSR, thereby risking her prestige as a superpower. In the late 1940s, while it still had a nuclear monopoly, the United States allowed the USSR to consolidate its control over Eastern Europe and North Korea.

In the 1950s and 1960s, while the United States could still play the role of the peacekeeper with its predominant strategic forces, it hesitated to protect the nations under its wings, such as Cuba, from the Soviet menace. In the 1970s the United States finally was outpaced by the USSR in war capability, despite its greater industrial capability, and began to lose control even over areas in which once the United States had unopposed hegemony. The U.S. image as a superpower was greatly shaken by the humiliating defeat in Vietnam. Accordingly, all the nations that had relied solely on U.S. protection had to seek alternative measures for their own survival. The stable bipolar world order of the Cold War era collapsed.

The transition from the stable U.S.-Soviet rivalry to the new anarchic disorder meant great danger for the peripheral nations of the old Free World community. With its shrinking power, the United States was forced to reduce its effective sphere of defense responsibilities to only the core members of its old bloc, namely the West European nations and Japan, leaving most of its old friends in the Third World undefended, even where treaty arrangements remained on paper.[12]

A recent survey conducted in the United States jointly by the *Dong-A Ilbo* and the Gallup Association revealed that only 43 percent of the U.S. public agreed to support South Korea in case of war (47 percent opposed). In South Korea, too, many security experts doubt the U.S. will as well as its capabilities to help South Korea in any new war. They are especially worried about the limited capabilities of the United States. In this situation, U.S. commitments to the defense of small allies are not accepted by friends and enemies alike to be as credible as before.

If war broke out in Korea today, we could expect prompt deployment of U.S. air and naval forces in the war zone. Could we expect, however, that the United States would and could send enough ground forces to stop North Korean aggressors?

According to an International Institute for Strategic Studies (IISS) report, the United States maintains an active army of 775,000 people, which includes four armored divisions, six mechanized divisions, four infantry divisions, one airmobile division, one airborne division, one armored brigade, four infantry brigades, and three independent armored cavalry regiments. If we add a marine corps of 188,100 men that operates three divisions, then the United States at the moment maintains roughly about a twenty-two-division equivalent ground combat strength.[13] Of these, only one infantry division is currently deployed in South Korea, and about three or four more divisions deployed in the Pacific and the West Coast may be available for prompt reinforcement.[14]

A more serious limitation in U.S. ability to intervene is its limited airlift capability. At present the United States maintains 218 C-130s, 70 C-5s, and 404 C-141 A and Bs.[15] The whole payload of these planes is 24,415 tons; therefore, even including extra cargo capacities of the civilian airplanes to be mobilized in an emergency, we can roughly estimate the maximum airlift capability across the Pacific to South Korea (about 6,000 miles from the West Coast) at no more than 2,000 tons per day.[16] This means that it would take more than a week to airlift an armored division from the continental United States to South Korea. Under these circumstances, it is natural that South Korean security planners are worrying about the credibility of the U.S. defense commitment.

Problems with the U.S. Strategic Concept

For the past thirty years the United States has spent enormous amounts on its defense and has maintained strategic nuclear forces superior to those of the USSR. As far as the ground forces are concerned, however, it has maintained an unbelievably small number of divisions, as pointed out earlier. The number of U.S. army divisions is about one-tenth that of the Chinese People's Liberation Army and even smaller than that of the North Korean People's Army. This means that the United States has never thought of ground battles as a means of checking Soviet challenges, at least outside the European theater.

The basic strategic concept of the United States seems to be based on the Klauswitzian doctrine of a concentration of power on the core of the enemy forces. In the bipolar conflict the USSR has been this core, with all other Soviet allies peripheral to the USSR. As the Soviet sphere of influence stretched from Europe across the Middle East and jumped into Africa and Asia, it might have been almost impossible to check Soviet expansionism all along the front line, since it would require more than a thousand divisions to build an effective blockade. Thus the United States must have chosen a strategy of deterrence in which it threatened the Soviet Union, the heart of the enemy forces, directly with formidable nuclear weapons.

Meanwhile the USSR, which was far weaker than the United States at the beginning of the confrontation in the late 1940s, seemed to respond with an opposite strategy, based on Lenin's indirect-war idea, a derivation of Sun Tzu's strategic thoughts—avoiding direct confrontation with the United States, the principal enemy, while nibbling at the isolated and weak peripheral areas, the loss of which was so negligible to the United States that it would not risk all-out war with the USSR.[17] The USSR intervened in Angola, the Congo, Somalia, Yemen, Afghanistan, Kampuchea, Guatemala, one by one; each time the stake was so small that the United States could not use its nuclear retaliatory power against the USSR.

Reviewing the past thirty years, we can say that the strategies of the United States and the USSR were both effective. The U.S. strategy of massive retaliation against the USSR was effective in that the USSR has been successfully deterred not to take any aggressive moves toward the key nations of Western Europe and Japan. On the other hand, the Soviet strategy of indirect and steady encroachment in peripheral areas, while keeping nonhostile relations with the United States itself, was also effective, since without arousing any serious retaliation by the United States, the USSR expanded its sphere of influence in Africa, Asia, and even Latin America.

The detente between the United States and the USSR that took shape in the 1970s meant strategically a shift from direct confrontation to indirect competition between the two antagonistic superpowers, which again meant that both agreed not to fight with each other directly. Thus theoretically the United States no longer has any deterrent countermeasures to Soviet expansion.

Probably the United States might have considered political and economic retaliation as a substitute for the old military retaliation to discourage Soviet aggression against allied nations and neutral Third World nations. Notwithstanding the validity of nonmilitary measures, however, it has become obvious that the new strategic concept of the United States does not work. The Carter administration tried to apply economic and political retaliation against the Soviet takeover of Afghanistan, but failed. With its reduced economic and political influence, the United States could not mobilize even its allies to take collective actions against the USSR.

The new U.S. strategic concept was interpreted by its allies as an indication of U.S. powerlessness, and the credibility of the U.S. security assurance rapidly eroded. In addition, the Carter administration shattered the image of a trustworthy United States, stating that the United States would reconsider its defense commitments and redefine its relations with old allies on the newly adopted criteria of political freedom. Carter's decision might have enhanced the U.S. image as the guardian of liberal democratic values, but it hurt its image as a faithful nation because the decision implied that even treaties signed by the U.S. government can be revoked unilaterally by the United States. In sum, the U.S. decision to shift from military countermeasures to political and economic means as the main retaliatory device against Soviet aggression, and President Carter's suggestion of unilateral alterability of U.S. defense commitments precipitated disillusionment in Korea about the value of U.S. protection.

New Dimension of the Korean Security Dilemma

The South Koreans who had naively taken U.S. support for granted were seriously shaken by President Carter's decision to withdraw ground troops from Korea. For the first time the South Koreans began to feel the urgent necessity of a self-reliant defense policy.

South Koreans now realize that the United States is no longer an almighty guarantor of their security, but only a helpful ally that can provide limited military and diplomatic support. Furthermore, South Koreans began to understand that not all the Free World nations that once presented a common front against communism would automatically support them in case of another war against the communist nations. Now they realize that there no longer exists a U.S. bloc or a Free World group. Their sudden awareness that the stable structure of the Cold War era has fallen apart aroused tremendous anxieties in the minds of South Koreans. South Korea hurriedly began to reassess its relations with each of the nations of the world, and tried to establish new relationships to adjust itself to the new multipolar international political system.

South Korea is engaged in an endless struggle with communist North Korea and thus cannot escape from the Cold War legacy of anticommunism. This means that for the foreseeable future there will be no chance for South Korea to improve its relations with the PRC and the USSR. South Korea, with its limited power, cannot confront the two giant communist neighbors by itself. It must rely on the United States for deterrents. A pro-Washington policy thus is a must for South Korean survival. Close association with the United States, however, hinders Korea's approach to the Third World nations as well as to all the communist nations. In the old days this was no problem because the U.S. assurance of protection was more than enough for security, and no additional help was needed. As the United States has lost its dominant position in global politics, however, this situation has changed.

The situation puts South Korea in a dilemma. If it chooses to remain under the U.S. defense umbrella in order to counter threats by the communist giants, it may lose access to new friends and allies that might help fill the security gap as U.S. power weakens. On the other hand, if it decides to dissociate itself from the United States, it would immediately be exposed to the menace of the USSR and its proxy, North Korea.

Economic Threats

During the Cold War era, South Korea had no difficulty obtaining necessary resources from abroad. It received most needed resources from the United States or nations under strong U.S. influence. As U.S. leadership in the world has eroded, however, this situation has changed. Now South Korea must acquire for itself what is needed for its industry. Oil supplies must be directly negotiated with the oil-producing Middle East nations. New markets must be explored with its own effort.

South Korea is figuratively an island, isolated from the outside world by the Pacific Ocean on the south and the Asian communist nations on the west and the north. As mentioned earlier, its conflict with North Korea deprives it of access to its communist neighbors; and its close relation with the United States disturbs its access to the nonaligned Third World nations.

South Korea is a newly industrialized country with a predominantly externally oriented economic structure. It has a very small territory with almost no natural resources. South Korea imports most of its raw materials from abroad and exports about one-third of its GNP. Thus its dependence on foreign trade is astonishingly high.[18]

Meanwhile, South Korea, with limited industrial capability and a small economy, does not have great influence on her trade partners. For example, 26.3 percent of South Korean imports came from Japan in 1980, but this accounted for only 2.3 percent of Japanese exports in that year. Exports to the United States in the same year constituted 26.3 percent of South Korean exports, but only 2.06 percent of total U.S. imports. In 1980 South Korea imported 93 percent of its oil from Kuwait and Saudi Arabia, but its exports to these nations amounted to only 2.2 percent of their total imports. Thus South Korea was not in the position to exert strong bargaining power on these major trading partners and oil suppliers.

With such a high economic dependence on the outside world, it seems to many Koreans that their economy is at the mercy of much larger trading partners. For instance, imposition of an import quota by the United States on color television sets alone or Japanese tariff increases can be a serious threat to the South Korean economy. An Arab oil embargo would suffocate the South Korean economy within a month or two. A precarious economy that is highly dependent on factors beyond South Korean control thus becomes another source of South Korean apprehensions about their future destiny.

Conclusion

The Koreans have a long history of hostile interactions with big neighbors. They have been invaded by the Chinese, the Mongols, the Manchus, and the Japanese. More recently the Sino-Japanese War of 1894 and the Russo-Japanese War of 1905 were fought on their territory. They were occupied by the Japanese for thirty-five years, until 1945, and by Russians and Americans for three years after the end of World War II. Throughout the two thousand years of its written history, Korea has lived under incessant threats from powerful neighbors.

Historically the most dangerous periods for Koreans have occurred when the power balance among the surrounding nations was shifting. Whenever a new power emerged in East Asia, Korea suffered the most. In the thirteenth century, when the Mongols defeated the Chinese, Korea was invaded. When the Manchus defeated the Ming dynasty in the seventeenth century, Korea suffered greatly. When Japan became the new power in East Asia after it defeated the Manchus at the end of the nineteenth century, Korea lost its independence and became a Japanese colony.

In the 1980s we anticipate another power transition, from U.S. dominance to Soviet superiority in East Asia. Thus the Koreans are very concerned about their destiny in the anticipated international turmoils this shift will bring.

As a relatively small nation surrounded by big powers, Korea has never been able to quell neighboring nations with military power to secure its own safety. With strong determination to resist foreign invasions, however, Koreans have successfully sustained Korea's independence and security, with only a few exceptions.

As the coordinated efforts of a crew can save a small ship in a stormy sea, so, with the fully integrated effort of its people as a whole, South Korea will be able to survive the treacherous sea of power transition in the 1980s.

Notes

1. The first informal contact between the Seoul government and the Pyongyang regime took place in 1972, and a joint communique in which both sides pledged peaceful unification of Korea was issued by the delegates of the two governments. The delegates, however, did not claim that they were representatives of the governments; they signed the document simply "upholding the desires of their respective superiors." Legally both sides still claim the entire Korean peninsula as their territory, ignoring each other.

2. On North Korean determination to achieve national unification, see Jong-ho Ho, *Chuchesasang-e Kichohan Namchoson Hyokmyong-Kwa Chokuktongil Riron (Theories on Revolution in South Korea and National Reunification Based on the Juche Idea)* (Pyongyang: Sahoekwahak Chulpansa, 1975). For the development of their belligerent unification policy, see In-Duck Kang, "Revolution and Reunification," in *North Korean Communism*, ed. Chung-Shik Chung and Gahb-Chol Kim (Seoul: Research Center for Peace and Unification [RCPU], 1980), pp. 282-341; and Sang-Woo Rhee, "North Korea's Unification Strategy: Review of Military Strategies," in *Politics of Korean Reunification*, ed. Young Hoon Kang and Yong Soon Yim (Seoul: RCPU, 1978), pp. 127-157.

3. The survey was conducted in the summer of 1981 by Kwan-shik Min of the Asian Institute for Public Policy. The sample includes professors, members of the National Assembly, business leaders, and journalists.

4. See Sang-Woo Rhee, "Public Opinion on the Reunification and Nuclear Armament," *Hankuk-ui Anbo Hwankyong (The Security Environment of Korea)*, vol. 2 (Seoul: Goshiyongu Company, 1980), chap. 29, pp. 425-451.

5. These statistics are not publicly confirmed by any authoritative agencies. I based the figures on the information I could obtain. The U.S. Department of Defense (DOD) also has confirmed North Korean military superiority to South Korea and the offensive nature of the former's military structure. In the 1981 *Annual Report*, the DOD concluded that:

Starting early in the 1970s, the North Koreans have engaged in a major military build-up, primarily of their ground forces. The North Korean Army now has a strength of around 600,000 men: a substantial increase over the 450,000 with which we had previously credited Pyongyang, and with more tanks and artillery than we had previously thought. The intentions of North Korea are unclear, but its military forces clearly are not geared for defensive operations. . . . [p. 50]

North Korean ground forces are now larger than those of South Korea, and they have advantages over the South in artillery and tanks. [p. 113]

In the fiscal 1982 report, the DOD stated that ". . . the balance between North and South Korea has shifted from rough parity in 1970 to Northern superiority, as North Korea's ground forces have nearly doubled" (p. 88).

6. For a detailed discussion of the methodology and source material, see Sang-Woo Rhee, "North Korea Today and Tomorrow: Ideology, Social Change, and Policy toward the South," delivered at Conference on North Korea, cosponsored by the Korean Association for Communist Studies and Institute of East Asian Studies, University of California, Berkeley, held in San Francisco, 23-28 February 1981.

7. A thorough survey of the U.S. attitude toward South Korea was recently reported at a Conference on Korean-American relations, 29-31 October 1981 in Seoul. William Watts, "The United States and Korea: Perception vs. Reality," unpublished draft.

8. See Kang, "Revolution and Reunification."

9. A survey conducted in 1978 revealed that 62.9 percent of the population regarded themselves belonging to the middle class, and another survey published in the *Chosun Ilbo* in March 1980 showed that 78 percent of the national sample considered themselves as being in the middle class.

10. Ray S. Cline, *World Power Trends and U.S. Foreign Policy for the 1980s* (Boulder: Westview Press, 1980), p. 173, table 34.

11. Ibid., pp. 136-137, table 31.

12. The U.S. Department of Defense (DOD) publicly recognized the reduced operational area of its land forces to the European theater, stating that "our land forces are designed primarily to counter Soviet/Warsaw Pact ground forces in Europe as part of the NATO alliance." See the *DOD Annual Report, FY 1981*, p. 150.

13. The *DOD Annual Report FY 1981* states that the United States retains a total of twenty-eight divisions: nineteen active divisions (sixteen army and three marine corps) and nine reserve component divisions.

14. These include the 25th Army Division in Hawaii, the 7th Army Division in California, the 1st Marine Division in California, and the 3rd Marine Division in Okinawa. For details, see Sang-Woo Rhee, "Tongpuk-a Kwanryonkuk dul-ui Chonryok Tongwonnungryok . . . " ("Mobilizing Capabilities of the Northeast Asian Nations . . . "), *Yonkunonch'ong*

(*Kukche Munche Ch'osa Yonkuso*), vol. 2, 1980, pp. 71-118. The author estimated that at the maximum the United States can deploy about three divisions in the first three days and an additional eleven divisions in ten days. Considering that the United States should retain reserves for a European contingency, the most likely reinforcement in a Korean war zone would not exceed four divisions.

15. Figures are taken from *Military Balance, 1981-82.*

16. This figure was calculated using data derived from the U.S. airlift records during the Yom Kippur War. The average airlift during the war was about 1,200 tons per day.

17. For an excellent analytic assessment of Soviet strategy, see R.J. Rummel, "Soviet and American Strategy, The Probability of a Soviet-American War, and Northeast Asia," delivered at International Symposium in Search of a Peace System in Northeast Asia, 15-17 November 1978, Japan Press Center, Tokyo; and idem, "Soviet Strategy and Northeast Asia," *Korea and World Affairs: A Quarterly Review* 2, no. 1 (Spring 1978):3-45. In this article Rummel points out that

> their [Soviet] goals and means are organized around a superordinate intention: the struggle to defeat capitalism and make Soviet communism globally dominant . . . the United States is perceived as the main enemy and arsenal whose defeat or neutralization would assure the final goal . . . and detente is a tactic to inhibit Western reactions to the success and advances of the anti-capitalist struggle.

And see also Amoretta M. Hoeber and Joseph D. Douglas, Jr., "Soviet Approach to Global Nuclear Conflict," in *The United States in the 1980s*, ed. Peter Duignan and Alvin Rabushka (Palo Alto: Hoover Institute, Stanford University, 1980), pp. 445-467. These authors concluded that

> their [Soviet] strategic objective is to acquire a combination of offensive and defensive capabilities that not only will support their expansionism, but will permit, should war come, a Soviet victory. The most important aspect of this strategy are superiority, surprise, survival, and clear and coherent goals. [p. 449]

18. In 1980 the total GNP of South Korea was $57,650 million, and it exported $17,050 million and imported $22,292 million. This means that Korea exported 29.58 percent of its total GNP. The data are from *International Economic Report (1981)*, compiled by the Korea International Economic Institute.

7

Indonesia's Security and Threat Perceptions

Jusuf Wanandi
and *M. Hadisoesastro*

This chapter discusses the main issues for Indonesia in assessing threats to its security in the future. In view of all the problems faced by Indonesia, it seems insufficient to use the words *security* and *threat,* with their emphasis on war, armed rebellion, civil war, and other violent actions.

For Southeast Asia, including Indonesia, the terms *security* and *threat* should have a broader meaning and should be interpreted more flexibly to include political, economic, social, cultural, and ideological aspects. These aspects have both domestic and external dimensions, which are closely interrelated. It should be noted that although military aspects are important, they are not the determining factors in Indonesia's perception of security and threat. This is clearly reflected in Indonesia's defense budget; it remains relatively low, although substantial increases were made in the last few years as a result of the objective need for improvements in training and hardware.

The general view in Indonesia remains that for the next ten years or so the challenge to Indonesia's security stems from internal problems that will have to be solved by Indonesia's national forces and leadership themselves. This is not to deny that international developments also affect Indonesia's security. This view has been reinforced by the fact that since 1975 Southeast Asia no longer has been an arena for direct great-power involvement. It is worth noting, however, that the conflict over Kampuchea since early 1979 does create a new opportunity for the great powers to involve themselves in the affairs of the region, particularly for expanding the Sino-Soviet competition into Southeast Asia. Possible U.S. involvement here should also be taken into account.

Despite the Indochina conflict, the general situation in Southeast Asia today differs from that of a few years ago. ASEAN member countries, individually and collectively, have developed successfully: they are stable politically, are progressing admirably in the economic field, and have greatly enhanced their self-confidence. They also have been able to overcome a variety of domestic problems by themselves and are playing an important role in determining Southeast Asia's future. Thus one can no longer speak of these countries as falling dominoes.

The following views are greatly influenced by our experience of Indonesian history and environment and thus differ subtly from the views of other ASEAN member countries.

Internal Problems

A major problem faced by Indonesia for at least the next generation is in dealing with the many societal changes arising out of the process of development. Success in national development brings with it great changes in value systems over a short period of time. Economic development and the introduction of modern technology, transportation, and telecommunication have opened the developing nations to the international world.

Essentially, all change is a source of instability in society. The question is whether changes can be channelled in such a way as to minimize their destabilizing effects and to balance these effects with stabilizing factors. These factors incude: (1) the existence of a national consensus on the direction and means of those changes; (2) the existence of political and social institutions that can channel the changes in an orderly way; (3) the existence of national solidarity regarding the development process and the just distribution of the gains of development; and (4) the existence of a national leadership that is capable of harmonizing traditional and new values.

There is optimism about Indonesia's longer-term development prospects because of the inherent ability of the society to undergo the process of acculturation with foreign cultures, as well as its resource base, both human and natural. The problems of the next ten to twenty years, however, will still be enormous and complex, primarily because of Indonesia's geographic factors, its huge population, the plurality of its society, and its relatively early stage of economic development. In fact, successes in Indonesia's development efforts to date have brought about new problems for which appropriate solutions need to be found.

Conscious development efforts in the developing world started only after World War II. Thus it is still too early to judge whether a development model exists that promises success in the longer term. Recently, South Korea, Taiwan, and Singapore have had successful development efforts. It is questionable, however, whether their development models can be emulated and whether their strategies will continue to be successful in the years to come. There are still no scientific methods to assess the process of development in the developing world. Thus no definite conclusions can be reached. The Indonesian case is no exception, and the development process in Indonesia is likely to continue to involve trial and errors. The challenge to the system as a whole is whether this learning process can be dealt with in an appropriate and dynamic fashion.

In more concrete terms, Indonesia faces the following problems.

National Unity

In the first twenty years after independence, national unity was challenged by a variety of separatist movements and rebellions through civil wars and attempted coups d'etat. Most of these problems have been overcome. Past experience has shown that separatism has little chance of success. In addition, both the bureaucracy and the armed forces have established themselves as strong integrating forces in society. Furthermore, the development of physical infrastructure, transportation, and communication (including outside Java), and improved regional distribution of economic activities, all have strengthened the sense of unity in the country.

Issues of minority participation—between various ethnic groups and of citizens from Chinese origin—are still alive and sometimes lead to social conflict, but these conflicts do not destabilize the government or the country as a whole. One area of concern relates to the phenomenon of extremist groups employing the banner of Islam and arguing that modernization has undermined religious life. These small and fragmented groups reject a priori Pancasila as the foundation of the state and the development strategy that has received a national consensus. The existence of such extremist groups often has been misread and misinterpreted as a manifestation of a growing conflict between the government, the armed forces, and Islam. Islam is the religion of the majority of Indonesians, but the national consensus arrived at by an absolute majority rejected the creation of either a theocratic or a secular state, and fully endorsed the establishment of a state based on Pancasila, in which religious freedom and interests are recognized and promoted.

Communism will not be an urgent problem for at least the next ten years because the traumatic effects of the 1965 attempted coup by the Indonesian Communist party (PKI) are still deeply felt in the society at large. The threat of communism will be minimized or eliminated if ongoing development efforts successfully improve the well-being of the Indonesian people. Organized communist activities could well attempt to frustrate development efforts by manipulating latent conflicts in society as described earlier. On their own, however, the communists do not have the power to destabilize the country.

Economic Development

It is only natural that the Soeharto government, which inherited an almost bankrupt economy, has emphasized economic development. This emphasis grew out of a national consensus that put a priority on increasing the well-being of the people (prosperity approach) as well as on safeguarding the country from internal instabilities (security approach). Economic development has been pursued systematically since 1969, with the formulation and implementation of the First Five-Year Development Plan.

The challenges faced by the economic planners were enormous in view of the size of Indonesia's population and its concentration on Java; the lack of physical infrastructure (especially outside Java); the lack of socioeconomic infrastructure in general; and low production capacities, especially in the rural areas that encompass about 80 percent of the population.

From a macroeconomic point of view, a number of problems needed to be resolved. The major task was to introduce fiscal and monetary discipline but at the same time to attain significant economic growth. In resolving this problem, the main features of the government's policy were: (1) to adopt a restrictive monetary policy and gradually to liberalize the financial system; (2) to increase the role of the government's budget as the main instrument for development and to strengthen the private sector so that it could play a greater role in economic development; (3) to provide subsidies to a number of economic sectors that were considered important in the provision of basic needs, such as food, clothing, and housing, without creating too heavy pressures on the fiscal system; (4) to complement scarce domestic capital resources with external funds, primarily foreign assistance and direct investment.

In the course of development, various criticisms have been raised about these policies. Monetary policies often have been regarded as too restrictive and therefore as not having helped to encourage greater production. The role of the government as an agent for development tends to go beyond what is considered healthy. Foreign capital is criticized, especially by certain political groups. These problems, however, are not specific to Indonesia but are inevitable in the development process.

Nonetheless, economic management and development in Indonesia for the last ten years have brought some significant results. The country has maintained general economic and monetary stability and has attained real economic growth of about 80 percent per annum on average. With the growth of domestic capital (savings), issues of foreign capital have become less controversial; in the 1982-1983 budget, project aid will constitute about 20 percent of the government's development expenditures, compared with about 80 percent in the 1969-1970 budget.

Still, although the macroeconomic performance of the Indonesian economy has been remarkably successful, questions remain on a number of microeconomic issues, of which income distribution is the main one. In the absence of reliable data, it is not easy to examine distributional issues. Despite the lack of such data for Indonesia, however, certain inferences can be made. The majority of the population has gained from development, but some have gained more than others. In some sectors, income distribution has worsened. From a developmental point of view, it is important to note that a large segment of the population has moved from below the poverty line upward. It cannot be denied, however, that unbalanced growth raises political problems.

The government understands that these problems need to be dealt with seriously. Although trickling down does occur in a number of sectors and regions, other sectors and regions lag behind. Political stability has contributed to economic stability, but economic issues also affect political stability.

Political development cannot be ignored because political issues that emerge from the process of economic development itself need to find their political expressions and to be channeled in an institutionalized fashion. In addition, with the emergence of a growing middle class as a result of progress in economic development, the process of institution building in general and political-institution building in particular has become a crucial element of national development.

The Third Five-Year Development Plan, starting in 1974-1975, gave greater emphasis to distributional issues, as demonstrated in the reallocation of government expenditures. Assistance to the so-called economically weak has been stepped up as well, both through the budget, with the expansion of basic need programs, and through the banking sector, in the form of a variety of small-scale credits. In many cases these programs have not proved as effective as planned, largely as a result of organizational and managerial problems.

Basic needs programs involved bureaucracies at the lower levels, in particular, the village level where managerial skill is still underdeveloped. Private participation and organization at this level—such as through cooperatives—need to be developed in an atmosphere of reduced government command. It is now recognized, especially since development programs have become more extensive and more complex, that managerial and organizational capabilities constitute a major bottleneck. In view of this, the 1982-1983 budget will allocate, for the first time, the largest amount of resources to the educational sector.

There is also a recognition that balanced economic development will require greater efforts to restructure the economy, primarily to eliminate various structural features that brought about dualistic development, the rural-urban gap, the gap between large and small economic units, and so on, which in turn cause fragmentation in the economy.

Efforts to restructure the economy will cause greater competition in the allocation of resources between the economic sector and other sectors. This is the greatest challenge of the current stage of development in Indonesia. Resolution of this problem requires not only political stability but also a more highly developed political structure.

Political Development

Political development has been recognized as an important task in Indonesia today because economic development alone cannot reach all strata in society in a short period of time. In the process of economic development and change, there are always groups that move ahead and those that are left behind. Thus there is an objective need to correct this process by formulating a more balanced national-development program to include social development, primarily in the fields of education and health, as well as political development to satisfy demands for participation of the growing middle class and the population in general.

In the realm of political development in Indonesia, there are two main issues. The first is the formulation of a national political system that is capable of harmonizing traditional values with new values that are strongly influenced by Western culture—namely, human (individual) rights—including political rights such as freedom of the press, academic freedom, and the one man, one vote principle—as well as the development of democracy, the rule of law, and limitations on government power.

These values have become more relevant as progress is made in the field of education, communication, and the mass media, and as there is an expansion of the middle class, comprising professional groups, intellectuals, technocrats, the bureaucracy, skilled workers, and entrepreneurs. Development often could lead to a clash with the traditional values and paternalism that are still prevalent in the society. This is a major challenge faced by the government and leaders of the society.

Japan's political system, which is capable of harmonizing traditional values with new (Western) values, is often called a model for political development. We question whether this model is applicable to Indonesia, given its pluralistic society, compared with the homogeneous Japanese society. It should be noted, however, that from an anthropological and sociological perspective, involving languages, customs, and customary law, and basic ideas and values, there are more similarities than differences among the various ethnic groups in Indonesia. As mentioned earlier, one can also discern a greater sense of unity in society today. A political system that gives all citizens opportunities to participate in national development is an absolute necessity to maintain and strengthen national unity.

The second issue is the building and consolidation of political and social institutions, including state institutions such as the People's Consultative Assembly, the House of Representatives, and the political parties, as well as professional organizations such as labor and farmers' unions, and journalists', women's, youth, religious, and enterpreneurs' associations.

Greater participation by a growing part of the population needs to be encouraged in implementing expanded and more complex development programs. The government and the bureaucracy are the main actors in the early stages of development, but this role must gradually be transferred to the private sector. Building and consolidating political and social institutions take time. The prevalence of paternalism makes two-way communication difficult to materialize. In developing societies, the role of the government and the bureaucracy tend to be so dominant that conscious efforts and policies by the government itself and the society as a whole are needed for developing the necessary private-sector political and social institutions.

Another important factor in political development in Indonesia relates to the role of the armed forces. Because of their history, originating with the revolution and the war of independence, the Indonesian armed forces play a unique role in national development, including political development. The significant contribution of the armed forces in creating the state gives them the right and responsibility to adopt a dual role or a dual function, and this role is accepted by the people at large. This dual role is performed by the armed forces according to the situation and condition at a particular period in time. Far fewer active military personnel occupy administrative positions in the civilian bureaucracy than was true ten years ago. The armed forces no longer allow active military personnel to take positions in the Golkar leadership, despite the fact that Golkar basically is the government's party.

The armed forces are now in the process of reducing their role in nonmilitary affairs. They have drastically reduced the number of active personnel in service, from about 660,000 in 1966 to about 300,000 (including the police force) at present. Questions have often been raised about the capability of the younger generation in the armed forces to perform this dual role because this younger generation consists of graduates of the various military academies and does not come directly from the people, as was the case with the 1945 generation. Generational changes within the armed forces have occurred continuously over the last twenty years, exposing each new generation to the theory and practice of the sociopolitical role of the armed forces in society. Outside observers also pose the question of how long the armed forces will continue to play a role in political life. This certainly will depend on developments in the two areas described earlier—that is, the political system and political and social institutions. On the one hand, modernization brought about by development will tend to lead the society toward greater specialization and differentiation, in which the armed forces' military role will receive greater emphasis. On the other hand, national development must be guaranteed its continuation before the armed forces can reduce their sociopolitical role, because development requires political stability.

The Problem of Succession

The succession problem in developing countries has become a favorite subject of many scholars and the media, who predict that a country that does not create an orderly mechanism for succession is doomed to collapse. Succession is an important factor but not the only determinant factor in security; its influence on security differs from one country to another, and no single model of succession applies to different countries. Singapore, for example, has made conscious efforts to prepare a new generation of political leaders, largely because of the very limited pool of political figures in that country. Not only is its population base small, but the interest of the younger generation lies mainly with the private sector. Indonesia, in comparison, has a large population base and a politically active elite. Thus preparing some individuals to be the next generation of political leaders in the Singaporean fashion has not been considered necessary. In due time the next leadership will emerge by itself. In addition, there is an institution within the Golkar—namely the supervisory board (*dewan bembina*)—comprising forty-five leaders of society, including retired armed forces figures; social and political leaders, and technocrats, headed by President Soeharto himself, which in due time will elect its candidates. This mechanism can provide the necessary political support for the candidate and legitimate the candidate as the party's choice.

In view of sociopolitical and cultural factors as well as progress made in economic development, it can be expected that whoever takes over the government in the next ten years or so will come from and receive the support of the present ruling coalition (the armed forces, technocrats, bureaucrats, professionals, and the middle class).

Developments in the Asian-Pacific Region

The external environment can affect Indonesia's security in two ways: (1) in the form of infiltration and subversion in support of internal rebellious groups, and (2) in the form of conflicts in the surrounding area that could divert attention and resources from national-development efforts. These two threats to security and stability are not urgent for the time being for Indonesia or the other ASEAN countries.

Increasing national resilience is the response to the first kind of threat. The problems of main concern in this realm were dealt with in the previous section. In dealing with the second kind of threat, Indonesia has adopted a positive and good-neighbor policy by promoting ASEAN cooperation as a priority in its foreign policy.

Cooperation within the ASEAN framework has not only served to overcome and prevent intraregional conflicts, but has also strengthened the position of the group in its dealings on extraregional relations, both politically and economically. ASEAN as a group has successfully created the basis for structuring broader relationships with other Southeast Asian countries—namely, the three Indochina countries—despite the Kampuchean conflict, as well as with the great powers that are present in the region and with the international world. This broader structure of relationships is to be achieved through the creation of a regional order for Southeast Asia, ultimately based on the ZOPFAN (Zone of Peace, Freedom, and Neutrality) idea and manifested in its initial effort in the Treaty of Amity and Cooperation. The ultimate aim is to enable the countries of the region collectively to determine their own destiny in the future.

The ZOPFAN idea is itself based on the achievement of a regional resilience of ASEAN as a group, with which it could negotiate with the three Indochina countries and offer them—with a great sense of self-confidence—a regional order for Southeast Asia. It is also through this idea that the ASEAN countries attempt to structure a balanced relationship with the great powers and to play a more active and constructive role in international forums, interregional organizations, and other multilateral cooperation schemes.

ASEAN has no illusions; the ZOPFAN idea cannot be realized overnight. In the meantime, however, each ASEAN country has successfully improved its national resilience and greatly increased its self-confidence in dealing with its own domestic problems. In addition, ASEAN's experiences in overcoming intraregional conflicts have greatly strengthened its sense of solidarity. These all provide for a strong foundation for pursuing the ZOPFAN idea further. ASEAN's efforts to structure its relations with other regional bodies, such as the European Communities, and to play an active and constructive role in the international forums and other multilateral bodies such as the various commodity associations, have shown significant results. These efforts have greatly improved the international reputation of ASEAN.

Nonetheless, there are two areas that deserve ASEAN's serious attention and efforts in promoting a regional order for Southeast Asia. First, the conflict in Kampuchea, which constitutes a real obstacle to achieving this regional order, must be resolved. Second, structuring of a balanced relationship with—and acceptable to—the great powers remains an intricate problem.

The Kampuchean Problem

The Kampuchean conflict is complex, and one cannot expect a solution in the near future. First, it involves Kampuchean factions that are divided among themselves. Second, it also involves Vietnam, which has invaded Kampuchea to support one faction and to destroy another faction, which is backed by China and therefore has been regarded as a threat to Vietnam's security.

ASEAN is not directly involved in the conflict, but its concern with the development in Indochina originates from the fact that the principle of national sovereignty has been violated, constituting a bad precedent for the region. The invasion by Vietnam also has upset the balance in mainland Southeast Asia and poses a problem for Thailand because of the presence of Vietnamese forces on its borders.

A third factor that complicates the conflict relates to the involvement of the great powers, primarily China and the USSR, which support different conflicting parties. The Kampuchean conflict, therefore, could bring the Sino-Soviet conflict into Southeast Asia and gravely destabilize the region. In addition, because of the rising tensions between the USSR and the United States globally, Southeast Asia—which since the Vietnam War has been able largely to free itself from the East-West confrontation—again could become an arena of conflict. There is also the danger that the great powers will exploit this conflict for their own interests without paying due attention to the interests and aspirations of the Southeast Asian countries.

For the time being, the situation in Kampuchea seems to be bearable to all the conflicting parties. Therefore, one is not likely to see the kind of significant changes in their policies in the near future that are needed for any real solution.

Despite the complexity of the Kampuchean problem, a protracted conflict is not in the interest of ASEAN for reasons discussed earlier. A protracted conflict could easily trigger large-scale Vietnamese incursions on the Thai border, perhaps with the aim of forcing Thailand to change its policies, which are considered to be too pro-China and anti-Vietnam. Vietnam may also release another wave of refugees to create burdens for its neighboring countries, although this can hurt Vietnam itself in the longer term.

Vietnam, on its side, also may not be able to sustain a protracted conflict in Kampuchea because of continuous deterioration of its economy, and may be weakened totally from within. There is no certainty, however, that a worsening situation internally would in itself force Vietnamese leaders to back down. Short of this, the USSR may be invited to step up its presence in the region, which in turn will intensify the conflict and complicate the great powers' political configuration in the region.

For the next six months or so, the Ad Hoc Committee of the International Conference on Kampuchea (ICK) should be given the opportunity to develop a new initiative to solve the conflict. ASEAN should also attempt to find other options toward reaching a solution on the Kampuchean conflict. In doing so, it must take certain steps.

First, it must make a comprehensive assessment of the situation in Kampuchea and the conflicting factions there, as well as of the influence of and positions taken by outside parties, including the great powers.

Second, it must come up with a more comprehensive ASEAN political framework (blueprint) based on the foregoing assessment, to be used as a guide for all ASEAN countries. A general ASEAN political framework was formulated at the ASEAN's Foreign Ministers Meeting in Manila in June 1981 in preparation for the ICK in New York. This framework is still valid but needs to be refined.

Third, to achieve the first two and to be able to pay continuous attention to the future development and solution of the Kampuchean conflict, an ad hoc planning committee is urgently needed to propose various alternative solutions to the ASEAN foreign ministers. Whether this committee is new or whether its task could be given to existing ASEAN institutions is up to the ASEAN ministers to decide. It would be ideal if the ad hoc planning committee were an interdepartmental institution so that all the institutions that play some role in the decision-making process of each ASEAN member could also be coordinated to a certain extent.

These three steps are especially important in preserving ASEAN's solidarity, integrity, and unity in its endeavors to participate in resolving the Kampuchean conflict. Whether there should be a regional conference or an international one is not certain. Vietnam proposes a regional conference to discuss regional problems, including the Kampuchean problem, with the five permanent members of the U.N. Security Council and the U.N. Secretary-General present as observers. ASEAN could agree to that proposal only if that regional conference were related to the ICK. ASEAN thinks that an overall solution to the Kampuchean conflict could be initiated but not achieved by a regional conference because of the involvement of two great powers: the PRC and the USSR.

ASEAN's initiatives, based on a common political framework, are probably needed in the near future to approach the main conflicting parties, Vietnam and the PRC. Indonesia, which is considered to have the closest relationship with Vietnam among ASEAN member countries, could approach Vietnam on behalf of ASEAN.

One element in ASEAN's efforts would be confidence building between ASEAN and Vietnam. ASEAN needs a viable Vietnam for the future of Southeast Asia; therefore, ASEAN is seriously seeking a solution that takes account of Vietnam's interests as well. This can be seen from the attention the ASEAN foreign ministers paid to Vietnam's concerns in their June 1981 Manila meeting and in the subsequent ICK Meeting in New York in July 1981, which clearly showed the differences between the PRC and ASEAN in solving the Kampuchean conflict. Indonesia believes that Chinese pressures on Southeast Asia in the future could be reduced and balanced effectively, if all the countries in the region support the idea of ZOPFAN. ASEAN would also try to convince Vietnam that a lasting solution requires that Vietnam too make concessions and accept a change in the status quo. Without a compromise from Vietnam there can be no solution to the Kampuchean conflict. This would only increase the burden on Vietnam rather than on ASEAN.

On the other hand, Thailand (and possibly Singapore) could approach the PRC to seek a compromise; up to now the PRC has shown no willingness to make concessions except in trivial matters, because it would like to use Democratic Kampuchea to destroy Vietnam. If the PRC is unwilling to compromise in the near future, ASEAN-PRC relations, which are showing a gradual improvement, would again deteriorate—to the disadvantage of both sides. In this complex problem the United States definitely has a role to play, mainly in the political arena.

1. The United States should give stronger support to ASEAN's policies in seeking a compromise to the Kampuchean conflict. It has not always done so—for example, in the ICK Meeting in New York in July 1981.
2. The United States should give more concrete guarantees to Thailand, to increase its self-confidence and its ability to seek a solution to the Kampuchean conflict without depending too much on the PRC position of continued support for Democratic Kampuchea. These guarantees could include air cover if Vietnam invades Thailand, more aid for military hardware and training, and security support to help compensate Thailand for the extra expenditures it must make for security reasons.
3. The United States should put pressure on the PRC to be more forthcoming in reaching an accommodation with Vietnam so that Vietnam will not be too dependent on the USSR and give the Soviets further opportunities to increase their presence in the region.
4. The United States could start to normalize its relations with Hanoi if the latter is willing to make some concessions in solving the Kampuchean conflict. This normalization process should be carried out in stages—for instance, by first initiating some economic relations with Vietnam, which could make Vietnam more flexible toward the United States.

All these possibilities, unfortunately, will not be realized because the United States has many limitations that reduce its flexibility, including the following:

1. The anti-Vietnam mood in U.S. public opinion is still very deep, and an accommodation with that country would not easily be accepted.
2. One should not expect the Reagan administration to be flexible toward Vietnam—especially toward normalization with Vietnam—unless it is clear that Vietnam is going to reduce Soviet influence. It is also difficult to expect such a flexible attitude from Vietnam vis-a-vis the USSR in the near future.
3. Although the so-called Vietnam syndrome is declining, there is little popular support for the involvement of U.S. forces in a Third World country, especially in Southeast Asia. This makes the U.S. administra-

tion hesitant to promise any direct military support, even in the form of air cover for Thailand.
4. U.S.-Chinese relations for the time being are troubled by the Taiwan issue; therefore, one can not be too optimistic about the potential for U.S. leverage on the PRC in the case of Kampuchea.

Only if all ASEAN members together insist clearly and candidly on U.S. support for a policy of compromise toward Vietnam will there be hope for a more flexible U.S. policy; in that event Vietnam's willingness to compromise also will be a most important factor.

What could be expected from a coalition government or a united front of the three anti-Heng Samrin factions? Basically, it is a tactic for the U.N. General Assembly to cover Democratic Kampuchea's bad image in international public opinion and in that way to get more international support for ASEAN's position, which constitutes political pressure on Vietnam. Whether such a move will get results or not remains to be seen. Indonesia clearly is not too optimistic that the coalition government or the united front will bring greater results.

Indonesia likes the idea of supporting an anticommunist or nationalist third force based on Son Sann's forces. Whether this idea is viable or not will depend on the kind of military support such a force could muster, and the Indonesian view is that Son Sann is unable to organize an effective force. Moreover, ASEAN is not an association created for military cooperation; thus it cannot support Son Sann militarily. Nonetheless, each member country of ASEAN has the freedom to assist Son Sann or the third force in accordance with its own capabilities.

Great Power Relationship in Southeast Asia

ASEAN's long-term political program for Southeast Asia, ZOPFAN, would permit all the great powers to be present but allow none to have a dominating role. The countries of the region would be able to decide their own future. From Indonesia's point of view the idea should be implemented through national and regional resilience, so that great powers' formal support would not be an absolute necessity. Although the presence of the great powers in the area should be in balance, the fact is that ASEAN's political and economic relations have been largely with the United States and Japan. For the time being, ASEAN is clearly closer to the United States and Japan than to the PRC or the USSR. The presence of the PRC and the USSR in the region is regarded as acceptable and unavoidable; but ideally that presence should be arranged through ZOPFAN in an orderly and balanced way, rather than in the form of an increasing military presence only.

Through ZOPFAN the ASEAN countries try to establish a kind of regional order for Southeast Asia that also takes into account the presence and relationship with all the great powers in the region.

The increase of the Soviet naval presence in the Asian-Pacific area, including Southeast Asia, because of the facilities at Cam Ranh Bay and Danang, in the longer term (ten years or so) will arouse apprehensions in the region if it is done continuously without any counterbalance from the United States and Japan. Soviet capabilities in Southeast Asia have up to now been intended primarily to collect intelligence data, to develop a capability to project power in the region and into the Indian Ocean in time of crisis, to balance the U.S. Seventh Fleet at Subic and Clark Field, and to balance the PRC along its southern borders. Thus an increase of U.S. Seventh Fleet presence in the Asian-Pacific region is needed as a counterbalance; the bases in Subic and Clark Field, which will be renegotiated with the Philippine government next year, constitute an absolute necessity for the U.S. presence in Southeast Asia. Reagan's strong policy of taking countermeasures to the increasing presence of Soviet Pacific Fleet is reassuring to friends of the United States and its allies in the region.

Japan

ASEAN would certainly support an increase in Japan's self-defense forces if it is intended for defense of the Japanese archipelago and its surrounding seas, even of sea-lanes a thousand nautical miles southward and eastward. It is understandable that without an increase of burden sharing from U.S. allies, U.S. public opinion will be reluctant to support a great increase in its defense budget in the longer future. If the United States intends to give some kind of regional role to Japan in the Asian-Pacific area, including the protection of Japan's vital sea-lanes through Southeast Asia, then a lot of discussion with ASEAN is need to make it acceptable.

The main problems are: (1) the ASEAN countries aspire to be capable of defending their own seas, including the right of free passage through their territorial waters in the 1990s; (2) the role Japan will play in the region is still unclear to U.S. officials and defense experts. Besides, the consequences for the United States itself of giving Japan a regional role have not been thought out. Because of history and past experience, ASEAN members will not easily accept an expanded role without serious consultation on exactly what the role might include and how it could relate to ASEAN's own plans for a regional order and regional defense.

The ASEAN countries also fear that U.S. credibility in the region will be again questioned if a regional role is given to Japan, and that the USSR might use this development to increase its own military presence.

There would clearly need to be some coordination between Japan and ASEAN regarding the future regional security of East Asia. In that context the problem of free passage through Southeast Asian waters should surely be included. For that purpose Japan should implement the kind of technology transfer that would increase each ASEAN member's ability to develop its own regional-security role.

Indonesian-Japanese relations have improved since the Tanaka riots in January 1974 because both sides are conscious that good relations are mutually beneficial. Compared with eight years ago, their economic relations are more balanced; Indonesia is now more self-confident, more capable, and relatively more successful in its development efforts. Meanwhile, strategic factors such as the passage of Japan's vital sea-lanes through Indonesia's territorial waters and Indonesia's position as one of Japan's sources of oil and raw materials make Indonesia important to Japan. On the Japanese side, the government in particular, but also the private sector, is consistently striving to attain a better relationship through all kinds of efforts, including some in the political field, such as Japan's support for ASEAN's policy toward the Kampuchea conflict, and in the sociocultural field, such as in training, education, and technology transfer.

China

The development of U.S.-Chinese relations is still unclear because of the intensification of the Taiwan issue. Indonesia appreciates Reagan's attentiveness to Taiwan's interests as an old friend and in accordance with the Taiwan Relations Act. From Southeast Asia it looks as though U.S.-Chinese relations have been a one-way street, profiting only the PRC, all of whose demands have been fulfilled by the U.S. On the other hand, Indonesians do not want new tensions to emerge in U.S.-Chinese relations because this would introduce a new factor of instability in the Asian-Pacific region. Indonesia understands that U.S.-Chinese relations have become an important element in the U.S.-Soviet balance in East Asia and in the global context. U.S. China policy in the region will be successful, however, only if the United States also takes into account regional interests, including the sensitivities and complexities of the ASEAN countries' relationships with the PRC. For example, a U.S. arms sale to the PRC would be taken very seriously by the ASEAN countries. A sale, though basically only symbolic and political, still could be used by the PRC against Southeast Asian countries, which still face insurgencies of local pro-Beijing Communist parties, supported by Beijing whenever it thinks it is in its interest to do so, as in Burma. Moreover, before announcing the possibility of an arms sale in June 1981, the United States did not consult ASEAN members; afterward was it explained to the ASEAN foreign ministers in Manila by Secretary Haig.

Chinese-Indonesian relations have not been normalized because of pending matters. There is still some ambivalence in Indonesia toward the PRC; the PRC is still unpredictable in its policies, and recently there are signs of a more assertive foreign policy. Geopolitical and strategic factors—namely, the role and influence of the PRC on the future of Southeast Asia, particularly in the short run in solving the Kampuchean conflict—are still very ambiguous. Although there are some improvements in the PRC's attitudes toward ASEAN members on such matters as Communist party-to-party relations, China's policies toward the overseas Chinese in Southeast Asia, and the Kampuchean problem, for Indonesia these improvements still seem too vague and peripheral to provide a sound basis for normalization. There is also no sense of urgency for Indonesia to normalize its relations with the PRC because the necessary contacts and dialogues are going on informally through many channels, especially at the United Nations. Eventually, Indonesian-Chinese relations will be normalized, but the exact time is still to be determined after the presidential elections in March 1983. A possible accelerating factor in this normalization process could be the PRC's willingness to compromise on the Kampuchean conflict. Such a basic policy change is difficult to expect in the near future.

United States

U.S.-Indonesian relations can be seen in three interrelated layers: bilateral, regional, and multilateral.

On the bilateral level, the previous warmth diminished in the last year of the Carter administration, even though relations remained correct and formal. Senior officials of the Carter administration in charge for this region seriously tried to improve relations, but President Carter himself never understood or gave attention to Indonesia. Finally, at the end of his presidency, there was just too little time to do so. The Reagan administration started to try to improve U.S.-Indonesian bilateral relations, but it is too early to draw a conclusion about the results. The attitude of the Reagan administration on security and strategic matters is basically more convincing. The question is whether its implementation will also incorporate national and regional realities, and the aspirations and complexities of U.S. friends and allies. This combination of global and regional interests will determine the results of U.S. policy in the future. Sufficient U.S. attention to Indonesian aspirations, views, and sensitivities—and vice versa—will constitute important factors that will determine U.S.-Indonesian relations in the future.

Second, on regional relations there are two problems that could affect Indonesian—U.S. relations in the future: first, Indonesian-Vietnamese relations and U.S.-Vietnamese relations; second, Indonesian-Chinese relations and U.S.-Chinese relations. Indonesia is of the opinion that the PRC potentially poses the main threat in the future because it is the only great power in Southeast Asia. Historically, the PRC has always taken this region as its sphere of influence through the tributary system toward the middle kingdom, which, to draw a modern analogy, is like the position of Finland toward the USSR or Burma toward the PRC. This is not acceptable for Indonesia. Thus Indonesia intends to create a regional order through the implementation of ZOPFAN in Southeast Asia, which includes the three Indochinese countries. Indonesia believes that only if all the Southeast Asian countries work together can they resist pressures from the PRC or any great power in the future. Vietnam will clearly play an important role in the implementation of ZOPFAN, and that is why Indonesia continues to seek a modus vivendi with Vietnam despite the differences in ideology and in social, political, and economic systems. For the time being the ZOPFAN ideals cannot be fully implemented between ASEAN and Vietnam because of the existing Kampuchean conflict. This does not mean that ultimately the ZOPFAN idea goes against the interest of ASEAN. In the final analysis, all ASEAN members have the same opinion about the future of Southeast Asia, despite some differences on the modus operandi to achieve it. These differences, which are attributable to different histories and geographic locations, are normal. To a certain extent they have already been surmounted, and they will surely be solved by the ASEAN members themselves.

On the other hand, the United States is of the opinion that the PRC is a strategic friend in its global rivalry against the USSR. Therefore, the United States will strengthen its relations with the PRC. In the implementation of this relationship there are differences of opinion in the U.S. government. The so-called pragmatists, especially in the State Department, seriously intend to increase the relationship into a quasi-alliance that includes the sales of U.S. arms, whereas the so-called ideologues, especially in the White House, never fully believe in a communist regime like the PRC and feel that they have a special relationship with Taiwan, which is considered an old friend. This dichotomy has not yet been completely overcome. Because of the growing U.S.-Chinese relations on the one hand and a growing dependency of Vietnam on the USSR on the other, Vietnam will never be fully accepted by the Reagan administration until it lessens its relations with the USSR. This difference of opinion may need a lot of dialogue and consultations in order not to become a problem between the United States and Indonesia bilaterally, and between the United States and ASEAN on a regional level.

Third, multilateral issues will become a more and more difficult subject between the United States and Indonesia, because there are basic ideological differences between Indonesia as a nonaligned developing country of the Third World and the Reagan administration, which is trying to implement capitalist and liberal principles in international economic relations. The most important problem for Indonesia is the resolution of the new Law of the Sea, which is now under review by the Reagan administration because of its ideological bias. Although U.S. vital interests (namely, free passage through Indonesian archipelago's seas and vital straits) have been included, there is no guarantee that the treaty will be accepted by the Reagan administration, although it is considered a matter of survival by Indonesia. There is also a problem over commodities such as tin and rubber. These multilateral problems will become more significant not only in international forums, but also for relations between Indonesia and the United States in the coming years. Therefore, capable and professional representations are needed on both sides to overcome these differences, besides the bilateral dialogues already mentioned.

Conclusion

U.S. strategy toward the USSR includes three principal elements: (1) how the United States arranges its relations with its allies—namely, NATO and Japan; (2) how the United States arranges its relations with the USSR, which is its main rival and with which the United States has to maintain a dialogue because of their capacity for mutual destruction; and (3) how the United States arranges its relations with the Third World.

Developments in international relations are such that although the United States and its allies are in totality very powerful, they still need new arrangements with the Third World in order to compete with the USSR globally. These arrangements could be multilateral (as in the North-South dialogues), regional (the U.S.-ASEAN dialogues), and bilateral (the Indonesian-U.S. dialogues).

Indonesia clearly is not an ally of the United States, but it is a friend that has parallel interests and opinions, particularly in the economic and political fields. The challenge the United States will face is whether or not it is capable of establishing new dialogues and institutions in its relationships with some important Third World countries (such as Indonesia) or with regional associations (such as ASEAN). This challenge is of prime importance for the United States in order to maintain good relations and a two-way flow of ideas with the Third World. Thereby U.S. policies and ideas can be better communicated, understood, and accepted by a majority of the developing countries. It is also important that through such continuous dialogues the United States can reach mutual understanding with Indonesia on some of the main issues of the new international economic order.

International public opinion among Third World countries after Afghanistan, Kampuchea, and the Polish crisis are advantageous to the United States. The problem is whether there is understanding, wisdom, and statesmanship on the part of U.S. leaders to use this favorable environment to maintain the kind of international order we all would like to see developed.

8. Malaysian Threat Perceptions and Regional Security

Zainal Abidin B. Abdul Wahid

Malaysian Security Perceptions

Since June 1948, when the Emergency was declared in Malaya, most Malaysians have perceived communism as a threat to Malaya's security despite the official ending of the Emergency in July 1960. Whether one considers the Malayan Communist party (MCP) or any of the communist splinter groups, most Malaysians consider them as contrary to Malaysian national interests.[1] Until now the military threat of the MCP and the other communist groups has not really been great.[2] The Malaysian government has been able to contain their activities. None of the communist groups has been able to establish a so-called liberated area. Acting on their own or even in concert, they would probably be unable to topple the present government and set up a communist republic in Malaysia at any time in the foreseeable future.

However, the very presence of the communist groups provides possible rallying points for those who are greatly dissatisfied with the government. It is in this respect that the communist groups, particularly the MCP, could become a serious threat to the security of the country. Every communist group in Malaysia consists mainly of people of Chinese origin. The MCP has the biggest membership and is Beijing oriented. In a multiethnic country like Malaysia, a communist party is important not only for its ideology but also for the ethnic composition of its membership and leadership, since this latter factor has wider implications.

As a result of British colonial policies, Malaysia now has a multiethnic population consisting mainly of Malays, Chinese, and Indians.[3] The Malays are the indigenous inhabitants; most of the Chinese and Indians were originally brought into the country by the British in order to exploit the country's economic wealth. Through the years of British colonialism, the Malays have been left far behind, especially in the economic and social fields.[4] Since Merdeka (independence) in 1957, and more particularly since the Incident of 13 May 1969, the Malaysian government has adopted a number of policies, in particular the New Economic Policy, in order to bring the economic and social positions of the Malays up to the level of the non-Malays. The government believes that a more equitable distribution of opportunity and wealth is necessary in order for the economic and social positions of the different ethnic groups in the country to become more balanced. The great existing inequality is not considered conducive to efforts to build a strong, united Malaysian nation. The argument follows that a failure of programs to provide equality could result in dissension and hence instability; this in turn would affect security adversely. Besides, such a situation could be exploited by the MCP; if the dissatisfied elements happen to be persons of Chinese origin, then the chances of success of the MCP would be greater.[5]

Another dimension of this situation pertains to the effect of dissension and instability on economic development. Except for the 13 May Incident, there has been no real conflict between the Malays and the Chinese since Merdeka. Relative harmony has prevailed because, among other things, the country's comparatively successful economic development has increased the size of the economic pie. The New Economic Policy is premised on an expanding pie of which the disadvantaged groups get a relatively larger share. Should there be economic difficulties that make the pie smaller, these could serve as a source of dissatisfaction, which in turn could sour relations between the two major ethnic groups, seriously jeopardizing national security.

Therefore, it is highly important that Malaysia succeed in its economic and social development programs. Although Malaysia is trying to industrialize itself, it is still very dependent on the proceeds from its primary produce. For example, it must have a stable price and market for its tin and rubber in order to maintain, let alone increase, the size of the pie. Any move that adversely affects the price and marketability of these two major Malaysian exports would have a politically destabilizing effect on the country. Every time the U.S. government decides to release rubber or tin from its stockpiles into the international market, ripples of dismay are set in motion that make the Malaysian government and the affected private sector wonder whether the United States really does consider Malaysian security interests when it makes such decisions.[6]

Another aspect of the danger from communism concerns its international nature. The composition of the membership of the MCP, its orientation toward Beijing, and the geopolitical proximity of China—especially the presence of overseas Chinese in Southeast Asia—have made the work of Malaysian security planners burdensome, to say the least. Moreover, the PRC's insistence on maintaining party-to-party relations with the MCP, coupled with China's involvement in the Kampuchean problem, makes the task of those in charge of Malaysian security even more difficult. The problem is not so much the direct participation of China in Malaysian affairs as it is the spread of the Sino-Soviet conflict into Malaysia.

Seeing the MCP as the biggest communist group in Malaysia and the PRC's maintenance of party-to-party relations, the USSR cannot be expected to remain quietly on the sidelines. Besides sponsoring its own militant communist group—the Communist Party of Malaya-Marxist-Leninist—the

Soviet Embassy in Kuala Lumpur has been actively attempting to recruit members from the Malay and Indian communities. One tactic used by Soviet agents is to paint a picture that blends Chinese communism with Chinese nationalism, making them at times indistinguishable and thus also playing to communalism. They have managed to arouse and in some cases to strengthen suspicion against the Chinese community. Some members of the Indian community have also been vulnerable to a Soviet approach that emphasizes Sino-Indian dispute. The logical consequence of the rivalry between the two communist giants can only be a threat to the national security of Malaysia. They heighten the feeling of communalism. Malaysians do not wish to see the Sino-Soviet rift transplanted into their country.

Realizing the multifaceted dangers of communism, the Malaysian government has formulated various policies to counter it. On the military front, the government has enlarged the military and police forces, improved their armaments, and increased their salaries and postretirement benefits. Steps have been taken to involve the military in community work. Such activities help to bolster the image of the military, which makes it easier to get cooperation from the people when the need arises.

The policies and activities of the government on the political, economic, and social fronts are too numerous to discuss here. Suffice to say that the government fully understands the relations between political, economic, and social policies on the one hand, and national security on the other. The New Economic Policy is a clear manifestation of this realization. Through this policy the government believes that it can achieve national solidarity by abolishing poverty and restructuring society so that no ethnic group will be identified by its economic function.[7] The stereotyping of ethnic groups by economic function had, in the past, helped to emphasize communal differences. In the process of achieving the objectives of the New Economic Policy, the backward segments of Malaysian society would be given extra help to bring themselves up to the level of their more fortunate fellow citizens. When the social and economic positions of the different ethnic groups become more balanced, each one of them will feel more secure. Such a situation would generate greater tolerance, a willingness to give and take, a readiness to work together and to cooperate. There would be a feeling of confidence, a belief that one group would not be overwhelmed by the economic and social superiority of the other. Once this is attained, there would be no further need for special position for any group. A satisfied, happy, united population is more of a sure guarantee against threats to national security of the country than merely a strong military force. A contented population cannot easily be manipulated to work against the interests of its country. In fact, it would fight for the defense of the motherland.

Two other possible threats to national security that could be regarded as internal are drug and religious extremism. The magnitude of the drug-addiction problem is causing alarm.[8] Despite efforts to eradicate the drug menace, it still is not under control. The number of drug addicts is greater than the number of places available in rehabilitation centers or even in prisons.[9] Drug addiction can sap the energy of a whole generation, making them easy prey to antinational elements. We should not miss the lesson of the Opium War of China, although this time it may be in reverse.

Besides the problem of addiction, the MCP has been known to finance its activities through the sale of drugs. The close proximity of Malaysia to the main source of supply, the Golden Triangle, makes control difficult. Various measures have been taken by the government and the private sector to eradicate the drug menace. Rehabilitation centers have been established by the government and by religious organizations. The government has also tried to educate the public about the dangers of drugs through television, radio, publications, and exhibitions. Youth organizations have been encouraged to offer constructive activities in order to keep young people away from drugs. Realizing the peril of drug addiction, the Malaysian government has introduced a law that would make serious drug offenses punishable by death.

Since the 1979 Iranian revolution, religious extremism seems to be in vogue whenever security threats are discussed. In fact, it has been said that the next country to follow Iran would be Pakistan; with Malysia not too far behind. It is clear, however, that conditions in Iran in 1979 were different from those prevailing in Malaysia today—politically, economically, or even socially.

Religious extremism is not an easy term to define. It is relative: what is extreme in one society may not be considered so in another. In Malaysia there have been cases of religious extremism, but they are more the exception than the rule. The general trend of religious development in Malaysia has been beneficial. In the case of Islam, the strengthening of Islamic consiousness among believers contributes a greater sense of responsibility, an insurance against corruption, and an abhorrence for communism. It also helps to fight against drug addiction.

Despite the many benefits that can be derived from Islam, there is still the possibility of it being abused. There have been such incidents, but they have been effectively contained by the government. As long as the communists or other antinational elements are denied the opportunity to exploit such abuses, they should not become a threat to national security.[10]

The Malaysian government has taken various steps to try to prevent abuses of Islam and the rise of religious extremism. It has spent large sums of money annually on Islamic education, both at schools and at institutions of higher learning. The government has established Islamic research and missionary institutes in order to provide reading materials for the public and to propagate Islam. The government also organizes and participates actively in Islamic religious activities, thus making it difficult for those who are inclined toward extremism to accuse the government of being anti-Islam or uninterested in Islam.

External Threats

Malaysians also feel threatened by events outside their country. Since Malaysia is the only ASEAN country that has common borders with all the other members of ASEAN, there are border problems such as irredentist movements. Malaysia has also been preoccupied with the Kampuchean problem, which it would like to see solved and contained within Indochina.

As a Malaysian, I see the Kampuchean problem as the result of great-power politics. Therefore, the solution must also come from the great powers. Each must be willing to accept a settlement that is not entirely to its satisfaction. This region has not seen real peace for the last forty years. Even more depressing, the conflicts and wars have not actually been initiated by Southeast Asians, but have been manipulated and sometimes conducted by powers external to Southeast Asia. The people of the region have been pawns of great-power politics.

The contention here is that Vietnam would not have invaded Kampuchea if the latter had not made incursions into Vietnam and China had not tried to establish itself in Kampuchea through the Pol Pot government. When Vietnam felt itself threatened from the north as well as the south, it had to take action to secure its borders. To move southward was certainly much easier than to go northward. Thailand regards Vietnam's invasion of Kampuchea as a dangerous threat to its national security, although Vietnam had given assurances that it would not violate Thai territory unless provoked. Nevertheless, Thailand, together with the other members of ASEAN and many other countries, has tried in various ways—including through the United Nations—to get Vietnam to withdraw from Kampuchea and then to allow the Kampuchean people to elect a government of their own choosing under the supervision of the United Nations.[11]

Vietnam has not responded positively to the request to withdraw either by the United Nations or ASEAN. This does not necessarily mean that Vietnam has closed the door on a political settlement. Unfortunately, that settlement, despite the independence of Southeast Asian countries, must still be dependent on stands taken by the great powers. ASEAN's attempts to promote a third force in Kampuchea could only serve as a respite and provide a semblance of greater legitimacy to the Khmer opponents of the Heng Samrin government in order for the latter to get wider support from the international community. In particular, a coalition would minimize the role of the Khmer Rouge. It is also a way to gain time, which sometimes has a healing effect. The first step toward a political solution, however, must really come from China, whose presence and pressure in Kampuchea sparked the Vietnamese invasion. If China could assure Vietnam that it would no longer involve itself in Kampuchean affairs and would lean less heavily on Vietnam, then the latter would be more accommodating on Kampuchea. Because of its past experience, however, it would be difficult for Vietnam to agree to a completely independent Kampuchea. The most that Vietnam could accept would be a guaranteed neutral Kampuchea, because Vietnam cannot afford to have a Kampuchea that might pursue policies contrary to the interests of Hanoi.

One might ask why China would agree to a neutral Kampuchea. It is believed that one reason that China wanted to make a pincer movement against Vietnam was the Soviet presence. The PRC would not like to see its southern border threatened by the USSR through the latter's connection with Vietnam. On the other hand, Vietnam could not afford to sever its dependence on the USSR, since throughout its history Vietnam was the victim of Chinese aggression whenever China was united. Even recent experiences have not inspired Vietnamese confidence in China. For example, Vietnam cannot easily forget China's flirtations with the United States in the early 1970s, even while Vietnam was fighting a bitter war against the United States. At that very moment, however, the USSR was standing by the side of Vietnam.[12] After all, the USSR is considerably farther away from Vietnam than China. If a choice must be made, it would be almost natural for Vietnam to align itself with the USSR. If the USSR were to become unbearable, then the chances of freeing itself from Soviet pressure would be greater because of the geographical distance and its logistical implications. In contrast, China is adjacent to Vietnam. Vietnam's historical experiences with China have proved that its current choice of an ally is the most logical. Is it necessary, however?

It would not be if there were a recalculation of interests and objectives by the great powers. Most of the Vietnamese actions have been taken because of a perceived threat from China. If there were a genuine undertaking by the PRC to respect Vietnamese sovereignty and territorial integrity, then Vietnam could gradually free itself from the Russian embrace. It is contended that after fighting for its independence from Western colonialism and intervention for about thirty years, suffering untold miseries and deprivations, Vietnam would be highly unlikely to be willing to place itself under the Soviet yoke. Vietnamese nationalism is a much stronger force. An alternative must be provided, however. Normalization of relations with the United States could contribute toward easing the situation. Raising Vietnam's status internationally could inspire greater confidence in the Vietnamese and inhibit China's desire to teach a lesson. Normalization would have to be followed by economic aid. In this respect, Japan, ASEAN, and other Western powers could play a constructive role. Intense pursuit of such a policy could help Vietnam to orient itself away from the Soviet embrace and toward Southeast Asia.

If that is achieved, China need not be unduly anxious about its southern border. Such a development could make Vietnam less intransigent about its policy toward Kampuchea and Laos. This would not only placate China but would also lessen Thailand's apprehension.

Would the USSR be willing to let Vietnam out of its clasp? It might. The continuance of the Sino-Vietnamese confrontation could prove to be highly expensive for the USSR. The U.S. experience in Vietnam illustrated the futility of any attempt to control Vietnam by force. An independent Vietnam need not necessarily be antagonistic towards the USSR. Moreover, the act of freeing Vietnam could be advantageous in terms of the Soviet image and relations with ASEAN. The USSR has many problems in its hands at the moment—for example, Afghanistan and Poland—and would probably be relieved at the removal of one.

In the interest of peace, the great powers must strive for accommodation. China should not be too hostile toward Vietnam, for this is only counterproductive. If China does not want a Soviet military presence in Vietnam, it must ensure that Vietnam feels secure from any threat from China. The United States and Japan would have to exercise their influence on China so that the latter could change its policy toward Vietnam. The United States could go a step farther in terms of getting the Soviets to cooperate in the interest of maintaining a kind of detente. To make this proposal more meaningful, the United States, Japan, and ASEAN must undertake a commitment to ensure the development of Vietnam so that it will not find it necessary to turn again to the USSR.

Although the USSR may look at this type of approach favorably for reasons stated earlier, China could also have grounds for not rejecting it. At present China would probably prefer peace so that its modernization program could be pursued with a greater chance of success. If China were to accommodate this approach, then it could be assured of greater international assistance for its modernization. For the moment, China cannot by itself confront the USSR militarily. A powerful ally or allies are needed. To get an ally or allies, one must find at least a congruence of interests. More often than not compromises are required to accommodate each other. Perhaps China's policy toward Vietnam could be one of these compromises.

A stable, independent, and reasonably strong Vietnam is important to Malaysia. Vietnam is not regarded as the most dangerous threat to Malaysian security. In fact, Vietnam could serve as a buffer against China, which does present the gravest long-term threat to Malaysia. Although it may sound contradictory, Chinese nationalistic communism, once strengthened, could make its presence felt in Malaysia and disrupt the stability and security of the country. Reference was made earlier to the various roles of the

MCP and the extra dimension of the Sino-Soviet rivalry. The parts played by the Indonesian Communist party and China in the Indonesian Communist party's attempted coup of 1965 serve as a grim reminder to be ever vigilant of China's declared intentions and unannounced motives, including its current (ephemeral, one hopes) understanding with Thailand on the Kampuchean issue.

In this respect, Malaysians are particularly perturbed by the U.S. friendliness toward China. For example, in January 1980, Harold Brown, then defense secretary, spoke of a parallelism of views between the United States and China over Indochina.[13] Then one hears about military assistance to be provided by the United States for China.[14] There also seems to be an understanding between the two countries to follow a bleed-Vietnam policy. This growing cooperation makes one wonder whether, in pursuing its global, anti-Soviet policies, the United States has not overlooked Malaysian interests.

Forty years is a long time even in the search for peace, but hope springs eternal. Thus Malaysia and its ASEAN colleagues have put forward the proposal known as ZOPFAN—Zone of Peace, Freedom, and Neutrality—as a framework for a peaceful Southeast Asia. Various attempts to achieve peace in the past were unsuccessful, whether they involved military alliances; self-proclaimed neutrality; or an active, independent foreign policy. ZOPFAN may provide the answer to Southeast Asian security.

The great powers should not be hesitant to support ZOPFAN because in the long run ZOPFAN would also serve their interests. ZOPFAN is based on the idea of the neutralization of Southeast Asia.[15] The specific terms of ZOPFAN cannot yet be delineated, but the range of possibilities can certainly be discerned. Briefly, at one end lies the hope of completely neutralized Southeast Asia, with the great powers guaranteeing that no Southeast Asian countries attack one another and that Southeast Asia will be defended against any attack from outside the region. Although the great powers could participate in economic activities in the area, they would have to stay out of Southeast Asia militarily and politically. The idea has also been expressed in terms of equidistance. It is a kind of self-imposed check and balance to be exercised by the great powers—a voluntary system of balance of powers.

The main merit of the neutralization proposal pertains to its ability to fulfill one of the major objectives of the three great powers—China, the USSR, and the United States—in Southeast Asia. Each of these powers would like to dominate the whole region by itself. If this is not achievable, then a power like China would rather have the United States continue its presence in Southeast Asia than allow the USSR to come in. Alternatively, each power would like to see the other two excluded from the region, even if this means its own exclusion. The neutralization proposal hopes to reduce the capacity for political and military meddling by all three great powers in Southeast Asia.

The ASEAN countries must not spare any effort in trying to establish a Zone of Peace, Freedom, and Neutrality. We hope that 1982 augurs well for the future of Southeast Asia.

Notes

1. Tan Sri Ghazali Shafie, *Malaysian Security: A Viewpoint* (Kuala Lumpur: Malaysian Centre for Development Studies, 1979), p. 5. Ghazali refers to the MCP, Communist Party of Malaya-Marxist-Leninist, and Communist Party of Malaya-Revolutionary Faction.

2. The MCP is regarded as the original and main group. It was responsible for the declaration of the Emergency in June 1948.

3. The term *Malay* here is used to refer to an ethnic group, including the Natives of Sarawak and Sabah. The alternative term is *Bumiputra,* meaning "son of the soil."

4. *Siaran Akhbar,* Jabatan Penerangan Malaysia, PEN./6/80/2 (PM), p. 6 (from the speech of the Right Honorable the Prime Minister of Malaysia in June 1980). The following figures are for 1979.

Profession	*Percentage Bumiputra*	*Percentage non-Bumiputra*
Architecture	11	89
Accountancy	7.6	92.4
Engineering	11.6	88.4
Medicine	8.6	91.4

5. L.A. Mills, *Southeast Asia: Illusion and Reality in Politics and Economics* (Minneapolis: University of Minnesota Press, 1964), pp. 116-117; A.C. Brackman, *Southeast Asia's Second Front: The Power Struggle in the Malay Archipelago* (New York: Praeger, 1966), pp. 185-186.

6. Last December the U.S. General Services Administration sold 1,415 tons of tin within four days. This caused the price to fall by 55 cents per kilo. Since 2 December, 1981, the price of tin had fallen by $1.10 per kilo. *New Straits Times,* 23 December 1981.

7. Kerajaan Malaysia, *Rancangan Malaysia Ketiga, 1976-1980* (Third Malaysia Plan) (Kuala Lumpur, 1976), p. 2.

8. A.F. Yassin, "Dadah" ("Drug"), *Dewan Masyarakat,* Dewan Bahasa dan Pustaka (DBP) (July 1972):2-4; Amir Awang, "Dadah: Menjadi Persoalan Ugama" ("Drug: A Religious Question"), *Dewan Masyarakat* (DBP) (May 1976):42.

9. *New Straits Times,* 12 October 1981, p. 8.

10. *Utusan Zaman* (a Sunday Malay newspaper), 11 October 1981, p. 16.

11. UNGA Provisional A/35/PV 44, 22 October 1980, *Thirty-fifth Session Provisional Verbatim Record of the Forty-fourth Meeting,* p. 28.

12. Ha Van Lau of Vietnam stated in the U.N. General Assembly, "During its thirty-five years of existence Vietnam could not have safeguarded its independence had it not had the precious assistance of the Soviet Union." U.N. General Assembly, Provisional, A/35/PV 36, 15 October 1980, *Thirty-fifth Session Provisional Verbatim Record of the Thirty-sixth Meeting,* pp. 53-55.

13. T.W. Robinson, "China's Asia Policy," *Current History* 79, no. 458 (September 1980):3.

14. *New Straits Times,* 3 October 1981, p. 11.

15. For a more detailed study of neutralization of Southeast Asia, see *Nusantara* 1, Dewan Bahasa dan Pustaka (Kuala Lumpur, 1972), pp. 134-143. (*Nusantara* is a journal of the arts and social sciences of Southeast Asia, published twice a year by the Dewan Bahasa dan Pustaka.)

9

National Threat Perceptions of Singapore

Lau Teik Soon

In most new developing states, national security concerns the preservation of certain vital values that a state considers essential to safeguard its independence, sovereignty, and territorial integrity. These values, which may be termed security issues, include political stability, national unity or interethnic harmony, economic development, and national defense. Often these issues are interrelated: without political stability there can be little if any economic development and national unity; without national unity and economic development there is little if any need for national defense. Certain Western writers espouse the view that political disorder may be a good thing for the long term unity of the state, or that national defense need not be effective or comprehensive for peace and stability. It is doubtful, however, that the leaders of most new states hold such contradictory views.

In Singapore, unlike many other new states, the security issues mentioned here are of the utmost significance because of the state's extreme vulnerability. The compactness of the republic, the limited amount of usable land, the small but heterogenous population, the lack of natural resources, and the country's very strategic location all contribute to the vulnerability of Singapore. Any major threat to national security can be catastrophic for the state and its people. For example, if there is widespread political chaos and disorder, the people will be in conflict with each other, foreign investors will desert the country, the economy will collapse, and this in turn will aggravate political instability. The state is so small that interethnic conflict in one part of the island spreads instantaneously to the whole country. Thus any foreign power gaining a foothold in any part of the country could quickly take over the whole country. In Singapore, therefore, national security means the very survival of the state itself.

In Singapore the People's Action party (PAP) has been in power since 1959. This remarkable continuity reflects the recognition that a strong and effective centralized government is essential in Singapore, and the strong popular support for the policies of the PAP. In discussing the perceptions of Singapore's leaders, therefore, the dominant role of the PAP and the government is evident.

This chapter will discuss the facts of Singapore's situation that contribute to its vulnerability and then discuss three major sources of threat to its national security: the Communist Party of Malaya (CPM), the communal or racial extremists, and the antinational elements. The ways in which the government has dealt with these threats will be mentioned. The chapter will conclude with a brief discussion of Singapore's perception of regional security, which is an important complement to the government's strategy of survival.

The Case of Singapore

Singapore is a small city-state with a land area of 617.8 square kilometers. The main island of Singapore, which is about 41.8 kilometers in length and 22.5 kilometers in breadth, has a coastline of 193.7 kilometers. There are fifty islets, about two dozen of which are inhabited. The island was colonized by the British and was under British administration from 1819 to 1955. In 1955 it was given partial autonomy in internal affairs. In 1959 Singapore achieved full internal self-government, and in April of that year the PAP was elected to power. In September 1963 Singapore became part of Malaysia, but less than two years later it was separated and became an independent country on 9 August 1965.

Singapore is not a homogenous nation. According to the census taken in June 1980, the total population of Singapore was 2,413,945. The population comprises three major racial groups—Chinese, 76.9 percent; Malays, 14.6 percent; and Indians, 6.4 percent. Other ethnic minorities account for 2.1 percent. They profess a variety of religions; for example, the Chinese believe in Confucianism, Taoism, and Buddhism; the Malays are almost all Islamic; and the Indians' main religions are Hinduism and Buddhism. The Western influence is reflected in the conversion of many Chinese and Indians to Christianity. Since independence, Singapore has been a secular state, which allows freedom of worship, use of the various languages, and promotion of the diverse cultures. Interethnic coexistence, cooperation, and harmony are vital to the stability of Singapore.

Singapore has no natural or mineral resources that it can derive from its land. There are insignificant rubber estates, fruit and vegetable plantations, and poultry farms; but all these are in danger of extinction in view of the demand for land. This means that the people of Singapore cannot live off the land but have to import almost everything, including water, for their needs. They cannot seek employment or better their standard of living through any form of agriculture or cottage industry.

Singapore's significance lies in its strategic location. It is situated at the crossroads of sea and air transportation networks and at the southern end of the vital Straits of Malacca, which connect the Indian and Pacific oceans. It is linked to Malaysia by a land and rail bridge and is within sight of Indonesia.

Singapore and its people have had a long association with Malaysia. Singapore, together with the Malaysian states of Penang and Malacca, formed the British Straits Settlements. Administratively and economically, Singapore was an important center for the Malay states. After World War II, Penang, Malacca, and the Malay states became known as the Federation of Malaya; Singapore remained a British colony. The political, economic, and social development of Singapore kept pace with that in Malaya, however, because the goal of the PAP political leaders in Singapore was to merge with Malaya. This came about in September 1963, when Malaya, Sabah, Sarawak, and Singapore formed Malaysia. Because of the intense political conflict between the ruling party in Malaysia, the Alliance (UNMO-MCA-MIC), and the PAP, however, Singapore was separated from Malaysia in August 1965. Thus from the beginning of existence as a Malay fishing village until 1965, Singapore and its people have had close symbiotic relations with Malaysia and its people. In general, what happens in Malaysia will affect Singapore in significant ways, and vice versa.

In view of these facts—its small size, the heterogenity of the population, the lack of natural resources, its strategic value, and its close symbiotic relations with Malaysia—Singapore's leaders have been keenly aware of the extreme vulnerability of Singapore. More significantly, the PAP leaders have had personal experiences of the traumatic events of the political development of Singapore between 1945 and 1965. Consequently, they have perceived that certain vital factors are needed for Singapore's survival: first, political stability; second, foreign investment, technology, and expertise; and third, a pragmatic foreign policy. Political stability has demanded of the leaders an acute sensitivity to any threat that can undermine the peace and order of the country. Economic development is dependent on foreign inputs. National security requires not only an effective defense force but also a stable regional order.

The Communist Threat

In the history of Singapore, there have been periods of violent and unconstitutional struggles threatening the nation as a whole as well as the party in power. The most serious of these threats is the Communist Party of Malaya (CPM). The CPM was formed in April 1930, and its goal is to overthrow the democratic system of Malaysia and Singapore through revolutionary warfare. Although the CPM is currently well-contained and does not pose an immediate threat, the memories of the disruptions it caused in the past and its efforts to exploit sensitive issues in Singapore and Malaysia make it a continuing and important concern of Singapore's leaders.

During the last phase of the colonial administration, Singapore was in a state of revolutionary ferment that was not unlike the condition of other Southeast Asian states emerging from colonialism and in the throes of a nationalist struggle for independence. The Cold War was developing; under the USSR's instigation, insurgencies were initiated by the local Communist parties in a number of states. Between 1948 and 1960 Malaya and Singapore faced the communist threat. The CPM waged war against the British (up to 1957) and the Malayan and Singapore governments. This was the so-called Malayan Emergency period. In Singapore the Communists were behind the student riots, industrial unrest, assassination, arson, and damage to persons and property.

A few examples of the turbulence of the period should suffice to illustrate the nature of the threat to the internal security of Singapore.[1] In February 1946 the CPM organized a massive general strike under the banner of the Singapore Labour Union: 173,000 workers stopped work. Between 1954 and 1956 the CPM successfully infiltrated the Chinese language schools, students' unions, teachers' organizations, and labor unions. The CPM exploited certain sensitive issues, such as Chinese language, education, and culture, which incited the students and workers to violence. On 13 May 1954 about five hundred Chinese-school students clashed with police over their protest against national service. About a year later the Communists instigated a riot during a strike by workers of a bus company. This resulted in the death of four persons and the injury of many others. In March 1956 the government took action against the Chinese-school students' union, which was a Communist front organization.

Between 1961 and 1966 the CPM was again active in organizing various disturbances, including a boycott of a Chinese-school examination in November 1961 and a demonstration against the arrest of left-wing extremists in April 1963. Finally, in October 1966 the pro-Communists decided to boycott Parliament and take their struggle to the streets. The extraparliamentary struggle consisted of demonstrations and acts of sabotage, including arson and vandalism.

After their defeat in 1960, the CPM in Malaysia retreated to the Malaysian-Thai border region, reorganized, and waited for the occasion to renew their revolutionary warfare. This came in 1968, when the CPM initiated the current phase of revolutionary war against the Malaysian and Singapore governments. In a document issued on 1 June 1968, the central committee of the CPM announced the return to a policy of struggle. The document was entitled "Hold High the Great Red Flag of Marxism-Leninism and Mao Tse-tung Thought and Courageously Forge Ahead!" and stated: "We must in all circumstances persistently take to the role of using the countryside to encircle the cities and seizing power by armed force. This is a most important experience gained by our party from the 40 years of hard struggle."

The document outlined a nine-point program for "the fulfillment of the new democratic revolution." The nine-point program included the overthrow of the government (of Malaysia and Singapore), the creation of a Malayan People's Republic, the confiscation of the enterprises of the imperialists and their so-called lackeys, the building up of a powerful People's

Armed Force, and support for the liberation struggles of all oppressed races and oppressed people. Since then the clandestine radio station of the CPM, known as the Voice of the Malayan Revolution, has continued to broadcast party statements, reiterating the exhortation to the people to persist on the correct road to armed struggle.

The implementation of the CPM's new policy has resulted in the establishment and expansion of the CPM military presence on Malaysian soil, the creation of an underground mass-support infrastructure in Malaysia and Singapore, and the launching of a campaign of terrorism and sabotage in Malaysia. From 1968 on, the CPM began to infiltrate Communist terrorists in small groups into the various areas in the northern states of Peninsular Malaysia. The campaign of terrorism from 1968 to 1975 resulted in a number of acts of sabotage and assassination in Malaysia.

In Singapore there have been no assassinations or attacks on military installations. According to Chua Sian Chin, the Minister of Home Affairs, however:

> The CPM is present in Singapore and its commitment to armed struggle is equally strong but it is engaged in the building up of an infrastructure from which it will move to violent activities if given the opportunity to do so. Both the satellite organizations of the CPM (central) under Ching Peng and the break away CPM (Marxist-Leninist), are operating in Singapore today. The CPM continues to regard Peninsular Malaysia and Singapore as one entity and there is no separate communist party for the Republic. In fact, important CPM leaders previously responsible for the CPM operations in Singapore are presently operating in Peninsular Malaysia maintaining direct liason even with various CPM guerrilla groups.

In Singapore the CPM strategy made use of various Communist united-front organizations. As noted earlier, in the 1950s and early 1960s these included the Chinese schools, teachers' organizations, trade unions, and political parties. After 1966, however, the CPM and its united-front organizations devoted themselves to subversion and terrorism, including arson and bombing. The Communist underground satellite organizations include the Malayan National Liberation Front (MNLF) and the Malayan People's Liberation League (MPLL). On occasion the Singapore government has exposed the activities of the subversive groups. In 1974 they arrested thirty people and seized arms and ammunition from members of the same group. Between 1969 and 1976 there were twenty-two incidents of arson and eleven bombing incidents committed by Communist and pro-Communist elements. In 1976 the Singapore police arrested fifty members of the underground satelllite organizations. Those arrested included persons of the upper strata of society—a ballerina, a business executive, journalists, and national servicemen. According to a Ministry of Home Affairs statement of 27 May 1976:

The police have arrested fifty persons under the Internal Security Act since January this year, and have uncovered plans by two factions of the Communist Party of Malaya (CPM) to regroup in Singapore for a new phase of subversion and terrorism. The police have also captured documents, including field directives, photographs of communist guerrillas in a training camp at the Thai-Malaysian border, booby trap paraphernalia, including detonations, cash for the funding of underground activities, and sketches of government buildings and military installations. Links have been traced, too, between communist agents in Singapore and a cadre central post in Kuala Lumpur; an ideological and military training camp in the Johore jungle; a guerrilla camp in Southern Thailand; contact points in Bangkok and Hong Kong; and a recruitment propaganda and fund-raising center, set up in Sydney to subvert Singaporeans and Malaysians in Australia.

The CPM and its united-front organizations constitute the major threat to the security of Singapore. The government stated that:

The reality of the communist struggle in Malaysia and Singapore is not a case of innocent peace-loving constitutional minded people bravely taking on oppressive and reactionary governments. It is a story of ruthless murders, assassinations, intimidations, booby traps and ambushes—in short, the use of revolutionary violence as a means to topple elected and popular governments in power.

In 1976 the Communist united front in Singapore collaborated with extreme leftist elements in the Dutch Labour party (DLP) and the British Labour party in an attempt to put Singapore in an unfavorable position in the democratic-socialist movement.[2] The Communist united front manipulated the DLP to put up a memorandum to the Socialist International that alleged that Singapore was a one-party state. Of course, this is incorrect. In Singapore there are more than a dozen political parties, although not all are active. General elections have been held since 1955; in all these elections except that of 1955, the PAP has been returned into power. The results of these elections are as follows:

Date	Uncontested Seats	Contested Seats Won by PAP	Percentage of Votes for PAP
2 April 1955	0	3 out of 25	8.6
30 May 1959	0	43 out of 51	53.4
21 September 1963	0	37 out of 51	46.5
13 April 1968	51	All 58	84.8
2 September 1972	8	All 65	69.0
23 December 1976	16	All 69	72.4
23 December 1979	37	*All 75	75.6

*In the by-election for the constituency Anson held on 31 October 1981, an opposition candidate from the Workers' party won the seat. The Workers' party polled 51.9 percent of the valid votes cast.

The DLP accused the PAP of repressive policies, including the detention of political opponents without trial, suppression of the trade-union movement, and control of the press. In a strong rebuttal, the PAP exposed the work of the Communist united front, subsequently the PAP resigned from the Socialist International on the ground that: "We cannot belong to an organization, some of whose social democratic members allow themselves to be made use of by communist elements in our society who are out to destroy democratic institutions."

From 1976 to 1980, the government continued to conduct police and security operations against the CPM and its underground organizations. For example, in 1980 thirteen persons were arrested and another twelve were questioned for involvement in Communist underground activities. In its annual report, *Singapore '81,* the government stated:

> The Communist Party of Malaya's (CPM) underground activities in Singapore remained in disarray after being crippled by security operations in 1976 and 1977. Nonetheless, the CPM continued their attempts to rebuild their networks.[3]

The CPM, therefore, is a permanent threat to Singapore and to the party in power. It has been well contained by the Singapore government, however. The CPM is an illegal organization. To deal with the CPM threat, the government has the provision of the Internal Security Act (ISA). Under the ISA, the government, mainly through the Ministry of Home Affairs and its police forces, can detain Communists and pro-Communists without the necessity of bringing them before a court of law. Between 1960 and 1976, 661 persons were detained without trial; of this number, 492 were released in Singapore, and 90 went to countries like China and Malaysia. In May 1976, out of the 64 detained, 53 were detained for MNLF and MPLL activities. All of those released were prepared either to renounce and disavow the CPM's use of armed force, terror, and assassination as means of securing political change, or to accept offers to send them to any country of their choice. One important reason that detention without trial is necessary is that individuals who dare to give evidence against the Communists and their supporters risk an assassin's bullet.

The Communal Threat

The second major threat to Singapore's security comes from the racial or communal extremists. In view of the heterogenous composition of Singapore, the government has promoted the pluralistic nature of its society—the various religions, languages, and cultures. The maintenance of the country's multiracial character and racial harmony is emphasized as vital to the stability of Singapore. Nevertheless, there are internal issues and external forces that can polarize the communities and incite them to racial confrontation, resulting in death and injury to the population.

Before independence, Singapore experienced racial strife on two occasions. In 1950 four days of rioting occurred over the Maria Hertogh case. In the end, fifty Europeans were killed and many more injured by Malays and Indian Muslims. The Maria Hertogh case invovled a Dutch girl who was given to a Malay woman to be looked after as the Japanese overran Southeast Asia. She became a Muslim convert. After the war, the attempt of the natural parents to recover her and the ruling of the British judge created resentment on the part of the Malays and led to the riots.

In July and September 1964 racial riots occurred, leaving about forty people dead and about five hundred injured. According to the government, the sustained campaign in a Malay-language newspaper, falsely alleging the suppression of the rights of the Malay and Muslim minority by the Chinese majority, led to the riots. Apparently, the Malay party, UMNO, wanted to regain Malay support that had gone to the PAP in the 1963 general elections.

The most recent example of the racialist threat to Singapore's security occurred in January 1982.[4] The government exposed the existence of an extremist organization known as the Singapore's People's Liberation Organization (SPLO). The SPLO's objective was to overthrow the government through communal unrest and sabotage. In order to achieve this, the SPLO planned to distribute pamphlets alleging government oppression of the Malays' language and culture, and to carry out acts of arson and bombing. It also intended to solicit support, including manpower and finance, from individual and foreign powers such as Vietnam and Libya. The SPLO exhorted its followers to remember that: "It is the duty of every Muslim to protect the morality of Islam by whatever means. True Islam does not fear death. Imbibe a political spirit among our people to crush the suppressive policies of the PAP fascists."

The SPLO members decided to distribute its propaganda pamphlets, which contained seditious statements calculated to stir communal resentment, on a Muslim holy day. The occasion was the celebration of the Prophet Mohammed's birthday at the National Stadium, where about 24,000 Muslims were present. Before they could do so, however, they were caught by the police. Subsequently ten members of the SPLO were detained. Five of them were brought to trial and pleaded guilty to the charges, including the possession of pamphlets containing statements that had a tendency to incite organized violence against members of the government of Singapore.

It is obvious that the threat from extremist racial elements is taken seriously by the government. Any race riot resulting in death and injury will not only create political instability, disorder, and lawlessness, but also shake the confidence of foreign investors and governments in the stability of Singapore.

Threats from Antinational Elements

In view of the multiracial composition of Singapore and its economic dependence on outside powers, the government considers political stability crucial to the maintenance of national unity and economic development. Hence it is extremely sensitive toward any group that intends to undermine the political stability of the country. Over the years the government has taken strong actions against certain antinational elements, including the press and liberal-minded neo-Marxists among the intellectuals. Some of these groups have been manipulated by foreign powers to cause disruption and trouble in the country.

In 1972 the government took action against three newspapers: a Chinese newspaper, the *Nanyang Siang Pau;* and two English newspapers, the *Eastern Sun* and the *Herald*.[5] The *Nanyang Siang Pau* was accused of playing up issues relating to Chinese language and culture, and glorifying developments in the PRC in order to create resentment against the government among educated Chinese. The *Eastern Sun* was a case of what the government calls a black operation, whereby a foreign power uses a local proxy to influence public opinion and thereby advance its interests. The government had proof that the newspaper was being used by Chinese Communist agents in Hong Kong to further their interest in the long term. The *Herald* was financed by foreign capital and was accused of publishing statements that undermined the national policies of the government and promoted the values of the counterculture of Western societies. The government action led to the detention of certain administrators of *Nanyang Siang Pau* and the closing down of the *Eastern Sun* and the *Herald*.

Following these cases of local newspapers being manipulated by foreign forces, the government introduced the Newspaper and Printing Act in January 1974. Under Section 10(i) of part III of the act, no newspaper can receive foreign funds without the approval of the minister for culture. Further, under the act it will no longer be possible for private or business individuals to control the editorial policy of a newspaper.

Regional Security and External Threats

The Singapore government has identified the following threats to internal security: first, the CPM and its underground organizations; second, the extreme racialists or communalists; and third, various antinational elements that seek to undermine government policies aimed at political stability and rapid economic growth. Beyond these, the government perceives regional peace and stability as part of an essential protective umbrella for Singapore's development. To this end the government has decided on a two-pronged policy to deal with regional security: first, a defense capability to contribute to any regional-defense arrangement, and second, alignments with like-minded governments in Southeast Asia and other major powers whose interests coincide with Singapore's strategy of survival.

Singapore's overall political stability and economic development have depended on a peaceful and stable Southeast Asia. Hence any destabilizing development in the region will be regarded as a threat to Singapore's national security. Singapore has been concerned with the changing balance of power in Southeast Asia. The change in the power balance between the United States and the USSR, and its effects on Southeast Asia, have been perceived as contributing to instability in the region. In general, Singapore's leaders have emphasized the need for a balance of power in Southeast Asia. In this kind of regional political system, the United States, the USSR, and China, through military, political, and diplomatic means, would deter one another from gaining dominance in the region. As for the Southeast Asian states, they would have to abide by an international code of conduct including recognition of and respect for each other's independence, sovereignty, and territorial integrity; the peaceful settlement of regional disputes; and the promotion of efforts to cooperate with one another.

Since the end of World War II, the only external power that has actually threatened Singapore's security has been Indonesia. Between 1963 and 1965 Indonesia, under the revolutionary leader Sukarno, refused to recognize the existence of Malaysia, of which Singapore was then a part. Indonesia's government then perceived the formation of Malaysia as part of the encirclement by Western imperialist powers. To break the federation, Sukarno conducted a strategy of confrontation through infiltration, subversion, and limited war against the Malaysian states. Throughout 1964 Singapore was the target of Indonesian sabotage and bombing incidents that occurred in various parts of the island. Attempts were made to blow up vital bridges like the Merdeka Bridge and the Johore-Singapore water pipeline. Sixty Indonesian saboteurs were arrested up to May 1964. In early 1965 a serious bomb explosion took three lives and injured thirty-three others in Singapore.

In recent years, Singapore's leaders have emphasized the external threat to the country's national security as emanating from Vietnam. Vietnamese aggression against an independent Kampuchea is seen as a violation of a cardinal principle of peaceful coexistence. More directly, the Vietnamese aggression threatens the security of Thailand and in turn the rest of ASEAN, of which Singapore is a member.

Threat Perceptions of Singapore

The Vietnamese aggression is encouraged and supported by the USSR as part of a Soviet effort to expand its power and more specifically to encircle China. The USSR has sought the opportunity to gain a strong foothold in Southeast Asia. The Soviet-Vietnamese Treaty of November 1978 is regarded as a hostile act on the part of the two Communist powers.

As far as the Vietnamese aggression and Soviet expansion are concerned, the Singapore leaders' view is that they should be contained by the United States and other Western powers. Toward this end, Singapore has been a strong advocate of the return of the United States to a dominant security role in Southeast Asia. Singapore supports the continued presence of U.S. forces and bases in the Philippines and the continuation of the Manila Pact commitments to Thailand and the Philippines. Prime Minister Lee Kwan Yew earlier suggested that the United States could work in concert with other like-minded states, including Japan, Australia, and New Zealand, to maintain a multinational naval task force to ensure a blance of power in Southeast Asia.

A long-standing source of external threat to Singapore's national security is China. China had maintained its links with the CPM and continues to provide the CPM with moral and material support. For example, CPM leaders reside in Beijing, and the party has been provided with a radio facility—the Voice of the Malayan Revolution—that has been located in the southern part of China. In various meetings between Singapore and Chinese leaders, the former have always pointed out that unless the Chinese government and party break off all ties with the CPM, China will continue to constitute a long-term threat to the national security of Singapore as well as that of other ASEAN states.

Conclusion

The Singapore government has managed very successfully to contain the internal security threats. The ISA and other security measures have been used to curb the activities of the CPM, the underground satellite organizations, the racialist groups, and other antinational elements.

With respect to regional security, the Singapore government has tried to build a defense capability that will contribute toward any regional-defense arrangements. For example, Singapore is a member of the Five Power Defense Pact, which comprises Australia, Malaysia, New Zealand, Singapore, and the United Kingdom. Singapore also has bilaterial exchanges of information and training with its ASEAN neighbors. Beyond all these, Singapore's strategy is to encourage the United States to maintain a strong presence in order to deter any potential external aggression against the non-Communist states of Southeast Asia.

Notes

1. The main material for the following discussion has been taken from C.V. Devan Nair, ed., *Socialism That Works* (Singapore: Federal Publications, 1976). See particularly the chapter by Chua Sian Chin (the minister for home affairs), "Communism—A Real Threat," pp. 12-25.

2. Refer to C.V. Devan Nair, "Statement on Behalf of the PAP at the May 1976 Meeting of the Bureau of the Socialist Internation," in *Socialism That Works*, p. 123-145.

3. Ministry of Culture, *Singapore '81* (Singapore, 1982), p. 122.

4. Refer to *The Straits Times,* 11 and 15 January 1982.

5. See Lau Teik Soon, "Singapore and Political Stability: The Press Incident," *Pacific Community* (Tokyo), 3, no. 2 (January 1972):378-388.

10 National Threat Perceptions in the Philippines

Carlos F. Nivera

Threats to national security are a concomitant of independence. In a world of virtually unceasing political turbulence, they are among the geopolitical realities nations and governments must live with—and surmount. No country on the face of the earth, big or small, mighty or humble, is immune to such threats. They may come from within or from without. Philippine President Ferdinand E. Marcos has been one with Singapore Prime Minister Lee Kuan Yew in saying that the prevailing threat to national security in the ASEAN region is insurgency. In the light of contemporary events, the assessment of the two ASEAN leaders is indisputable. It also is clear, however, that there are external threats to the national security of ASEAN member nations. The Philippines, for one, is faced with such dangers from different directions, as will be shown in this chapter.

External Threats

The Philippines, which lies in one of the most strategic areas of the globe, is what one U.S. military expert has called "a natural pawn in the game of empire." Current regional and world affairs tend to accentuate the strategic importance of the Philippines. It must be underscored at the outset that U.S. involvement in any war in the Asian-Pacific theater would unavoidably entail a real risk for the Philippines. The presence of two major U.S. bases in the Philippines—Clark Airbase and Subic Naval Base—make this inevitable.

The security arrangements between the Philippines and the United States confer certain benefits on the Philippines. The philosophy of such arrangements—namely, that an attack on the Philippines is an attack on the United States—has historically served the Philippines in good stead. The alliance between the two countries has operated as a powerful and effective deterrent to aggression against the Philippines. On the other hand, the alliance has also made of the Philippines an actual or potential enemy of the enemies of the United States. This is a fact of life that no amount of diplomatic cosmetics can hide or obscure. It is thus of the utmost importance that points of possible U.S. involvement in military conflict within the Asian-Pacific theater be carefully examined in a study on threats to Philippine national security.

Soviet Union

The USSR poses a threat to Philippine national security on several different scores. Its manifestly expansionist policy presents a present and imminent danger to the Philippines; the Philippines lies in the trajectory of Soviet expansionism and imperialism, and the foreward thrust of Soviet strategy in Asia brings the peril of Soviet aggression increasingly near to this country. In concert with its client state, Vietnam, the USSR has established a formidable and ominous presence in Southeast Asia. It has fallen heir to the modern and sophisticated naval facilities set up by the United States in Vietnamese bases during the Vietnam War. From these bases the USSR has the capacity to harass the sea-lanes between the Indian and Pacific oceans. The USSR has a major naval contingent deployed in the Indian Ocean—and in strategic waters close to Japan.

The outstanding roadblock to Soviet expansionism in Asia and the Pacific is China. That the Soviets are concerned about the state of their relations with the Chinese is amply shown by the massing of many Soviet divisions on the Chinese-Soviet border. The USSR is gradually encircling China, however; it has massive forces north of China; and Vietnam, Laos, and Kampuchea—all supported and armed by Moscow—are steadily building up military potency south of China. Using Vietnam as a proxy, Moscow has established a foothold in the South China Sea.

Any military confrontation between the USSR and China would place peace and security in Asia and the Pacific in jeopardy, and raise the danger of U.S. involvement. It must be borne in mind that, to begin with, Moscow believes, and has publicly claimed, that the entente cordiale among the United States, China, and Japan is a weapon of aggression fashioned to serve U.S. designs on the USSR.

U.S. involvement would likewise be a distinct possibility if a full-scale war were to break out between China and Vietnam. The USSR would not stand idly by while its ally proxy, Vietnam, is locked in military conflict with China. Nor would the United States be likely to stand above the battle while the power balance in Asia and the Pacific is at stake.

The dispute between Japan and the USSR over continued Soviet occupation of Japanese islands seized toward the end of World War II is also a source of potential danger to peace and security in the Asian-Pacific region. If hostilities break out between Japan and the USSR, the chances are more than even that the United States would be involved. Japan is the chief U.S. ally in Asia and the Pacific. It is logical that a military threat to Japan is, by extension, a similar threat to the U.S. position in the Asian-Pacific region.

Vietnam

According to the International Institute of Strategic Studies in London, Vietnam today has the third largest army in the world. It inherited an enormous modern and sophisticated arsenal when the U.S. forces withdrew from South Vietnam. It has a convenient jumping-off base in Kampuchea. These facts, together with Vietnam's alliance with the USSR, raise the possibility of Vietnam becoming an actual threat to the Philippines and other non-Communist countries in Southeast Asia. Any military incident or serious diplomatic issue between the Philippines and Vietnam could be exploited by both Vietnam and the USSR to spur larger operations by their comrades-in-arms in the Philippines. Should a war between Vietnam and Thailand eventuate, the Philippines and the other ASEAN colleagues of Thailand would be in immediate peril of involvement.

It is well to consider that Vietnam, even with Soviet support, could not marshal the economic and complementary resources required by a major, protracted military effort overseas. Repeated crop failures, the slowness of economic recovery in what used to be South Vietnam, almost complete isolation from the financial capitals of the world—not to mention the multilateral banking agencies controlled or dominated by the United States—and continuing lack of access to current technology—these inveigh against further Vietnamese military adventures, at least in the foreseeable future. Even with enormous Soviet contributions in money and material to the maintenance of Vietnamese forces in Kampuchea, Hanoi is encountering serious problems of peace, order, and economic cooperation among the Kampucheans. Stories appearing in the European press on the steady deterioration of public utilities in Kampuchea attest to the enormity of the problems of occupation confronting Vietnam.

It is highly debatable whether Vietnam could, with Soviet support, undertake a military expedition against the Philippines, particularly while the United States maintains a significant military presence in the Philippines and on the Pacific littoral. Then, too, it is doubtful that the USSR would, on account of Vietnam, risk a major military confrontation with the United States in the Pacific, where the United States indisputably is predominant. Moreover, the USSR must reckon with Chinese retaliatory measures should it unleash Vietnam. The consensus among impartial observers is that the USSR could not, at this point, accept the cost of military confrontation with China. An added risk for the USSR is that the entente cordiale among the United States, China, and Japan may very well come into play once Peking and Moscow are engaged in combat.

China and North Korea

Because of the tendency of the new Chinese leadership to live with the rest of the world, which has stripped China of its old warlike image, there is a marked inclination among Filipinos in high places to think that the Chinese threat is behind them. This may prove an extremely dangerous delusion.

As pointed out by leaders of the Malaysian government and others, the refusal of Chinese leaders to disavow fraternal ties with Communist parties and Communists overseas presents a constant danger to peace and security in the ASEAN countries, where insurgency rather than threat of aggression is the immediate problem. What do fraternal ties encompass? It is well known that, in communist lexicon, fraternal ties stand for comradeship, which in practice means alliance.

At this stage of its economic development, China appears too engrossed in pressing and vexatious domestic problems to engage in any major military adventure overseas. Yet China could really hurt the Philippines were it to extend more than moral support to the insurgents in the country who are wedded to Chinese communist doctrine and dogma.

U.S. military presence is without doubt a deterrent to any military move against the Philippines from China. Add to this powerful deterrent the consuming desire of the Chinese to build up an anti-Soviet coalition of nations, which must count on U.S. support to come to fruition. Therefore, there is no discernible external threat to the Philippines from China.

There is, however, a potential Chinese Trojan Horse in our midst. Chinese nationals have a decisive say on the course of the Philippine economy because of their control of vital sections of business, industry, and finance. The Chinese community is also a fertile source of intelligence.

One factor cannot be ruled out in assessing possible problems with the large, sprawling, and potent Chinese minority in the Philippines: the majority of the affluent and well-placed Chinese in the country still are beholden to Taiwan and have vast interests there. Nor can one brush aside the fact that the bulk of the Chinese population of the Philippines is of ancient lineage. Naturalization and assimilation may have gone far to discourage them from playing the role of patsy to Peking.

Another danger to peace and stability in the Asian-Pacific region is the presence of North Korea, one of the most intractable communist states, in China's acknowledged sphere of influence. A fresh attempt by North Korea to go into South Korea would almost instantly draw into the ensuing conflict both the United States and Japan. In such an eventuality, what would become of the entente cordiale among the United States, China, and Japan—admittedly one of the stabilizing influences in today's world?

Distance from the theater of conflict would not confer immunity from involvement on the Philippines. One only has to recall that Philippine forces fought in the Korean War.

The objective evidence shows that both Peking and Moscow have consistently discouraged North Korea from embarking on another military expedition against South Korea, and that North Korea is bankrupt, with no further access to international credit of any consequence.

Threat Perceptions in the Philippines

Will U.S. Bases Invite Attack?

In a total war, the presence of U.S. bases in the Philippines certainly would invite attack. As the USSR would in all likelihood be the enemy in such an eventuality, it must be recognized that the bases are open to assault from the air—and also from the Soviet Far Eastern fleet of nuclear-powered submarines. In a limited war, more likely in Europe than in the Far East, the bases might well be spared attack—that is, if the USSR is averse to the idea of bringing the war to another theater.

The justification for the bases, from a national standpoint, is primarily strategic but partly economic. The Philippine government has consistently taken the position that the bases serve the end of protecting the Philippines from external aggression. With U.S. bases here, an attack on the Philippines is also an attack on the United States. Employment opportunities in the bases and their vicinity and significant foreign-exchange earnings from these establishments contribute to the economic well-being of the country.

The importance of the U.S. bases in terms of regional security can readily be appreciated. They are an integral part of the system of defenses in Asia and the Pacific that protect the lifelines of the Free World in these strategic areas. Thus President Marcos is right when he says that the Philippine-American bases agreement contributes to the maintenance of the balance of power on which regional peace and security rests.

The psychological climate for continued alliance between the Philippines and the United States draws considerable warmth from history and shared experience. In the Philippines, public opinion strongly supports the continuing security arrangements between the two countries. Polls conducted in the United States also have invariably indicated strong public support for the alliance.

Some Filipino political personalities and competent observers entertain doubts and misgivings, however, about the tenacity of U.S. public opinion. Such reservations do not appear illogical and unreasonable when one recalls that adverse U.S. public opinion at the height of the U.S. war effort in Vietnam led to the first and only military defeat ever sustained by the United States in its two-hundred-year history.

In the Philippines, as in other ASEAN countries, the possibility of Japanese rearmament on a large scale, which becomes increasingly urgent because of U.S. prodding, cannot but give rise to grave concern. A militarized Japan, wedded to the Bushido, would be, to put it charitably, a potential threat to peace and stability in Southeast Asia. Yet the fact must be faced that Japan cannot long remain a major economic power without also becoming a major military power. Moreover, the United States is right in demanding that Japan assume commensurate responsibility for the maintenance of the balance of power and the reinforcement of the lifelines of the Free World in the Asian-Pacific region.

Because of the intimate relationship between the U.S. bases in the Philippines and the U.S. military outposts and stations in Japan, the rearmament of Japan would necessarily involve a restructuring of the system of U.S. military alliances in the region. As long as the United States remains the dominent power in the Pacific, it can provide effective safeguards against a resurgence of aggressive Japanese militarism.

There is a distinct need to consider the possibility of letting the bases agreement lapse. At the time the term of the agreement ends, the objective conditions for the maintenance of the bases may have ceased to exist.

In the absence of a continuing strategic justification for the presence of U.S. bases in the country, the Philippines should not countenance moves for their retention. The strategic need is the only justification for the limitation on Philippine sovereignty that the bases accord represents in substance. Consider the undeniable fact that the bases are constant sources of irritants in Philippine-American relations.

Although there is a growing movement to abolish the bases, this is not likely to progress in the next two or three years—not while President Marcos remains in power, which will be true for at least five years if he stays the course. This means that the Marcos regime should concentrate attention and energy on its internal security—the building of a sound economic base and the neutralization of the Moro National Liberation Front (MNLF) and the New People's Army (NPA).

Internal Threats

The consensus among the Filipino people is that President Marcos has succeeded in establishing a politically stable government. It is also perceived, however, that several factors are undermining this stability. The Moro National Liberation Front remains a thorn in the government's side. A graver danger comes from subversion as a result of the growing broad opposition front led by the NPA and composed of rightists, the Christian left, the infiltrated labor and student organizations, and various other anti-Marcos elements.

The next two years are crucial. If the economy fails, or does as badly as it did in 1981, the subversive movement would gain further ground, perhaps enough to destablize the government.

The Moro National Liberation Front

The Moro National Liberation Front (MNLF) today is down but not out. Its fighting force has been reduced to considerably less than 10,000 from some 60,000 combatants at the height of the Muslim rebellion in the early 1970s. Bickerings, personality clashes, and intrigues have split the MNLF leadership, which in turn has stymied its recruitment program and organizational expansion. The government puts the number of MNLF returnees to the government at 40,000. From a movement that sent shock waves not just through the south but across the entire archipelago when it burst on Mindanao with such strength and intensity shortly after the proclamation of martial law, what can be called aftershocks are the sporadic encounters and ambuscades, brigandage, piracy, kidnappings, and other terrorist attacks, mainly on civilians, and the recent bank robberies.

The MNLF deception—which, according to Admiral Romulo M. Espaldon, then highest-ranking military commander in Mindanao and now minister of Muslim affairs, accounted for the foreign material and moral support that were the primary source of the MNLF's organizational strength—has started to lose its magic. Some funds still come from radical foreign supporters, but Nur Misuari's demand to create an independent Moro Republic has been firmly rejected by the Islamic Conference.

In a dialogue with foreign correspondents on 5 January 1982, the Central Mindanao commander, Major General Delfin Castro, said that the situation in the south has improved considerably over the past two years, prompting the military to remove six battalions from Mindanao, with two or three more slated to be taken out. He said that MNLF strength now is much less than the 10,000-15,000 figure the foreign press cited as an unofficial estimate of the rebel force at present.

An example noted by General Castro to show how considerably the situation has improved was that in the last eight months not one soldier has been killed in Tawi-Tawi. As a result, the garrison there has been reduced from three battalions to two. Tawi-Tawi and Sulu, then a single province, was practically overrun by the rebels before January 1973. In Sulu itself, General Castro said, the military forces have been reduced from nine battalions to five.

Although the Cencom commander regards the rebellion as under control, however, he himself indicated that the MNLF cannot be counted out. General Castro said that the Digos bank robberies were staged by a Misuari faction of the MNLF from zone 5 of the Lanao del Sur Revolutionary Command, better known as the Kudarat Special Zone. (On 16 December 1981, thirty-seven Muslim rebels in army fatigues raided four commercial banks in Digos, Davao del Sur, and escaped with more than P1 million cash.) To offset the impact of the government's reconciliation and rehabilitation programs, which saw the surrender of many MNLF commanders and their supporters, Castro said that the Misuari faction thought of undertaking some activity to show that the MNLF is still around and functional enough to attract attention. He added that the MNLF has responded to the successes of the administration's policies by engaging in other extralegal activities such as holdups, kidnapping, and piracy.

Does the MNLF continue to be a force that threatens the nation? For now, an MNLF show of force or a confrontation with the military is out of the question. Nevertheless, the MNLF will continue to be a big thorn in the side of the government's pacification campaign, as evidenced by the Digos raid, the Pata massacre, kidnappings, piracy, and other extralegal activities.

That the MNLF can sustain this role—to harass the military, keep a considerable number of troops on alert, and prevent the return of peace and order in Mindanao—is undeniable when one considers the quality and level of training and orientation of the rebels, their organizational command and setup, the efficient and effective intelligence and communications systems, the weaponry, their familiarity with the terrain and mass base, plus a continuing foreign material and moral support. Even among the returnees, the inefficiency, indifference, graft, and corruption in the bureaucracy have caused considerable disenchantment. Many are fed up and ready to go back to the front. A number have since done so.

Is settlement of the conflict in sight? By admitting from the start that there is no military solution to the kind of problem the MNLF poses, the government can only seek a final settlement of the conflict. Although the other side appears to continue to be adamant and to spurn calls to return to the conference table since the collapse of talks in April 1977 under the Tripoli accords, the past year saw Misuari lose what may well be a last-ditch attempt to have the Islamic Conference support his demand for an independent Moro Republic. The Baghdad meeting ignored his plea entirely and instead called for new contacts with the Manila government regarding the implementation of the Tripoli agreement of December 1976, which unconditionally states that any settlement of the Mindanao problem must recognize the national sovereignty and territorial integrity of the Philippine republic.

Again although there have been only denials from government officials, the reported reconciliation between Misuari and former Congressman Rashid Lucman of the Bangsa Moro Liberation Organization (BMLO) last year might well prove to be a step toward unification of all the secessionist factions in the south (with no following, the Hashim Salemat faction has been written off). Thus a common Moro Front will be all the more ripe for a return to the table. Indeed, the settlement processes would have started last year had it not been for a last-minute change of mind by Malacanang. Following feelers from the MNLF central committee that settlement could be reopened only through direct contact between Misuari and President Marcos, a secret mission was dispatched by Manila to the Middle East to arrange the direct contact. When the moment of truth came and the overseas phone connection was ready, the Malacanang end—not necessarily the president—refused to make contact. The emissaries were frustrated and blamed the palace cordon sanitaire and those who stood to gain by keeping Mindanao aflame for the snafu.

The bright side of 1982 was that the initiatives and channels for settlement from all parties remained alive. The hope was that the Islamic Conference could get the parties together again early in the year to finalize and thrash out the details of implementing the Tripoli agreement. Should events conspire to thwart a settlement in 1982, what then? The continuing unstable situation in Mindanao, occasioned by operations—however limited—of the MNLF plus the depredations of the New People's Army and other outlaws will emasculate the economic program now under way for the south and consequently make the entire country's economic viability and recovery that much more difficult.

In the meantime, all government efforts and projects to win over the rebels are anchored on the administration's policy of attraction and reconciliation and its socioeconomic amelioration and development programs.

The task of winning over the rebels was from the outset a struggle to bring the government closer to the people, to compensate for the neglect and deficiencies the region has suffered through the past decades, to eradicate the feeling of alienation, and to advance the realization "of our common and long cherished aspirations as a nation: a peaceful society, a self-reliant nation, national understanding and unity, a society of equals, political stability and a national consensus."

Specifically, the government promoted understanding among the cultural communities, particularly among the Muslims and Christians, to eliminate any and all vestiges of divisiveness among Filipinos. In the drive to win the hearts and minds of the Muslim population, the emphasis was put on respect and awareness for Islam, its culture and heritage, and the Muslim role in the struggle for sovereignty and in nation building. This included respect for the Islamic way of life through the construction of mosques and madrazahs, the codification of Islamic laws, and the official proclamation of Muslim holidays. Thus the feelings of alienation precipitated by the patronizing postures of the past were erased, and the Muslim Filipino came to realize that he no longer was detached from the mainstream of Philippine society.

On the political front, the creation of the two autonomous regional governments showed the central government's sincerity in transferring certain powers to achieve a more responsive, dynamic, and effective administration. One of the most effective methods employed in the south to work out a consensus is the person-to-person consultation. It was there that the expedience of the dialogue was most crucial, intense, and unprecedented. The consultations were between commanders, the general public, civilian officials, and a government panel, and the rebels and returnees—even at the national level, when cabinet members visited areas of conflict periodically. A monument to this device to bring the government closer to its people is a building in Calarian, Zamboanga City, designated by President Marcos as the so-called Malacanang of the South.

To redress the lack or absence of equality in the pursuit of economic opportunities, the government stepped up the socioeconomic development of the south to bring it up to the level of growth and progress in other regions. Thus liberal policies and opportunities were extended by way of loans, government positions, training, grants, and scholarships. Innovative programs included "the barefoot doctors, medical outreach mission, the Guam medical mission, the barefoot teachers, 'Magbasa Kits,' and other livelihood projects in a bid to eradicate economic disparity."

By late 1979 livelihood programs with P100 million funding each for the two autonomous regions were announced. All officials concerned were briefed at live-in seminars, and the entire countryside was electrified by the promise of jobs and economic opportunities. The disappointment that swept the people when the programs could not get off the ground for lack of funds tended to erode a nascent credibility and cast doubts on the government's efforts and sincerity. The New Republic's KKK program (Kilusang Kabuhayan at Kaunlaran, or the National Livelihood of Progress Movement) is seen as the implementation of those initial livelihood schemes in the autonomous regions two years ago. The KKK itself, however, is short of funds. Its earlier promise of no-collateral, low-interest loans is gone.

The Communist Party of the Philippines,
New People's Army (CPP/NPA)

Of the internal forces threatening the nation, insurgency by the reestablished Communist Party of the Philippines and the New People's Army (CPP/NPA) specifically has come full cycle in the span of a decade.

The year 1981 saw CPP/NPA activities peak to alarming levels from the sporadic attacks and ambuscades of the mid-1970s, when the Maoist dissidents first started to resurface from the debacle they suffered with the imposition of martial law in September 1972. The daring, tenacity, and crescendo of armed operations were indicative of the strength and spread of the movement's influence, even into nontraditonal areas such as the Ilocos provinces, Eastern Visayas, and Mindanao. Complementing rural and urban guerrilla warfare was the heightened tempo in campus activism and labor unrest nationwide, culminating in the violent student demonstration at Manila's Liwasang Bonifacio on 7 October 1981 and the many violent workers' mass action and strikes in the wake of the lifting of martial law on 17 January 1981.

For the Maoists, 1981 was a time for consolidating their dominant role in seeking to forge a broad alliance of all antigovernment forces led by the

Christian left, the rightists, and the Moro National Liberation Front (MNLF). The parliamentary/political struggle that subversives waged simultaneously with protracted people's war was typified by the orchestration of the boycott of the 1981 referenda/plebiscites and the presidential elections, and the emergence of front groups among the youth, labor, the poor, religious, and those based abroad under the National Democratic Front (the umbrella organization).

A significant aspect of the efforts to unify the antigovernment elements was the overture of the CPP/NPA to link up with the Muslim rebels. Although the MNLF still has to openly accept the offer—and there are many who do not expect a formal link because communism and Islam cannot coexist. Already there have been growing tactical cooperation and collaboration at certain lower echelons of the subversives and the secessionists.

The escalating violence and terrorism of the war of national liberation against the backdrop of bold and relentless agitation and propaganda was reminiscent of the revolutionary mood of 1971-1972, which eventually led to anarchy, virtual paralysis of government, and near collapse of the economy. With the communist insurgents literally knocking at the gates of Malacanang, President Marcos proclaimed martial law "to save the nation and the Republic."

Thus, having seen how such a revolutionary mood could get out of hand, military authorities have taken appropriate steps to blunt what they now consider the most serious threat to the nation. The unrestrained boldness and tenacity of the Maoist concept of protracted people's war, together with the supportive parliamentary struggle, has caused the military to give the CPP/NPA due consideration if not priority attention over the Mindanao problem. With an ever expanding manpower and mass base that underscores the depth of its influence across the archipelago, the CPP/NPA has shown the capacity—as it has indeed started—to rally all the antigovernment forces to form a broad united front.

How the Maoist menace managed to rear its ugly head anew and come full cycle in just a decade, more than eight years of which were under martial law, is ironically attributable to a large extent to the situation spawned by the end of martial law. This opened the floodgates to make the urban struggle, recruitment, agitation, infiltration, mass action, politicization, and propaganda campaigns that much easier. Martial law had quelled the communist uprising and effectively forced the CPP/NPA to go into hiding. It is the same mailed-fist policy, however, that sparked the Muslim rebellion in the south with which the armed forces and the central government were preoccupied for the rest of the 1970s, leaving the CPP/NPA movement to thrive unmolested.

Admittedly, martial law resulted in an upturn in the economy, a more vigorous land-reform program, infrastructure growth, breakthroughs in rice and agricultural production, social development, a tourism boom, and other benefits. Yet the regimentation abetted by controlled mass media and external forces—foremost of which was the continuing oil crisis—bred military abuses and graft and corruption at all levels of the bureaucracy, exploitation by multinationals and conglomerates reputedly owned or controlled by palace kin and cronies, and an ever widening gap between the rich and poor made more pronounced by unchecked inflation and galloping prices of prime commodities.

Outside the revolt-racked areas of the southern Philippines, the peace and order achieved by so-called constitutional authoritarianism started to falter by 1975, when the rise in the crime rate was first registered. The volume has since continued to increase with syndicated or organized crime such as bank robberies and kidnappings being a major concern. The crime rate for 1981 stood at 50.6 incidents per 100,000 population per month, a 33-percent increase overall from the volume in 1980.

Given such a deteriorating atmosphere, with the armed forces spread thin and held down by the MNLF, and with the administration preoccupied with politics and an image-saving foreign policy in the name of the normalization process to restore democracy in the Philippines, the CPP/NPA, having adapted to martial law, had ripe conditions and a receptive public to work with to expand organizationally and deepen its influence. In just a few years following the Marcos clampdown, the NPAs have restored and strengthened their hold over traditional areas of the Cagayan Valley, Central Luzon, and the Bicol Peninsula. Soon the exploited tribes, especially those in the Chico River basin in the mountain provinces; the peasants in Abra and Ilocos provinces; Samar and then Leyte in Eastern Visayas and in Mindanao, Zamboanga del Norte, and the Davao provinces mainly, became prime targets and operational areas and are now the labeled hot spots on military maps. The main reason cited by military authorities for the revitalization and expansion of the CPP/NPA is its skillful use of propaganda and its infiltration of and agitation within the ranks of the youth, labor, and farmers.

The 1981 estimates of the armed forces place the strength of the communist insurgents at less than 6,000 regulars or card-bearing members, 16,000 active support elements and a 200,000-person mass base in thirteen regional commands. From the December issue of the party organ, "Ang Bayan," the figures given were 27 guerrilla fronts spread over 4,000 barangays in 400 towns of 43 provinces. To show how daring and tenacious the Maoists have become, military sources said that of the 1,188 violent incidents in 1981, 65 percent or 775 were the handiwork of the NPAs. In 1980 there were some 670 incidents, of which 380 or 55 percent were attributed to the subversives. There was a 103 percent jump, from 380 incidents in 1980 to 775 in 1981 in NPA-inspired violence. The sure sign of the deteriorating situation was the rise in military-recorded violence from 670 in 1980 to 1,188 in 1981, a jump of 77 percent.

Of the incidents perpetrated by the NPAs, the statistics showed that nine out of 10 were ambuscades. Disarming and liquidation were next in that order. There were 78 instances of ballot-box snatching in 1981. In terms of lives lost to NPA armed operations, military casualties rose from 128 in 1980 to 277 in 1981 (116 percent) and those of civilians from 205 to 343 (67 percent). Weapons lost to the dissidents numbered 394 in 1981 up 91 percent from 206 in 1980.

The rapid growth of armed operations and the emboldened orchestration of civilian disturbances in urban centers (the NPAs were involved in 90 percent of all such disorders nationwide in 1981) prompted fielding of more troops in NPA-infested areas. The Central Mindanao command chief announced early in January 1982 that six battalions, or some 6,000 soldiers, had been pulled out of Mindanao, with three or more battalions ready to be redeployed. Fortunately for the military, the leadership crisis in the MNLF, the lukewarm attitude of foreign backers, and the mass surrenders and punitive government action have reduced the MNLF to small pockets of resistance. Incidents blamed on the secessionists went down 21 percent, from 1,377 in 1980 to 1,088 in 1981. Troop casualties also dropped by 15 percent, from 516 to 439, with a similar drop in civilian casualties. As for the wounded, there were 48-percent and 42-percent decreases for government men and civilians, respectively.

Regarding the NPA strength in Southern Philippines, General Castro said there were less than 700 NPA regulars and that the foreign press report of 4,000 hard-core Maoists were unrealistic. As for funds, the dissidents have their own taxation methods in areas under their influence augmented by *tong* from extortion and terrorism. It is interesting to note that captured documents in the Bicol region included liquidation and accounting reports for thousands of pesos, which represented amounts far in excess of the normal revenues. With China's avowal that it is not supporting the local communists, the military's conclusion is that the CPP/NPA is drawing financial support from the rightists. Such funding support comes at a time when the CPP/NPA has shown that it is the only group with the strength, force, and base to be the rallying point in unifying all the opposition into a broad united front to disperse government forces and resources.

With such a dominant role, the CPP/NPA will continue to pose the most serious threat in the months ahead and perhaps up to the general elections scheduled for 1984 and even beyond. With good reason, the military is worried but is determined to go all out in routing the dissidents, as the late Ramon Magsaysay did in the early 1950s.

The Economy

For the Philippines 1981 was the worst year in over a decade. Confidence in the economy was badly shaken. So serious was the erosion in confidence that there are fears it may affect the very stability of the government unless the national leadership moves swiftly to alleviate the situation.

One out of every four Filipinos was out of a job by year end. Mass layoffs were resorted to as industries and commercial houses desperately attempted to stay alive. Trade unions were restive all year. Some 255 labor strikes took place in metropolitan Manila and 50 in other regions, four times more than in 1980, or an average of 17.35 strikes a month. The strikes involved 76,555 workers and cost industry production man-hour losses of 3.04 million. The labor ministry, in a report to the cabinet, disclosed that unemployment in metropolitan Manila, which more or less follows the national trend, had reached an alarming 26 percent during the first six months of the year, and estimated that it could reach 30 percent by year end. The gravity of the situation may be appreciated in the light of the fact that unemployment rate in 1979 was only 6.5 percent, and in 1980, 14.6 percent.

The labor ministry also reported that actual employment decreased in absolute terms. It estimated that by year end 1981, shutdowns and retrenchment had forced more than 70,000 out of jobs. Layoffs for 1980 totaled 63,335, and for 1979, 52,411. Each year there are about 750,000 additions to the labor force.

Part of labor's surge of activity may be attributed to the lifting of martial law on 17 January 1981, when both unions and management began adjusting after nine years of martial law to a relatively freer period of free collective bargaining and trade unionism. The labor ministry spearheaded the campaign of the Batasang Pambansa (National Assembly) for a new labor relations law that fully restored the workers' rights to strike and lockout. If the rate of unemployment and underemployment continues, labor's restiveness will be difficult to control, and grave social problems could result.

Jesus P. Estanislao, executive director of the Center for Research and Communications and one of the Philippines' leading economists, has listed five indicators of a depressed Philippine economy in 1981: (1) the drop in the real volume of imports; (2) stagnant investment; (3) low growth in real consumption; (4) negative growth in many manufacturing industries; and (5) reduced inflation in Meropolitan Manila, presumably reflecting depressed conditions.

Another indicator of how badly the Philippines fared in 1981 was the drop in GNP. Preliminary estimates of the National Economic and Development Authority (NEDA) place a 5-percent growth in the country's 1981 GNP—the value of goods and services produced during the period—or from 1980's P92,930 million at constant 1972 prices to P97,577 million. *Business Day* (a national business daily), on the other hand, is projecting a 4.9-percent growth, with GNP reaching only P97,455 million.

Early in the year, government planners projected a GNP growth rate of 6 percent for 1981. This was later scaled down to 5.5 percent and much later to only 5 percent, as it became apparent that external pressures—such as the recession that hit the country's major trading partners like the United States and Japan—and internal problems, particularly those that confronted the financial system, were taking a heavy toll on the economy's performance.

For example, preliminary estimates of the Central Bank show that 1981 exports, on which hopes for an economic recovery during the year were pinned, will amount to only $5.91 billion, or only 2 percent better than the previous year's output of $5.79 billion. On the other hand, imports are expected to reach $8.4 billion, or 9 percent more than the preceding year's figure of $7.7 billion, resulting in a trade deficit of $2.5 billion.

Central Bank Governor Jaime C. Laya late last month said that a factor contributing to the country's trade imbalance was the deterioration of the peso-dollar exchange rate which, as of the last week of December 1981, had already hit P8.20 to $1. Economic Planning Minister Placido L. Mapa, Jr., shared Laya's views, saying that exchange-rate instabilities have stunted the growth of industrialized countries, which prevented them from absorbing much of the produce of developing countries, including the Philippines.

The year 1982 could be as bleak as 1981, depending on how positively national leaders will tackle the problems at hand. President Marcos and government economists have issued guarded statements of optimism, but much will depend on how swiftly government programs can get off the ground. The situation is such that the private sector, despite its desire for recovery, cannot do much without a massive government infusion of money into the economy.

Private and government economists agree that the Philippines has reached the end of the road insofar as foreign borrowing is concerned. External debt may reach P18 billion in 1982, after which there will be nowhere to turn for more money. In such an event, economists point out, the nation's international reserves may have to fall. This may endanger the possibility of limited growth.

One economist warned that there would be a bleak future unless a serious program was immediately launched to attract foreign investment, backed up by a commitment for its success. Fortunately, even in the depressed year of 1981, foreign investment during the eleven-month period ending in November totaled P64.49 million, up by P8.5 million or 15.21 percent during 1980 (SEC figures).

With this encouraging trend, the national leadership should now review its investment-incentive policies, remove features that have proved discouraging, and introduce additional incentives. The lifting of martial law has contributed to a large degree to the return of confidence among foreign investors. The national leadership, however, must follow this advantage with a serious and immediate study, through consultations with foreign investors, of the factors that have in the past discouraged old investors.

Agriculture will continue to play a vital role in propping up the economy. Sustained increases in agricultural output will have to be maintained. Rice, now an export product, will serve as the mainstay in the agricultural-stabilization program.

The government has launched a massive corn-production program that should begin to see results toward the end of 1982. The corn-production program's success will stimulate other industries dependent on corn, such as the livestock business. Coconut, today's largest foreign-exchange earner, will have to be given greater attention. Something positive should be done with the large portion of rural purchasing power derived from coconut prices received by farmers; farmers should be given back as income subsidy the large amount accumulated from the special tax they had been paying for years. This will increase rural purchasing power. Also, the government should consider giving a subsidy for coconut as a food source to prop up demand for coconut oil.

Philippine agriculture has markedly suffered from excessive state control in certain critical aspects. Sugar and coconut products have to be stripped of government fetters to be in a position to find their proper places in the domestic and world markets. Philippine agriculture, too, is ailing from what may well be called a crisis of production. This problem must be addressed; otherwise the Philippines will not be able to fill the normal demands of its markets.

Experts on political economy are wont to say that economic problems are, at bottom, political. This is a source of strength for the Philippines; for there is no doubt that the political authority, the political knowhow, and the political instruments for the solution of the country's economic problems are fimly lodged in the hands of the national leadership. That leadership has a long history of success in solving problems of political economy.

The external political and economic factors—particularly in Western Europe, North America, and Japan, where the Philippines has its major export markets—may not be as bleak and unfavorable as they are portrayed in some sections of the world press. The quicker those markets survive the doldrums that now engulf them, the better for the Philippine economy.

Stabilizing Factors

Leadership

A crisis in leadership could bring down a nation like a pack of cards. In the Philippines, President Ferdinand E. Marcos has been able to establish his leadership firmly and beyond question. He was first elected in 1965. After four years as president, he was reelected in 1969—the first Filipino president to be so reelected—and with the highest majority ever recorded in Philippine history. After sixteen years as president, Marcos is today the only visible and acceptable national leader on the Philippine scene. No one else of consequence is in sight, neither among the younger men being groomed by Marcos nor among the opposition leaders in the Philippines or abroad. If Marcos goes suddenly, the average Filipino fears that he will leave a vacuum and that confusion will follow in the ensuing struggle for power and leadership. This fear persists despite Marcos's effort to establish an orderly line of succession.

On 17 January 1974, the first anniversary of the ratification of the new Constitution, President Marcos announced a decision about presidential succession. He said: "Should anything happen to the President, I have already provided for an orderly succession. This has been done by virtue of a decree I have kept in order not to sow envy and disunity. If anything happens, that decree would be immediately implemented." Later he initiated a move in the Interim Batasang Pambansa to pass what is now known as the Law of Succession.

The next presidential election is scheduled for 1986. It is hoped that by that time some worthy new leaders will have emerged to vie for the presidency —assuming, of course, that Marcos will decide to retire.

Meanwhile, no serious challenge to Marcos' leadership is anticipated. The timely lifting of martial law in 1981 and the creation of the Philippine-style parliamentary system, which allows for a strong president, were strategic moves that further entrenched Marcos in power. Through these moves, Marcos legitimized his continuance as head of state at least until 1986. Moreover, his position has been strengthened by the open endorsement of Marcos's leadership by the Reagan administration.

The next two years are crucial for Marcos, however. If the country is plunged into a grave economic crisis leading to a civil disorder, if the NPA succeeds in seizing such an opportunity, then the New Society and everything that Marcos has built in his sixteen years as head of state could be wiped out. If the country can keep the law-and-order situation in check, then Marcos may stand in history as one of the greatest leaders of the Filipino people.

The Military

To a large extent the internal security of any nation depends on the military—its background, training, and indoctrination; its position in the community as a stabilizing force; its posture and potency. The military in the Philippines has a total armed strength of about 308,000: 63,000 army, 20,000 navy, 16,000 air force, and 45,000 in the reserve corps. Its paramilitary forces of 65,000 include 40,000 men in the Philippine constabulary (national military police) and 25,000 in the Civilian Home Defense Force. Its budget of U.S.$680 million in 1979 represented less than 15 percent of the national budget.

The Philippines is fortunate in having a military that, by training and tradition, places civilian authority over and above the military. The military command is drawn from graduates of West Point like Lieutenant General Fidel Ramos, AFP Vice-Chief of Staff, or from the Philippine Military Academy, whose curriculum, discipline, ideology, and idealism are closely patterned after those of West Point. Some top-echelon officers are graduates of Annapolis, and quite a few are from the Philippine Reserve Officer Training Corps set up before World War II under the aegis of General Douglas MacArthur. Throughout the years since World War II, the armed forces of the Philippines have maintained a high degree of professionalism.

Unlike in other Asian countries, the military in itself in the Philippines has never played an active political role; it has always served as the civil government's law-and-order arm during political campaigns and in many cases has been a stabilizing factor. Military leaders have kept themselves in the background, emerging into the limelight only on special missions for the civil government.

Because it has kept itself aloof from politics, the military is regarded with considerable respect by most of the people. Although there have been isolated instances of military abuses, the military has shown its mettle by instituting prompt corrective measures.

Among the currently recognized senior military leaders, there is not one whose loyalty to the republic and to President Marcos may be questioned. Among the junior officers and the rank and file, there are no indications of the existence of radical elements or potential troublemakers. No one among the top-echelon officers is capable of taking over leadership to unite the armed forces against civil authority.

In the foreseeable future, the military will remain a passive force politically, committed to the support of legally established authority. It is, therefore, difficult to conceive of a military-led coup. Even in the event a vacuum is created by the demise or disability of President Marcos, most informed Filipinos feel that the military would not take sides in a political struggle but would stand firm behind established legal authority and serve as a stabilizing force.

At present the only two military leaders who may be capable of swinging the armed forces into some kind of unified political action are General Fabian Ver, chief of staff, and his vice-chief of staff, Lieutenant General Ramos.

The other generals are relatively new and do not yet command mass support among officers and rank and file. Although there may be professional rivalry between the two, both are blood relatives of President Marcos, Ver on the mother's side and Ramos on the father's side. Their loyalty to the president is unquestioned, and both proved this during the difficult days of martial law (1972-1981). Should the president go, it is unlikely that Ver and Ramos would break up. Because of their friendly relations with each other, despite professional rivalry, and their affinity through Marcos, they are likely to continue to team up behind the forces of law and order. Both are credited with sobriety, and neither is touched with ambition. More important, both believe in the legitimacy of the present government setup.

The Armed Forces of the Philippines (AFP) and the Philippine Constabulary (PC) are highly trained for combat and guerrilla warfare. They have proven their capability by keeping the MNLF in check and by neutralizing the sporadic NPA nuisance raids.

Conclusion

There seems to be no doubt that the Philippine national leadership has the proper perspective and is on the right course in solving the country's economic problems. In pre-martial-law days the best of intentions and plans usually were victims of political ambush, with the central government unable to move without political interference.

Martial law ushered in a new era more conducive to efficiency and serious work. With this distinct advantage, plus his continuing authoritarian position, President Marcos will have little excuse if he fails to pull the country out of the morass that 1981 created. He has the support of the majority of the people now, but failure to solve the economic threat may lead to an uncertain future for the country.

11 National Threat Perceptions: Explaining the Thai Case

Sarasin Viraphol

At present, Thailand's foremost perception of threat comes in the form of external threats to political and military security.

Geographically, Thailand occupies a strategic position separating the communist states in Indochina from the noncommunist ones in Southeast Asia. Because of its relative size, national endowments, and membership in ASEAN, Thailand is considered vital by all countries with important interests in the region, both those that are seeking to undermine its present political order and independence, and those working to preserve the status quo. Currently Thailand is the focus of a struggle related to external and local power rivalries. Historically, Thailand has lived among adversaries and rivalrous states. Clashes of security interests have been a recurring feature of its environment. In most instances it has managed to survive the test of safeguarding its independence. Over the past four decades Thailand has been subjected to foreign invasion, threats of invasion, and subversion—both locally and externally induced. The communist threat experienced by Thailand during the past three decades has been both direct and indirect. Notably through the introduction of the unique struggle for national liberation into Thailand via the foreign-supported Communist Party of Thailand (CPT), Thailand was one target of the communist attempt to seize political powers by force in the region. These efforts to link up activities of various Communist parties in the name of proletarian internationalism were directed from Moscow and Beijing and created the double threat of indigenous communist struggles assisted by external communist powers.

Thailand's recent alliance with the United States was predicated on national-security considerations. Joining the Manila Pact and the newly created Southeast Asia Treaty Organization (SEATO) in 1954 were means toward that end. Thailand was less concerned about the larger U.S. objective of containing global communist expansionism, but it joined hands with the United States primarily with its own specific security interests and well-being in mind. As the political situation in Laos was deteriorating, the issuance of the Thanat-Rusk Communique in 1962, stating that Manila Pact commitments are bilateral as well as multilateral, was an explicit response that the formal alliance could satisfy Thailand's security preoccupation.

Paradoxically, as the U.S. involvement in Southeast Asia deepened and as U.S.-Thai security relations developed further, the threat against Thailand also tended to grow, with external communist powers carrying out hostile acts essentially through indigenous communists they supported and trained. Hence, the Communist Party of Thailand (CPT) declared the start of armed struggle in Thailand in 1961, and Peking publicly endorsed the people's war against Thailand in 1965. By 1970 the CPT claimed to have a fighting force of more than 10,000 in the various regions of Thailand.

While continuing to rely on the U.S. arrangement for its security, Thailand began to experiment with the novel concept of promoting regional cooperation as a means for conflict resolutions; it joined in creating the Association of Southeast Asia (ASA) in 1961 and helped in the establishment of the five-member Association of Southeast Asian Nations (ASEAN) in 1967. The urgency to create ASEAN as a viable nonmilitary organization for satisfying the member states' national-security interests was heightened when the United States, hitherto the mainstay of Thailand's security, discontinued its military posture and acceded to a communist victory in Vietnam. Heads of government of Thailand and the other ASEAN countries met in Bali in early 1976 for the first ASEAN summit to determine how best to deal with the political situation in the region following the armed takeover of Indochina by the communists. The Treaty of Amity and Cooperation that resulted from their deliberations provided the framework for seeking expanded and better cooperation among the Southeast Asian countries.

Thai Security and the New Developments in Indochina

The U.S. withdrawal from mainland Southeast Asia meant that Thailand was deprived of its sense of being able to depend on a close great-power ally as it stood exposed to the new communist threats from Indochina. Thus it was with some satisfaction that Thailand was soon to find a counterweight in a China increasingly alarmed by the prospect of Vietnam's seeming readiness to challenge Chinese influence in Southeast Asia by drawing on Soviet support. The simmering internecine quarrels symptomatic of the deep-seated schism among the communist states found a regional expression in the ultimate armed conflict between the Khmer Rouge and the Vietnamese, which was replete with its own proxy element as evident in the backing of the respective sides by the Chinese and the USSR.

In such a milieu, Thailand is essentially confronted with an ominous three-way threat: by the presence of Vietnamese forces in neighboring Kampuchea, the aggravation of intraregional tensions resulting from the intensified extraregional rivalry, and the continuing indigenous insurgency that exists both dependent on and independent of exogenous elements. These factors vary in intensity and significance at any given moment. Consequently, Thailand's security has been made more precarious, although it can still count on the inner strength and resilience made possible by the homogeneity of its people, a tolerant religion, an enlightened and popular monarchy, a basically surplus agricultural economy, and a relatively strong sense of nationhood.

Thailand has always been conscious of the security threat because of its long northern and eastern borders (more than 2,000 kilometers) with Laos and Kampuchea and, beyond that, its proximity to Vietnam and China. In geopolitical terms, an enemy could enter Thailand through Laos and dominate the vast northeast region or sever it from the rest of the country. On passing through the flat plains of Kampuchea, an enemy could seize the heartland of Thailand after entering the country through the Wattana Nakorn Pass at Aranyaprathet.

With the communist victory in Indochina in 1975, Thailand adjusted its external policy and earnestly sought a modus vivendi with the new Indochinese regimes. Despite incessant irritations and nuisances that marked its relations with the new governments in Laos and Kampuchea, initial progress was made in establishing and improving relations with Vietnam on the tacit understanding that both sides would seek normal diplomatic relations without upsetting the existing power balance. Thailand was also encouraged by the consolidation of links among the ASEAN countries; China's endorsement of the existence and purpose of ASEAN; and the gradual change in attitude from outright hostility to cautious acceptance by Vietnam and the USSR of the noncommunist grouping and its political program of ZOPFAN (Zone of Peace, Freedom, and Neutrality).

Nevertheless, Vietnam's invasion of Kampuchea on the heels of premier Pham Van Dong's so-called goodwill tour of ASEAN and Thailand in late 1978 revived the Thai apprehension about Hanoi's real intentions toward other noncommunist states, particularly Thailand. The Vietnamese political and military domination, backed by some 200,000 Vietnamese troops, is especially disturbing because Thailand has no substantial deterrence capability of its own to deal with such a threat on its doorstep. Thailand and its ASEAN partners, however, have been able to galvanize significant diplomatic-political support to dramatize the widespread opposition to the Vietnamese invasion. Equally important, the Chinese administered a devastating punitive strike against Vietnam, which in effect has held down the main Vietnamese elite forces close to the Sino-Vietnamese border and has constrained the Vietnamese military action in Kampuchea. Nevertheless, the fighting rages on between the foreign occupying army and the Khmer Rouge forces close to the Thai-Kampuchean border; the frequent border incursions by Vietnamese regulars—the most serious being the Non

Mak Moon incident of 23 June 1980—highlight the danger to Thailand's national security. The precarious border situation has been aggravated by the problem of hundreds of thousands of Kampucheans crossing into Thai territory or gathering along the border as a result of the ongoing conflict. Their plight and its implications for Thailand cannot be solved simply by international humanitarian aid. It is rooted in the military-political configuration within Kampuchea. Thailand's security will be affected as long as the fighting in Kampuchea persists—very likely for a long time.

Vietnam has argued that its action in Kampuchea was needed to assure its own security by eliminating the Chinese threat as personified by the Khmer Rouge regime. In the process of trying to ensure maximum security for itself, however, Vietnam has not only trampled on Kampuchea's sovereignty and independence, but also violated the security interests of other states—Thailand in particular. It is questionable whether Vietnam has indeed added to its own security, since Vietnam's entry into Kampuchea has pitted China squarely against it while also earning the animosity and ill will of the international community—not to mention the enmity of the Kampuchean people. By virtue of seeking the support of the USSR in its invasion of Kampuchea, Vietnam has given China a pretext to conduct a sustained course of punitive action (military, political, and economic) against Vietnam and Vietnamese-dominated Laos, which is highly vulnerable in geopolitical terms. Vietnam also has alienated neighboring noncommunist countries and the international community at large by confirming generally held suspicions about its expansionist ambitions in the region. In relying solely on the USSR, Vietnam cannot be certain that it will always be in control of the situation it has created for itself. Already there are signs of friction developing between Vietnam and the USSR, as the latter, having found a golden opportunity to establish a firm foothold in Indochina, is eagerly stepping up its own activities in all spheres in the three Indochina states. An enfeebled, isolated, and dependent Vietnam is in no position to prevent this serious Soviet encroachment.

Vietnamese-controlled Laos represents an added security problem for Thailand as well as a burdensome responsibility for Vietnam. Relations between Bangkok and Vientiane have been blowing hot and cold since 1975; there is a general recognition on both sides, however, of the virtue of coexistence. Despite periodic border troubles, Thailand wants peace with Laos for strategic reasons—to demonstrate a willingness to conduct normal relations with the Laotian government and maintain friendly ties to the Laotian people. On the Laotian side there is an acute counsciousness of the looming Chinese threat, which forces the Vietnamese-backed regime to try to avoid creating a two-front security situation by neutralizing the potential Thai threat. Moreover, Laos remains economically dependent on Thailand, which controls its important access routes to the sea and thus to much of the

Explaining the Thai Case

outside world. In addition, the seemingly independent line assumed by Laos in international forums is a desirable projection by Hanoi of an image negating the popularly held suspicion that Laos has become an integral part of a putative Indochina Federation.

The Vietnamese occupation of Kampuchea has intensified external power rivalries by means of proxies. China is determined not only to conduct a lengthy war of attrition against Vietnam, but also to contain the growing Soviet presence and influence in Southeast Asia. To this end, China seems to have a good pretext for containing the threats by the USSR and Vietnam, especially when it publicly endorses ASEAN's effort to seek a comprehensive political settlement of the Kampuchean problem—which Vietnam has consistently rejected. The Soviet support of the Vietnamese adventures—which in turn has permitted the use of Vietnamese port facilities by Soviet ships and planes, as well as a growing Soviet presence in Indochina—has been an important factor in prompting the United States to enter into a strategic relationship with China. Ipso facto, the United States has acquiesced to a prominent Chinese role in facing up to the Kampuchean problem. This has neutralized the United States as a viable factor in shaping the course of peace and stability in Southeast Asia, although there are also strong indications that the United States was neither willing nor able to assume such a role in the first place.

As a result, the regional states' freedom of action is greatly restricted, especially since ASEAN's proposed political solution is inevitably entangled in the question of external-power involvement. Nevertheless, the Kampuchean conflict does involve China directly and hence cannot be settled strictly within the regional context without at least China's participation. The deepening external-power involvement leads to greater tendencies toward proxy wars and the widening of the current Kampuchean conflict.

The Communist Insurgency

As a front-line state that has been confronted with a serious insurgency problem in several regions—particularly the north, northeast, and south—Thailand must be wary of the new implications brought about by the aggravation of the regional-security situation. The open hostility between Beijing and Hanoi has greatly affected the CPT in its orientation, tactics, and operations. The loss of base and staging areas together with logistical lines in neighboring Laos and Kampuchea; the cutback of material support from China; Beijing's new approach to relations with the Thai government; and the friction between the hard-core elements in the CPT and the new recruits and allies that swelled the ranks of the CPT and its united-front organization following the 6 October 1976 Incident in Thailand, as well as the disenchantment among those who joined the communists as fugitives and as exploited minorities (like the Meo tribesmen in Northern Thailand) have resulted in serious morale problems and massive defections. For this reason, the current Thai government's open-arm policy of granting former political fugitives safe passage out of their jungle hideouts has been very successful. The CPT, however, may be down but not out. Beijing has gone to great lengths in placating the Thai government as a result of the Kampuchean conflict, including shutting down the CPT's Yunnan-based radio broadcasts. It could, however, easily revert to its former policy of directly aiding the CPT; for one thing, China has so far refrained from definitively renouncing its two-tiered (government/party) approach to its relations with Thailand and other countries confronted with a similar problem. What is alarming is that the issue of the foreign-backed CPT is now inextricably involved with the larger regional-security issue and could be used as a bargaining chip by the antagonists. CPT operatives continue to be active in Southern Thailand and have stepped up their acts of defiance against the Thai government. In the north, the CPT is reportedly collaborating with the Burmese Communist Party (BCP) in opening up new logistical routes for supplies from China. In eastern Thailand along the Thai-Kampuchean border, where the main Khmer Rouge forces are now concentrated and where the local Thai communists were collaborating with the Khmer Rouge in conducting illicit and subversive activities inside Thailand during 1975-1978, the situation regarding the communist insurgency is also volatile. Given the fluid security situation in this part of the country, there is always the possibility that external communist elements of whatever affiliation may be in an ideal position to link up with the local communist factions if and when the opportunity arises.

Thai-Vietnamese Relations

Taken as a whole, the present political-military security situation with which Thailand is confronted gives cause for concern. Although a number of factors are within Thailand's control, many others are not. Thailand is basically a relatively homogeneous society blessed with natural abundance. It has viable institutions such as the monarchy and religion, a continuous and independent history, and a good-sized educated elite capable of assuming the demanding and specialized responsibilities of national development. Moreover, Thailand has a mutually beneficial regional partnership within ASEAN and has pursued a sensible foreign policy, befriending all countries regardless of differences in ideology or in socioeconomic and political institutions. Such factors do lead to viability and resilience. The Kampuchean problem, however, remains crucial in determining whether Thailand's future course will be further orderly progress and development or greater political-military tensions leading to the further destabilization of not only Thailand but also the rest of Southeast Asia. Kampuchea is seen as the test of Vietnam's intentions toward Thailand; nothing short of a durable settlement will be acceptable. The Vietnamese should perhaps treat Thailand's insistence on the threat emanating from their occupation of Kampuchea as just as genuine as the imperative invoked by them to contain the so-called Chinese threat in Kampuchea.

Given that the Khmer Rouge might have been used by the Chinese to threaten Vietnam's security, Kampuchea was in fact too far inferior in strength to Vietnam to have warranted such a massive military invasion and a continuing occupation that, as has been pointed out, has drastically upset the regional power balance. In addition, ostensibly to ensure the success of its Kampuchean operation, Vietnam introduced the Soviet factor into the regional-security equation. These Vietnamese moves have inevitably invoked memories of the Vietnamese intentions allegedly contained in the Ho Chi Minh Testament. It has given credence to the widespread assumption that Vietnam is bent on creating its own empire in Indochina. Finally, the examples of past Vietnamese determination to employ every available means to achieve its objectives are looked on with apprehension by those whose security interests happen to be tied in one way or another to Vietnam's.

Because of the wide-ranging implications for Thailand, the region, and the world, the Kampuchean question has earned the widespread attention it has received during the past three years. There are only two alternatives: a continuation of the present tension, which will inevitably lead to a wider conflagration, or a compromise requiring the interested parties to cooperate sincerely.

The first alternative is clearly unacceptable to Thailand because those who stand to gain are the external powers, at the expense of the regional states. The second choice is more attractive since it offers all parties involved something in return for the genuine sincerity and effort they must offer to arrive at a settlement. Thailand and ASEAN have proposed a framework that should be tried for this purpose because it assumes that every involved party's interests will be taken into consideration. The heart of this proposal is that Kampuchea must be restored as an independent, neutral, and nonaligned state that would not threaten the security interests of Thailand, Vietnam, or anyone else.

Southeast Asia has recently witnessed successive waves of external-power rivalry and conflict, almost always to the detriment of the independence and well-being of the indigenous people. Thailand has always been fortunate enough to escape colonization, but it has suffered the effects of foreign hegemonism. In the past, external powers have tried to project and promote their interests in the region. During brief periods in the 1960s and 1970s, indigenous forces attempted to assert themselves in order to gain better control of their own destiny and to escape from perennial external influence and domination. ASEAN has proved to be exemplary of these aspirations. Shortly after 1975 there was hope that the Indochinese peoples, with their destinies now firmly in their hands, would dedicate themselves to the crucial task of national reconstruction and to cooperation with the previously estranged noncommunist nations of the region in realizing mutual desires for stability and progress. They could have accepted the ASEAN-proposed framework for cooperation, as embodied in the Treaty of Amity and Cooperation.

Economic Threats

For the past two years the Kampuchean question may have justifiably preoccupied Thailand's threat perception. With the prospect of an acceptable solution still nowhere in sight and the likelihood of a continuing stalemate over the next few years, the political-military aspect of security will continue to be paramount.

Meanwhile, Thailand is also buffeted by other strong winds, not least a lackluster economic performance that is having adverse effects on Thailand's overall prosperity and security. The unstable political-military situation in Southeast Asia necessitates a continued heavy commitment of Thailand's resources to defense. For the past five years Thailand's allocations for national defense have constituted one-quarter of the annual national budget. The trend calls for larger expenditures as demands and price tags for weapons continue their swift upward spiral. Being almost exclusively an importer of arms, Thailand, like many other developing countries, is at the mercy of Western arms manufacturers and dealers.

Energy, particularly oil, is another major item for which Thailand pays enormous sums. The previous fiscal year saw Thailand spend about U.S.$2.7 billion for oil imports—equivalent in value to 20 percent of the country's total imports and 42 percent of its total export earnings. Although the country has recently begun to tap offshore natural gas and has started exploration for oil on shore with initially encouraging results, it will be a long time before Thailand can benefit from these finds in real terms. In the meantime, as the consumption of energy continues to spiral, Thailand will have to allocate more of its already strained foreign exchange to import oil and gas.

Thailand is basically an agricultural country whose main income is derived from the export of primary commodities (rice, tin, rubber and the like). In addition, it has to rely to a considerable extent on foreign investment, particularly to develop the labor-intensive manufacture or assembly

Explaining the Thai Case

of secondary products for export or reexport. If the trend over the past year is any indication, Thailand will be facing mounting problems in these areas as well. By the end of 1981, high production in Thailand and elsewhere in the world, as well as unexpected competition from some quarters (including the United States, which unleashed its surplus stocks of tin and rice on the world market), Thailand found itself with an unsold surplus of rice and other products in the face of falling prices. The situation has seriously affected national income, which in turn causes ripple effects on national development and security. Foreign investment in manufacturing has also been in the doldrums for a variety of reasons, including the decrease of available capital, rising costs, falling purchasing power, and investor uncertainty about the country's stability. The temporary—one hopes—pause in the development of labor-intensive industry has also slowed progress toward the shift to technology-intensive industry, which is a vital step to modernization.

Although Thailand continues to enjoy a high rating in its international credit standing, it is facing growing difficulties in securing stable external financial credits with favorable long-term arrangements. Certainly the continuing trade deficits are a major contributing factor to the unstable financial position of the country.

The foregoing economic difficulties adversely affect Thailand's effort to improve its security posture through sound and steady development. The recurring problems of rural poverty and inequity in income distribution, which are the root causes of popular discontent and political instability, cannot be alleviated while these external economic threats persist. Thailand's current Fifth Five-Year Plan (1982-1986) has targeted a number of remedial measures, such as the acceleration of exports, slowdown of imports, and reduction of energy consumption. These, however, are meant to tackle only the symptoms, not the causes of the problem, which reflect international economic conditions beyond Thailand's ability to control or influence significantly.

12 Thai Security Perceptions in Historical Perspective

Somsakdi Xuto

This chapter provides a general overview of Thai security perceptions and responses to perceived threats. For the sake of convenience, it is divided into two periods: the pre-World War II period and postwar developments. These are preceded by an observation on the Thai notion of security.

The Thai Concept of Security

The word *security* encompasses a great deal and is subject to a wide variety of definitions and interpretations. Any particular definition of *security* gives rise to a set of associations that may be more or less threatening or more or less externally directed. This is true of the Thai word *kwam maant kong*, which is the accepted rendering of *security*. Literally, this Thai equivalent to the word *security* conjures up a notion of strengthening, stabilizing, or fortifying; but it has no specific meaning and no particular implied notion unless there are additional qualifying adjectives. The two sets of adjectives commonly used to qualify the word *security* are (1) *internal* as opposed to *external* security, and (2) *political, economic,* and *social* security.

Although these qualifying adjectives are often used, all of them, used either singly or in combination, are less important than *national security*, rendered in Thai as *kwam maant kong hank chart*. National security is perceived as taking precedence over other kinds of security and is in fact a kind of absolute term, integrating and combining all aspects of security into one all-important and supreme whole. It is thus perceived as an all-embracing term of unsurpassed significance.

The Thai tend to overuse the term *national security*, thus somewhat exaggerating threats. Particularly for internal consumption, national security has been rather loosely mentioned, with the consequence that its credibility is eroding. Nevertheless, frequent invocation of national security still tends to have a desired effect (from the standpoint of those responsible for such frequent use) of widening public perceptions that there are real and growing threats to Thailand.

Because of this, it is perceived that there are problems of national security that have a direct effect on national survival and independence. In effect, national security, national survival, and national independence have become so closely identified with each other that they seem to have acquired the same meaning. If the degree of threats to national security can be raised to such a level, particularly in the public view, then national security has priority over all other issues. In other words, the Thai perceive threats to national security as jeopardizing the very survival of their nation.

Because of this identification of national security with national survival and independence, the Thai do not consider the question of national security lightly. Only major threats would influence their perceptions. This helps explain why, although various groups in Thailand since the end of World War II have invoked national-security fears, it is the ruling power groups—that is, the military and governments in power—that are decisive in shaping public perceptions on national security. Other sources have little impact on the thinking and perceptions of the Thai public.

The role of ruling power groups in shaping national-security perceptions may reflect the notable Thai trait of pragmatism. It also represents an inclination to accept authority and power, although not necessarily agreeing with it. These traits do not encourage broadly based serious discussion and debate on national-security issues. Discussion and debate do take place, of course. National security has been a favorite theme lately, and there is a diversity of Thai opinion on the nature of the threats and the appropriate responses. These discussions are confined to the elite, however, and have little impact on the public. Moreover, such discussions are rarely analytical in the sense that is taken for granted in the West.

Consequently, the multifaceted complexities of national security have yet to be examined systematically in Thailand. The Thai approach could be characterized as intuitive rather than based on rational analysis. The effect of such an approach on thinking about national-security problems is to simplify complex matters.

Thus specific issues and events are first perceived as representing threats to national security. This perception of threats is followed by attempts to identify their sources. Here the complexities usually give way to simple categorization. Accordingly, threats to national security have been perceived intuitively as coming either from the outside or from within the nation. This neat division into external and internal threats not only oversimplifies, but also influences responses to these well-defined threats.

In sum, Thai perceptions of threats affecting national security have usually encouraged an intuitive simplification of security matters into fairly identifiable issues-oriented questions. This process mainly involves those with actual responsibility for security questions, and there is a tendency for the public to accept the views of those in authority.

Prewar Threats and Responses

Modern Thai history began with the founding of Sukhothai as the first capital in A.D. 1237. Throughout a history of nearly seven and a half centuries, Thailand has had two distinct political regimes. The absolute monarchy, which lasted nearly seven centuries, gave way to a constitutional monarchy after the revolution of 1932.

Until the arrival of Western colonialism in the latter part of the nineteenth century, Thailand was a traditional society. It was relatively stable and well endowed with natural resources. Western colonialism, however, brought the dynamics of change into the hitherto relatively static society of Thailand. Since then Thailand's development has been a continuing process of adjustment between the challenge of change and the continuity of tradition.

Despite the increasing impact of change, however, the Thai national-security perception had not been affected by Thailand's more complicated environment. In general, before the end of World War II, the Thai perception of threats to national security was still guided by the dominant characteristics of simplicity and intuition.

What were the Thai responses to perceived national-security threats during this long period of more than seven centuries? This chapter cannot do justice to this question. It does provide a short, generalized account of some characteristic patterns of response to threats to national security.

It will be recalled that in the Thai perception, national-security threats are regarded as originating from either internal or external sources. Throughout this long period, the Thai perceived a clear distinction between internal and external threats, which in turn would call for different responses. In general, this perception accorded with realities.

Thai history up to the end of World War II reveals innumerable instances of responses to perceived national-security threats. Although all these instances obviously differed in terms of details, a general consistency characterized the Thai responses. On the whole, perceived internal threats to national security generated either internal reform and/or internal power struggle. In response to perceived external threats to national security, by contrast, there would be a rallying of national sentiment and a combined utilization of political, diplomatic, and military means.

During this long period of Thai history, there were also many instances of internal power struggle, which was not always peaceful. This might indicate that responses to perceived internal threats had a mixed record of success. On the other hand, responses to perceived external threats must be regarded as a success. The fact that Thailand has been able to maintain its independence almost uninterrupted for so long is a testimony to this successful record.

Postwar Threats and Responses

Thailand emerged after World War II with its independence intact, another instance of successful response to external threats to its security. The postwar international environment differed from that of the past, however. In the early days of the Cold War period, the Thai believed there was a serious external national-security threat from the communist world, led by the USSR. This perception of external threat led Thailand to side with the Free World, led by the United States. Although this is now history, many critics have continued to argue against the Thai commitment to the Free World. In the context of the Cold War struggle, however, when the choice was perceived to be between the Free World and the communist world, Thailand's decision appears to have been inevitable.

Although the Thai external-threat perception during the Cold War period was justified, the responses of successive governments have raised reasonable doubt about whether the complexity of the postwar national-security problem was fully recognized. First, concentrating on external threats permitted internal problems to be blamed on threats from outside. These problems were then neglected and needed reforms postponed. Of the succession of governments in power at the time, there was only one exception. This was the government of Field Marshal Sarit Thanarat during the first half of the 1960s, which inaugurated and accelerated planned economic development (albeit in the absence of other noneconomic reforms). Second, the focus on Cold War-related external threats extended over a long period of time. Not until 1973 could it be said to have really come to an end.

This was the result of an internal political upheaval brought about by the so-called Students' Uprising of October 1973. For the next three years Thailand underwent an unprecedented experience in democracy. As far as threat perceptions were concerned, there was a swing to the opposite extreme. Threats from the inside dominated, and these could be resolved only through far-reaching structural reforms. This inward-looking and self-critical period coincided with the U.S. military withdrawal from South Vietnam, which—though heightening concern and anxiety elsewhere in the region—was accepted with relative equanimity in Thailand. In fact, the increasing North Vietnamese domination in Indochina did not cause any undue alarm, except perhaps at the very time of the fall of Saigon and Phnom-Penh in April 1975, when there was genuine fear about the possible intentions of the conquering North Vietnamese armed forces. Fortunately, no direct threats materialized; and Thailand soon reverted to its preoccupation with internal problems. Throughout this three-year period of democracy, Thailand turned inward and attempted to remove sources of internal instability through reforms. For those external threats that remained, especially the implications of the historic change in Indochina, reliance on political and diplomatic solutions was considered the answer. Because of political instability during a period that in three years had involved five government changes and two general elections, however, needed internal reforms could not be realized.

The military takeover in October 1976, staged under the name of the National Administrative Reform Council, put an end to the full-democracy period. With the Thanin government in power, the old Cold War framework for assessing threats reappeared, even more rigidly than in the past. The Thanin government held office for only a year, but it created an unusually high degree of internal divisiveness.

The military intervened in October 1977, and the Kriangsak government came into power. Its first priority was to attempt to undo the rigid anticommunist policy of the Thanin government through a policy of national reconciliation; in this it was extremely successful. General Kriangsak, though aware of possible external threats from the Vietnamese ascendency in Indochina, was encouraged by the prospects of peaceful coexistence to pursue a policy of promoting good-neighbor relations with all the communist states in Indochina. Unfortunately, this policy of promoting good relations between the communist and noncommunist countries of Southeast Asia on the basis of peaceful coexistence has not been reappraised or adjusted since Vietnamese troops moved into Kampuchea in December 1978.

In promoting good relations as a response to possible external threats from the communist countries of Indochina, General Kriangsak could be criticized for being too optimistic. In his successful handling of the national-reconciliation policy, however, General Kriangsak correctly perceived the need to eliminate sources of internal security threats—which would have undermined the long-term security of the whole nation—as a precondition for effectively uniting the Thai nation to face external danger.

From the time of the Kriangsak government through the current Prem government, the Thai political leadership, despite—and perhaps partly because of—heightened concern about external security, has increasingly recognized the importance of attending to sources of internal instability. There has been a growing appreciation that unless internal-security threats are reduced and removed, overall national security is weakened. In other words, the complicated interrelationship between the internal and external dimensions of security is better appreciated, though still more intuitively than analytically.

One compelling reason for increased recognition of internal threats is that the internal problems can no longer be ignored. Since the end of World War II, Thailand has already lost too much time in confronting these internal problems.

After vacillating between preoccupations with external and internal threats, the thinking of the current Thai leadership seems to be achieving a sensible equilibrium. A more balanced national-security perception entails a realistic acceptance of change. For Thailand, it requires an ability to accommodate change without losing sight of traditional strengths and values. A sense of balance is crucial. Taking into consideration a good past record, it is possible that Thailand can achieve this sense of balance.

13 The Indigenization of ASEAN Communist Parties

Donald E. Weatherbee

The 1975 triumph of communist forces in Vietnam, together with the related victories of their revolutionary comrades-in-arms in Laos and Cambodia, at first seemed to presage the realization of the worst-case scenario for noncommunist Southeast Asia. The strategic frontier had been shifted to the west. The Indochinese Marxist-Leninists' capability to provide direct assistance to fraternal movements elsewhere in the region appeared to be increased. A psychological lift had been given to the long-embattled armies of the Communist parties (CPs) of Southeast Asia. Noncommunist states readied defensive and accommodating postures to deal with a looming communist threat. Southeast Asia's remaining dominoes were wobbling. Yet later revolutionary fruits have been denied, not least because of all the contradictions existing in the region, the greatest existed in the communist world itself.

The congruence of the Sino-Soviet conflict with Sino-Vietnamese competition spilled over into the politics of revolution elsewhere in the region. The principal noncommunist-communist interaction has pitted the members of the Association of Southeast Asian Nations (ASEAN) against Vietnam in a political and diplomatic confrontation over Vietnam's invasion and occupation of Kampuchea. The People's Repbulic of China (PRC) has successfully identified its anti-Vietnam policy with ASEAN's, although there are significantly different interests at stake. In doing so, however, the PRC has had to publicly eschew its promotion of revolution in the ASEAN states. Vietnam has not yet benefited from China's ideological dilemma, since the leadership cadres of the ASEAN CPs have for the moment accepted the Chinese line that Vietnam is a Soviet surrogate in the latter's drive for hegemony.

Even while the ASEAN states review and upgrade their conventional war capabilities and toy with supporting insurgent warfare in Kampuchea, however, their leaders still maintain that the primary security threat is internal. In three of these states part of that security concern is a resource-sapping internal war sponsored by Marxist-Leninist-Maoist parties with their associated armed forces: in Malaysia, the Communist Party of Malaya (CPM) and its Malayan National Liberation Army (MNLA); in Thailand, the Communist Party of Thailand (CPT) and the Thai People's Liberation Army (TPLA); and in the Philippines, the Communist Party of the Philippines

(CPP) and its armed wing, the New People's Army (NPA). (Indonesia and Singapore are largely excluded from this analysis. There is no Singapore CP since Singapore is in the ambit of the CPM. In Indonesia the domestic infrastructure of the PKI was crushed in 1965-1966. Neither Singapore nor Indonesia has an armed CP insurgency.)

The ASEAN CPs and their insurgent warriors have been forced by the changed international environment and the impact of the Sino-Vietnamese conflict to become more self-reliant in terms of material morale, strategy, and tactics as the vision of international revolutionary solidarity receded and the prospects of increased support from Asian CPs in power dimmed. Moreover, the impetus to self-reliance has forced CP elites, particulary in the CPM and CPT, to begin to address the question of the appropriateness of Maoist policies that have kept them in the jungles for decades with little real prospect of winning a classical people's war.

There is truth in the Soviet criticism of the Maoist doctrine for people's war: that it is a falsified version of the Chinese revolution that "completely ignores the objective conditions in the world and the subjective factors" that decisively contributed to Mao's success in China.[1] The tactical scheme forced on the Communist parties in China's assumed natural sphere consisted of: (1) the armed struggle as the main form of struggle, regardless of conditions; (2) the creation of revolutionary bases in remote rural areas; and (3) the encirclement of the towns from the villages.

As long as the Chinese connection seemed firm and while the Indochina conflict could be represented as an example of people's war, the often ethnic-Chinese or Chinese-trained cadres of the ASEAN CPs remained true to their Maoist precepts. Neither of these two conditions can be fully met today. The ASEAN CPs' process of adapting to the new international circumstances and reexamining conditions in their own domestic environments is what we are calling here *indigenization*. The indicators for the existence of indigenization that will be surveyed suggest that younger or nonethnic Chinese Marxist-Leninists, not bound up in their own long-march myths, are critically comparing their own domestic conditions with the externally derived, a priori revolutionary model of Maoist leaderships.

China, Vietnam, and the ASEAN CPs

In pursuing its strategic goals in the region, China has relegated to the background the interests of the Maoist parties formerly under its patronage. The PRC's interest in wooing the domestically anticommunist states of ASEAN has caused Beijing to disavow any substantive tie to communist movements in the ASEAN countries. Premier Zhao Ziyang's 1981 swing through ASEAN capitals attempted to defuse the question. Everywhere he went, he promised noninterference in the internal affairs of the host government. The newly articulated Chinese position is summed up in the repeated proposition that the PRC relationship to the ASEAN CPs is only a political and moral one.

Not every ASEAN leader is convinced of the sincerity and effect of the Chinese statements. Malaysian Prime Minister Mahathir warns that China still supports communist subversion in Malaysia and that party-to-party relations between the CCP and the CPM constitute foreign interference in Malaysian affairs.[2] The Malaysian foreign minister, Tan Sri Ghazali Shafie, put it more colorfully in a U.N. speech in which he accused Beijing of serving ASEAN a "sweet and sour dish of rotten fish" by continuing commitments to terrorist groups that are continually striving to overthrow governments by violent means, yet shaking hands on a government-to-government basis.[3]

For those leaders in ASEAN who are unwilling to accept at face value the philosophical basis of PRC-ASEAN CP relations, Beijing has a more immediate pragmatic justification: it is in the current interests of the ASEAN states themselves that a "political and moral" link be maintained, since at China's urgings, the CPs of ASEAN could become allies in the patriotic struggle against Vietnamese expansionism and Soviet hegemonism. A major theme of both CPM and CPT propaganda since 1979 has been the call for the united front of all national forces against the Vietnamese-Soviet threat, suggesting that the refusal of the anticommunist governments to heed the call was antinational. The governments' response has been that if the CPs' major concern truly was building a strong national defense, they should lay down their arms and come out of the jungle. A second Chinese rationale for continued political and moral links with the ASEAN CPs, which is somewhat inconsistent with the first, is that if there were no Chinese connection, then the Soviets or the Vietnamese would seek to gain influence over the parties.

As a practical matter, direct Chinese material support to client parties in Southeast Asia, which was never as great as some would claim, has diminished, in part because former intermediaries are now enemies. The most directly touched by this is Thailand. Thai appraisal of the change is ambiguous. The Thai supreme commander General Saiyud claimed at the end of 1981 that there was no evidence that China was supplying military aid to the CPT or the CPM.[4] On the other hand, General Saiyud decried on national television the activities of a superpower that "is backing and directing the activities of the communist insurgents in the country."[5] In this thinly veiled reference to the PRC, the supreme commander voiced his concern about the political link, even if the logistic line may have become attenuated. China has cut back on propaganda support for the Southeast Asian revolutionaries, turning off the Voice of the People of Thailand (VOPT) in 1979 and the Voice of the Malayan Revolution (VOMR) in 1981. In the latter case, however, the next day the Voice of Malayan Democracy (VOMD), came on the air in a smooth transition. The New China News Agency and other Chinese media no longer republish for world consumption the antigovernment diatribes of the ASEAN Communist parties. The Voice of the People of Burma, however, does continue to provide a communication vehicle for Southeast Asian CPs. The ASEAN CP exile groups in Beijing are kept out of the limelight. Although the promise of continued PRC political and moral support means that the ASEAN Maoists have been orphaned, they have been made stepchildren.

Whereas the PRC tries to distance itself diplomatically from the ASEAN CPs, Vietnam insists that its once fraternal comrades-in-arms are Maoist bandits. Hanoi poses the not so rhetorical question: "Haven't the terrorist gangs set up and supported by China been posing a threat to ASEAN countries all these years?"[6] "It should be recalled," the Vietnamese admonish, "that Beijing caused an overthrow of government in Indonesia in 1965 and a revolt against the government in 1968. Beijing also did similar things in Thailand, the Philippines, and Singapore."[7] Whereas the Vietnamese excoriate the Maoist cadres of the Southeast Asian CPs as bandits, terrorists, and gangsters, these same cadres, who have been waging war against what they describe as U.S. imperialism and the reactionary cliques that govern the ASEAN states, now learn from China that they are part of a joint struggle, along with the United States and ASEAN, against Vietnamese and Soviet aggression. Cognitive dissonance must abound in the central committees of the various ASEAN CPs.

Although the fallout from the Sino-Vietnamese dispute has certainly accelerated doctrinal reinspection, it was not the sole cause. Other elements include the process of regeneration in the CPs, changed counterinsurgent strategies by governments, the growing impact of non-CP intellectual radicalism, and simple frustration at not being able to break out of the jungle. All these factors in varying degrees of importance have had a role in the indigenization of ASEAN's Marxist-Leninists.

The Communist Party of Malaya

Now in its fifty-second year, the Communist Party of Malaya (CPM) is the oldest active CP in the ASEAN states. The CPM was once the most extensively organized and influential political force on the peninsula. Its warriors celebrated their party's fiftieth anniversary in their jungle hideouts, isolated for a generation from the country's political mainstream. They could take only bitter comfort in the anniversary message that proudly boasted of the party's achievements, morale, and courage, with the prospect of ultimate victory in the revolution.[8] Theoretically the CPM's revolution encompasses peninsular Malaysia and Singapore. It seeks to overthrow the People's Action Party government in Singapore, as well as the Kuala Lumpur government. Realistically, however, the separation of Singapore from Malaya is acknowledged by the CPM in its program calling for the "reunification of the Malay peninsula and Singapore through consultations." In Singapore itself the CPM's infrastructure was routed in the 1960s. East Malaysia, on the other hand, is considered by the CPM as an area for "national liberation" by the North Kalimantan Communist Party. The CPM supports a voluntary union of North Kalimantan with the people of Malaya. There are still about 120 guerrillas of the People's Army of North Kalimantan (PARAKU) operating in Sarawak.

The remnants of the once 14,000-16,000-strong Malayan National Liberation Army, the armed force of the CPM, are largely contained on the Thai side of the Thailand-Malaysia border in a guerrilla zone or sanctuary that in the past half decade has become increasingly less secure for them. Politically split since 1970 over issues of loyalty and tactics, the MNLA has between 2,000 and 3,000 adherents of both sexes. The main CPM group—still apparently led by Chin Peng, who took the party into the jungle in 1948—may be between 1,500 and 2,000. Based in the Betong salient, where southern Thailand juts into Perak state, as well as the Waeng district, it is effectively blocked by the Malaysian Tenth Brigade headquartered in Kroh. To their north is the CPM-Marxist-Leninist, which may have as many as 600 guerrillas with whom the CPM sporadically skirmishes. The CPM-Revolutionary Faction, which bore the brunt of the joint Thai-Malaysian sweeps of 1977-1978, consists of fewer than 200 men in the Sadao region of Thailand, where across the border at Padang Besar it faces the Malaysian Twelfth Infantry Brigade. (Despite speculation about a possible Soviet connection for the rump factions, the intelligence consensus is that all three CP groupings are pro-Beijing.) Bottled up, harried, sometimes hungry and dispirited, the forces of the CPM seem to have little capability to mount any serious military action in Malaysia. Kuala Lumpur claims that there are only 230 CPM guerrillas still at large in the remote areas of Perak, Kelantan, and Pahang, the battered remains of the CPM's 8th and 6th Assault Units. Though still able to mount ambushes and isolated attacks at border points, the CPM must devote its energies to survival in competition for resources and recruits in its base areas with the Patani United Liberation Organization (PULO), or to fighting among themselves.

If over the years of its revolutionary struggle the CPM has experienced only military setbacks, this has not daunted its ideological ardor or its unswerving allegiance to Maoist doctrine. In its fiftieth-anniversary message of 28 April 1980, which has been elevated to a basic precept, the correctness of the Maoist strategy and tactics was reiterated:

> Our experience tells us that in order to achieve victory in our revolution we must take the road of using the countryside to encircle the towns and seize political power by armed force, and *not that of the so-called parliamentary democracy, armed uprising in the towns, or urban guerrilla war.*[9] [Italics added.]

The explicit denial of alternative strategies may indicate differences within the party.

For the CPM the crippling fact of its history has been the essential inhospitality of the countryside, peopled as it is by Malay peasants. Despite the party's self-identity as class based, the CPM from its inception has been identified as a Chinese party in terms of its ethnic recruitment, propaganda appeals, and perceptions of non-Chinese. In the words of one analyst, "There could be no possibility, in Malaya, of the successful application of the strategy of mobilizing the peasantry to surround and isolate the towns."[10] The vertical social cleavage of race limited the CPM to a minority community from the revolution's onset. The few Malays who joined the party were not fully accepted by Chinese cadres. Even the vaunted Malay 10th Regiment had its basis of recruitment in the particularistic discontents of Malays in Pahang State, not in Marxism-Leninism. The 10th Regiment, which even by the CPM's own statements never exceeded 400 men, had already been badly mauled by the end of 1950 and was reformed with Chinese cadres, though with visible Malay commanders. The antagonism of rural Malays, together with effective British-Malayan intelligence and suppression (which cut the link between the CPM in the interior jungle and its natural urban base) reduced the CPM to impotence, which persisted in part because of the party leadership's own ideological rigidity in the face of social and demographic realities.

Though certainly conscious of the complexity of the so-called nationalities question, the theorists of the CPM have persistently placed it on an ideological procrustean bed:

> Marxism-Leninism-Mao Zedong thought teaches us that a nation is divided into classes. National oppression is in essence class oppression and in the final analysis a national struggle is class struggle. The National problem is a part of the general problem of the proletarian revolution.[11]

The party has recently been preoccupied by the nationalities question, perhaps as a consequence of interparty disputes and of the need to come to grips with the *bumiputra* policies economically favoring ethnic Malays fostered by the Alliance government. A new nationalities special program was adopted by the central committee on 25 June 1981, which hewed to the established line.[12] The CPM is declared the "glorious heir" to the tradition of the revolutionary struggle of the oppressed people of all nationalities. Taking up the question of special privileges for the indigenous Malays, the special program claims that policies favoring the bumiputras are cruel, exploitative tools of the reactionaries' divide-and-rule tactics, which have "reduced millions of poor Malay peasants and workers to greater poverty." It goes on to assert that "the question of poverty is not a national problem but a class problem." The basic policy guidance is that: "In approaching the national problem, we should adopt the proletarian viewpoint. We should stress class unity and not national difference" in creating a common front against both the reactionary Alliance government and hegemonist aggression.

Although the guidelines of the special program are viewed by their framers as providing the equality necessary for the formation of a worker-peasant alliance cutting across nationality (racial) boundaries, in practice the special program is still ideologically divorced from the reality of the dominant structure of communal politics in Malaysia. It is doubtful that any front led by a Chinese organization will attract Malay followers. Even in the few cases where Malay leftists have attempted organizational cooperation with like-minded Chinese, the autonomy of the Malay structures was maintained—for example, in the PUTERA-AMCJA alliance in 1947, or—after independence in 1957—the troubled electoral alliance called the Socialist Front between the Malay Partai Rakyat, and the Chinese Labour party, which floundered on the Chinese-education issue.

The issue of the relationship between the CPM and the Malay community became acutely focused in 1981, following the defection of Musa Ahmad, who from 1956 had been prominent in Beijing as the chairman of the CPM and head of the party's delegation abroad. Although the role had little substantive importance, the presence of a Malay chairman was visible evidence of the CPM's multiracial pretensions. Musa, once trained as a religious scholar and a founding member of Hisbul Musliman, the first Malay Islamic party, had come to the party through the Malay People's Anti-Japanese Army (MPAJA). He had been a founding member of the radical Malay Nationalist party and headed the MNP's Barisan Tani (Peasant Front) until he and other communists in the MNP went underground in 1948 at the declaration of the emergency. Musa spent seven years in the jungle with the 10th Regiment before being named CPM chairman as part of Chin Peng's efforts to give a multiethnic image to the party's leadership in advance of the 1955 Baling truce negotiations with Tengku Abdul Rahman.

Musa was spirited away from Beijing to Kuala Lumpur in late 1980 under circumstances that are still unclear. In a nationwide TV appearance on 7 January 1981, the erstwhile leading Malay communist struck at the raison d'être of the CPM and the vain sacrifices of ethnic Malay comrades at the behest of Chinese chauvinists.[13] Musa claimed that the CPM did not work for the interests of the people but was instead an instrument of the

Chinese Communist party and Chinese expansionism. He accused the Chin Peng leadership of prolonging for Chinese ends a struggle that was futile from the beginning. Musa warned that the party existed not for revolution but to make Malaysia a Chinese satellite.

It was hoped in Kuala Lumpur that Musa's public utterances would strike a serious psychological blow to the CPM's efforts to advance its cause under the antihegemonist united-front banner. Musa obviously struck a nerve, given the reaction of the communists. The CPM's official response was quickly forthcoming over the VOMR.[14] In reviling Musa's betrayal of the party, however, the author of the CPM's reply may have revealed more about intraparty disputes than was intended. The reply acknowledged that by 1967-1968 Musa and others were already engaged in a polemic (antiparty activities) in which Chin Peng's leadership was criticized for not actively mobilizing Malay peasants to the armed struggle. It is now the CPM's position that Musa was then stripped of his party responsibilities, although this had never been made public before and may reflect an ex post facto downgrading.

A much more virulently ad hominem attack on Musa's vilifications and slanders was ostensibly penned by his former 10th Regiment comrades and ethnic-Malay cohorts Abdullah C.D. and Rashid Maidin, Malay member of the CPM's central committee.[15] Their CP connections, like Musa's, go back to the MPAJA and through the MNP. After 1955 the 10th Regiment was led by Abdullah, and Rashid became the first ethnic-Malay member of the central committee and the only Malay to accompany Chin Peng out of the jungle at the Baling talks. The CPM commentary, broadcast in Malay by the VOMR, was intended to limit Musa's attempt "to sow dissension among the people of various nationalities." In a defensive statement the CPM denied that the party did not respect Malays. To Musa's call for his 10th Regiment fellow Malays to surrender, Rashid and Abdullah rejoined, denying that the cadres and comrades were shaken and averring that "Even when there are setbacks in the revolution, all the comrades are determined to carry the revolution through to the end." They argued that Musa's effort to shake the confidence of the Malay masses in the CPM was futile.

Fultile or not, the Malay masses have not flocked to the banner of revolution as articulated in the CPM's Maoist terms. Even the 10th Regiment is a hybrid organization now on the Thai side of the border in the Betong salient, comprising 60 percent Thai Muslims or Chinese. It is estimated that only 5 percent of the guerrilla forces of the MNLA are Malay. The question is not the relevance of the CPM's programs to Malaysia, but whether the CPM can and will develop the structures that accommodate the fact of communalism needed to reach a potential Malay constituency.

The CPM has historically rejected the communal framework, but there are growing signs of an effort to Malayanize front efforts: an ethnic indigenization of the Marxist-Leninist movement in Malaysia. Certainly a constituency is there. Although Malaysia, along with its ASEAN partners, has experienced rapid economic growth, as elsewhere in the region, the distribution of rewards has been uneven and the semiauthoritarian framework of the state has created tensions among students and intellectuals. The latter has been expressed in the criticisms of the nonparty group known as Aliran. The government has been surprised in recent years by demonstrations of discontent from impoverished rural Malay supporters—for example, the Baling riots of 1974, the 1980 Alor Setar disorders, and the FELDA (Federal Land Development Authority) protests. Though quickly labeled by the government as communist inspired, these examples demonstrate that secular economic, political, and social issues can mobilize Malays. All politics among the Malays is not simply bumiputraism.

It is from the 10th Regiment's Malay leadership that initiatives have come to broaden the base of CPM support by sponsoring front structures for the mobilization of Malays as other than simply part of the oppressed masses. Rashid Maidin is behind the central committee of the Islamic Brotherhood Party (Partai Persaudaraan Islam, or PAPERI), whose propaganda leaflets and clandestine radio broadcasts cite the Quran to justify the struggle against the enemies of Islam in Malaya—the Malaysian government and the Soviet-Vietnamese hegemonists. PAPERI seeks to capitalize on the growing importance of religion, particularly among large numbers of youthful, urban Malays for whom Islam's social and political message defines the problems of their age and existence. PAPERI's appeals are relevant in this context, as they attack the corruption, depravity, and exploitation attributable to the false Islam of the government:

> We are grateful to Almighty God for the growing reawakening of the Muslims. We are totally convinced that the Muslims will launch a struggle against ignorance in accordance with a teaching by our great prophet, Muhammad—may the Lord bless him and give him peace—which says: if you are faced with ignorance you must convert it by using your hands. If you fail, use your tongue, and, if you still fail, use your heart.[16]

In some respects PAPERI's message, in its analysis of the evil of the secularizing forces unleashed by capitalistic development, is akin to that of Angkatan Belia Islam Malaysia (ABIM: the Muslim Youth Movement of Malaysia), which has galvanized Islamic social thought in Malaysia. PAPERI's appeals conform to those of the group of Malay Muslim reformers who, in trying to reconcile and rationalize Islam in a plural state, "stress universalistic ideals of mankind and causes such as social justice, land reform, and corruption free government, which transcend exclusively Muslim concerns and embrace problems which confront all citizens."[17] It should be noted, however, that ABIM as an organization rejects socialism as an alternative, having its own vision of an Islamic state.

A new and potentially significant front effort was signaled in the announcement of the founding on 24 May 1981 of the Malay nationalist Revolutionary Party of Malaya (Partai Kebangsaan Melayu Revolsioner Malaya), whose manifesto was broadcast by the VOMR on 11 June.[18] Not until late October, however, did the Malaysian government publicly acknowledge that a new CPM front had been sending hundreds of propaganda pamphlets to Malay individuals and organizations. The Malay community was warned not to come under the influence of the MNRPM.[19]

The mission claimed by the new MNRPM is:

> to unite the Malays of the various strata and to work side by side with the Chinese, Indians and others of various strata, so as to form a broad national united front in the fight against the imperialists and reactionaries and for the full independence and genuine liberation of our country.

In fulfilling this mission, the MNRPM claims to be the "continuation of the Malay National Party in the present historical state. Therefore its struggle cannot be separated from the MNP of the past." The MNP was the radical, secular Malay-based party ally of the CPM in the anti-British, anti-UMNO struggle before the Emergency. The MNRPM calls on Malays of all ideological persuasions to forge unity and cooperation among all groups struggling for political freedom and economic justice: nationalists, religious groups, socialists, and communists.

Its program is specifically directed toward the Malay community, targeting Malay peasants and intellectuals. It also appeals directly to noncommunist supporters of the old MNP and what it stood for, as well as other Malay opposition groups such as the supporters of the Parti Rakyat Sosialis. The call is to "Malays of various strata and ideological beliefs" to "rally around the MNRPM to realize this program," as well as to "support and join the MNLA, especially the 10th Regiment." The chairman of the MNRPM is Abdullah C.D.

The twin appeals to secular nationalism and Islam by PAPERI and the MNRPM are now heard over the Voice of Malayan Democracy (VOMD), whose inaugural broadcast was on 4 July 1981. The VOMD, though in a sense a carefully sequenced handoff from the VOMR and still clearly an arm of the CPM, carries more Malay-language broadcasting than the VOMR did. The relationship between PAPERI and the MNRPM was made clear in a VOMD broadcast of MNRPM *Id* greetings on 3 August 1981, calling for a continued struggle to form a broad national democratic coalition government in Malaya, followed in the same broadcast by PAPERI's announced support for the MNRPM.[20]

There is reason to believe that the new Malay-front efforts represent a shift in orientation of the party, perhaps a reflection of disenchantment with Chin Peng's leadership. This has been speculated on since 1976. Obviously the revelations of the Musa affair give evidence of intraparty discord on the problem of Malays and the CPM. The new emphasis on Malay-led organizations and democratic coalition government may be new tactics as well as concessions to Malay CPM cadres.

In its guerrilla zones the CPM still must vie for recruits with the PULO separatists, whose appeals are narrowly particularistic. Willingly or unwillingly, the CPM has been drawn into the battle for South Thailand and has condemned PULO and what it stands for:

> Facts show that PULO is an armed separatist movement which is nurtured, protected, strongly supported and directly manipulated by the Malaysian ruling circle. This movement displays the banner of the so-called Pattani Republic. It frantically carries out anti-Thai, anti-communist, anti-popular activities. Its aim is to realize the expansionist ambitions of the Malaysian ruling circle. These armed rebels have robbed property, burned houses, and even committed mass murder of innocent people everywhere. . . . We strongly condemn the bloody cruelty committed by armed rebels who continue disturbing security.[21]

Though perhaps reassuring Thai authorities that they have an ally in their opposition to PULO activities, the CPM position is not likely to enhance their Malay image with the many Malay sympathizers with the PULO, particularly in the border areas.

Ever alert to CPM tactical shifts, the Malaysian government has not let the new front activities go unremarked. Public statements of concern about the Malayanizing of the CPM have been few but to the point, indicating a growing concern in Kuala Lumpur about potential communist influence among the Malays. Barring serious economic difficulties, however, the threat does not seem great. The Malaysian government has shown itself repeatedly to be both efficiently suppressive and accommodative. The potential seems slight for Malay CPM-front structures to arouse true class consciousness bridging the communal gap.

The Mahathir government in its few short months in office has shown a startling vitality and willingness to attack problems of corruption, bureaucratization, and official arrogance. Public approval for reform in Kuala Lumpur could preempt part of the new CPM challenge. The Mahathir government has also kept the CPM's Chinese connection in the headlines. Kuala Lumpur's supposed hard line on the PRC, playing up China's continuing role in supporting subversion in Malaysia, can be interpreted in part as a domestic demonstration to Malays that the CPM is still a Chinese apparatus.

The structure of repression is firmly in place. The Internal Security Act is a weapon that is used freely. The recent, controversial Societies Act is a new barrier to political activities by groups that are not officially registered political parties, including ABIM and ALIRAN. The police special branch is ubiquitous. Still technically in a state of emergency, the government has far-ranging powers to cope with perceived subversive activities. In fact, some would say that the amount of resources devoted to defense against the CPM is far disproportionate to the CPM's actual threat. The government's position on stringent internal-security measures is unyielding, because (1) there is still an armed communist threat at the border; (2) it claims that underground subversive elements are still out to poison the minds of the people; and (3) certain individuals are bent on creating chaos.[22] According to the government, to ease up on the basically authoritarian controls would invite CPM penetration.

The Communist Party of Thailand

Of all the ASEAN CPs, the Communist Party of Thailand (CPT) was affected the most by the Sino-Vietnamese rupture. The CPT's insurgent capabilities have been critically impaired by the loss of Chinese logistical support through Laos. At the same time, the party's inability to capitalize on the political upheaval in Thailand after the October 1976 coup has provoked radical-left challenges to the CPT's continuing adherence to Maoist strategy. The CPT's Maoist line was laid down explicitly at the party's Third Congress in September 1961, when the delegates adopted a resolution "to resolutely take the course of armed struggle to seize power, using the countryside to encircle the cities."[23] This was seen as evidence that the party's theoretical level had deepened in its integration of Mao Tse-tung Thought, gaining a "firmer and more profound understanding of the revolutionary path of using the countryside to encircle the towns and the role of the peasantry."[24]

The CPT's people's war is commonly dated from 7 August 1965, when an armed clash occurred at Na Kae in the Phupan hills of northeast Thailand.[25] In the years that followed, the insurgency spread from the northeast to the north and south of Thailand. By 1978 the TPLA had well-established base areas and guerrilla zones from which they could mount tactical actions in over half the country's provinces. There was slow but steady growth in the size of the TPLA and the extent of the CPT's influence in the rural areas where the TPLA operated. The estimated size of the guerrilla force increased from 1,500-2,000 in 1968 to 12,000 by 1978, with political influence in over 5,000 villages. Within the framework of their own strategy, however, the TPLA never got beyond the stage of strategic defense. They were never able to mount a sustained campaign that could capture even a district town. On the other hand, despite repeated Thai military counterinsurgent assaults and a variety of so-called hearts-and-minds programs, the government was not able to dislodge the guerrillas from their bastions in the northeast; the tri-province area (Phitsanuloke, Loei, and Petchabun); the north (Nan and Chieng Rai); or the south (Surat Thani and Nakhon Sri Thammarat).

Since 1979 the situation has changed dramatically. The TPLA's very existence as an organized, centrally controlled military force is threatened in the northeast and the tri-province area. The slow growth of the insurgency has been reversed. Successful government operations into the CPT strongholds of the northeast and tri-province area this year led the Thai Army's chief of operations, Major General Chaowalit, to claim that the sixteen-year-old insurgent war was approaching an end, with almost all the major bases of the TPLA destroyed and the insurgents in disarray.[26] In the CPT's Phupan fastness, where once up to 4,000 insurgents were active, the government now estimates that there are only about 800. The once impregnable Red Triangle in the Khao Khor mountain complex of the tri-provinces has been stormed. The CPT's political infrastructure has been badly hurt by defection. Although greater media coverage has been given to the return of the students and intellectuals, perhaps more damaging for the party has been the loss of cadres. In 1981, for example, in the northeast the CPT lost through defection a regional committee member, six provincial committee members, eighteen members of district committees, four *tambon* committee members, and sixteen commanders of operational units. The great increase in defections tends to confirm the Thai government's thesis that "The Thai communist terrorists are now in a state of confusion. Their morale is low. The Communist Party of Thailand has been demoralized and is losing its men to the government."[27]

Part of the government's success in the recent months has been the implementation of the C-P-M—Civilian, Police, and Military—strategy, providing a broader-based concept of security and in a sense surrounding the jungle from the villages. Just as important, however, is the fact that collapse of the people's war in the north and northeast of Thailand reveals the extent to which the CPT was unable to adapt to the loss of its external support and sanctuary. Unlike the party's organization in the south, which was from the very beginning of its armed uprising fairly self-sufficient, the CPT in the north and northeast looked across the border for assistance. When the Vietnamese accession to power lifted the artificial requirement of communist solidarity, Hanoi attempted to use its control of the supply lines as leverage to persuade the CPT to modify its pro-Chinese, anti-Soviet line. The CPT's pro-PRC central committee (at least half of whose members are ethnic Chinese) held the party on a collision course despite increasing pressure from the Vietnamese through Laos. As the CPT showed no willingness to shift clientage, the Vietnamese in 1978 adopted a posture of opposition to the CPT.

When Pham Van Dong visited Bangkok in September 1978, he had no trouble with his promise that Vietnam would not support insurgency in Thailand. Whereas the PRC would maintain "moral and political" links with the CPT, the Vietnamese simply disowned them as Maoist bandits. Even though subsequent Vietnamese actions in Kampuchea made a mockery of Vietnam's pledges to ASEAN with respect to the general principle of noninterference, it should be pointed out that the break between Vietnam and the CPs of ASEAN occurred before the Vietnamese invasion of Kampuchea.

In November 1978 the Laotian party formally demanded that all CPT bases be withdrawn from Laos, denying any fraternal facilities. The CPT lost not only its weapons connections, but also schools, supply depots, training sites, a hospital, and so on. In short, they were expelled from the sanctuary. This was followed in April 1979 by what CPT sympathizers saw as Vietnam's ultimate betrayal—the so-called Laotian antiterrorist pact with Bangkok. This undertaking, in the joint communique issued at the end of Laotian leader Kaysone Phomvihane's first visit to Thailand, provided for "urgent and efficient measures to check and smash all activities of saboteurs who might make use of the border as places of refuge to carry out their subversive acts and disturb the security of the people along the common border."[28]

Vietnamese criticism of the CPT was not limited to the Thai party's pro-PRC alignment in the Sino-Soviet conflict. The Hanoi communists warned the CPT against slavish attachment to a Maoist strategy of rural encirclement through a peasant-based armed struggle. That this was an error was proved by the CPT's inability to take advantage of the urban turmoil in the essentially middle-class upheaval of the 1973 democratic revolution. Ideologically unprepared, the CPT was isolated from the main events of the Thai domestic political process. The Vietnamese argued that the Thai communists had to broaden their strategy to include the plains and urban areas.[29]

The Vietnamese attacks on the CPT's ideological inflexibility have been echoed for different reasons by the disillusioned Thai radicals who fled to the communists for refuge after the October 1976 coup, which brought to power the repressive Thanin regime. Although given refuge by the Maoists, the students and intellectuals were distrusted by the party because of their class background, lack of discipline, and poor revolutionary credentials. The urban radicals, on the other hand, found the party's Maoism sterile in its unthinking application of the Chinese experience to Thai circumstances. Furthermore, the CPT's acceptance of violence and armed struggle was difficult to integrate into a Thai Marxist framework, which historically had attempted to reconcile Marxism with traditional Thai values rooted in Buddhism.[30] Of the more than 3,000 students, intellectuals, socialists, labor leaders, and the like who took to the jungle, only a few of the more prominent were surfaced by the party in propaganda-making activities such as the Coordinating Committee of Patriotic and Democracy Loving Forces (CCPDLF). Headed by politburo member Udon Srisuwan, the CCPDLF was subordinated to the party's peasant-war mentality.

Many of the radicals filtered back out of the jungle after the Kriangsak government's blanket amnesty. Their statements in interviews and interrogations provide a comprehensive radical critique of the CPT.[31] Basically, the radicals gave up on the CPT because of the party's effort to impose the Chinese communist experience on Thailand unthinkingly, without relating it to Thai historical, social, or cultural conditions. Radical thinkers and activists like Seksan Prasertkul, Thirayut Boonme, Pridi Boonsue, and Therdphum Jaidee looked to the urban middle class as the potentially revolutionary force in Thai society. They argued that the CPT's simplistic transference of the Maoist class analysis to Thailand was fundamentally fallacious because of both its failure to recognize the degree of penetration of capitalism and its nondifferentiated depiction of the Thai peasantry. Strategically, Maoist armed conflict failed to take into account the relatively small size of Thailand and the consequent inability of the party to build base areas remote from the government's suppressive capability. Furthermore, although the CPT mouthed the slogans of the united front, particularly after 1976, the party's insistence that it be the sole leader, and its subsuming of front activity in the armed struggle, led to the alienation of the urban middle class, who could ask: Where was the party during the events of 1973 and 1976? In the jungle, not the town.

A last straw for the more critical urban radicals was the CPT's drawing of an analogy between Vietnam in Kampuchea and the Japanese in Manchuria, and its expectation of a united front with the government in anticipation of a Vietnamese invasion of Thailand—Chinese history, again, misapplied to Thailand. In an effort to operationalize such a united front with the Bangkok government, tentative overtures were made by elements of the CPT in mid-1981 for truce negotiations. A cease-fire was to be arranged so that a common fight could be made against the Vietnamese. It was the consensus on the government side that the initiative was Chinese inspired. It was not pursued.

More than ideological differences drove the urban radicals away from the CPT. There was also the unwillingness of the party leadership to communicate with the new recruits on other than a command basis. The CPT elite would not adapt. The CCPDLF had no input into decision making. The conflict between the members of the CCPDLF reached the breaking point when the CPT "refused to be responsive to suggestions of changes."[32] The rigid, doctrinaire Maoism of the CPT did not admit of revision. Ultimately, many radicals became convinced that the CPT was not a vehicle for Thai interests but rather an instrument of Chinese policy—a view previously shared by both the government and the Vietnamese.

Today, even to the party rank and file, doubts about the strategy of an armed conflict premised on rural encirclement must prompt defection in the face of successful government operations. The CPT leadership is aware that allies might be found in the towns, allowing them to shift their struggle from the military to the political front. Given the experience of Thailand's last decade, the decisive political forces are urban based. What the Thai radicals could not persuade the CPT elite to do may be forced on them by the necessity of survival.

The continued postponements of the CPT's Fourth Party Congress suggest that the leadership is still having trouble adapting to new ideological and physical circumstances. The congress was supposed to take place in October 1979 and to center on future strategy. Party regional units were requested to prepare recommendations. It is believed that many members, particularly younger ones, were calling for a break with the past, including new leadership. For whatever reason, the congress had not yet been held by 1982.

Speculation has been rife about the role and whereabouts of the CPT's secretary-general, Charoen Wanngarm. He has been reported dead, although a November 1981 story had him hospitalized outside Beijing.[33] Thai intelligence sources say that the real power in the politburo is held by Virat Angkhatavorn (alias Chang Yuan), an ethnic Chinese. It is perhaps his resistance to the forces of adaptation that has led to the stalling of the congress, because of fear of an outcome that the old-line Maoists could not control. Some Thai officials argue that the delay in holding the congress is evidence of a split in the central committee along ethnic lines.

Even in the absence of a party congress, a shift in tactics has been detected. General Pamoj, RTA chief of staff, noted in 1981 that the party now appeared to be following a doctrine called Three Strategic Zones on Two Battle Fronts—the jungle, plains, and urban centers on the military and political fronts.[34] This is the advice the Vietnamese party tendered to the CPT as early as 1976. The discovery of large arms caches in Bangkok has reinforced Thai military concerns about a new urban link. The CPT's grudging response to the new conditions may be in part a response to a challenge for revolutionary leadership in the northeast. Already in July 1979 it was rumored that a Vietnamese-sponsored rival had set up shop in Vientiane—a so-called Thai Northeastern National Liberation Party. Some reports have it that the TNNLP core membership included Thai radicals who had left the CPT, seeking alternative revolutionary venues. If so, the return to Bangkok of such leading figures would have seriously damaged the Thai credentials of the counter-CPT political structure. Yet still in mid-1981 the Thai government cautioned against the activities of a pro-Vietnamese, Laos-based Communist party.

Continuing uncertainty about the future of democratic government in Thailand underlines the CPT's dilemma. The implications of the abortive military coup attempt of April 1981 and the speculation surrounding the ascendency of General Arthit are fresh evidence that to influence the direction of politics, the party must have an urban base. The emphasis on the armed struggle in rural areas has confined the party's influence increasingly to the periphery of the state. The shift of the TPLA's operational headquarters to remote Tak Province, though perhaps providing a new link to Chinese material support via the Communist Party of Burma, illustrates the problem faced by the CPT. The pressure from lower ranks of the party, combined with the effectiveness of the Saiyud-Prem political-military counterinsurgent tactics, will probably force the leadership to reevaluate its priorities. The return of the radicals to the urban centers did not mean that they had abandoned their commitment to revolutionary change—only to the CPT's Maoist strategy. It is significant that the party did not denounce or openly confront the views of the urban radicals. Furthermore, more than a thousand of the 1976 urban recruits remain with the CPT. The door was left open for future cooperation and coordination. The degree to which the party moves to accommodate these views through circumstance and regeneration will be the mark of the CPT's indigenization. This will be known only when consensus is reached and the Fourth Party Congress is finally held.

The Communist Party of the Philippines

Of all the ASEAN countries, the Philippines seems to have the most widespread revolutionary and prerevolutionary opposition to the incumbent authority. Perhaps more than in any other ASEAN country, there is a real potential for the mobilization to armed struggle of diverse political groupings, by social forces and ideological symbols identifying the incumbent regime as the enemy. According to party doctrine, the CPP should be in the vanguard of that struggle. In fact, it is only the CPP among the ASEAN CPs that has increased the strength and the capabilities of its armed wing, the New People's Army (NPA), presenting a security challenge that, though not crucial as a military threat, is nevertheless resource draining. More important, however, in the Philippines—as opposed to Thailand and Malaysia—the Communist party's program does relate it to actual Filipino conditions. The CPP, though Maoist in origin and pro-PRC in the Sino-Soviet conflict, has been Filipinized in leadership and strategy.

Estimates of the NPA's strength vary, depending on the reporting source. The Philippines government uses the figure of 3,000-6,000, of whom one-half are armed. The party claims an armed strength of 10,000. There could be as many as 5,000 armed NPA guerrillas, with an equal number of paramilitary supporters. The official estimate of the number of

NPA sympathizers is 50,000. In contrast to the Hukbalahap movement, which was largely limited to the Pampango-speaking areas of Central Luzon, the NPA, which inherited the Huks armed struggle, has expanded its insurgent activities. It is strongest today in northern Luzon (Cagayan, Kalinga-Apayao, Isabel, and Abra provinces); Bicol; Samar; and the Davao provinces on Mindanao. According to communist sources by the end of 1980 the NPA had created twenty-six strategic guerrilla fronts (an operational zone around a base camp) in forty provinces,[35] which now have expanded to thirty guerrilla zones.[36] The CPP is said by officials to be organized in every one of the country's seventy-three provinces, and the party claims membership of 80,000 in its revolutionary organizations. The CPP-NPA has come a long way from 60 men in Pampanga province in 1969.

The present incarnation of the CPP was formed in 1968-1969 from the wreckage of the Hukbalahap revolutionary movement led by the old, Moscow-aligned Philippines Communist Party (Partido Komunista ng Pilipinas [PKP]) and its Stalinists. Under the political leadership of José Sison (alias Amado Guerrero) and the military leadership of Bernabe Buscayno (alias Commander Dante) the new CPP-NPA sought to adapt Maoist strategy to the situation in the Philippines. From the outset the Filipino Maoists recognized that a classical people's war could not be fought in an archipelago. There could never be a Yenan. The military strategy thus was one of mobile warfare, seeking to maximize the *political impact* of guerrilla forces that were scattered and operationally independent:

> As a rule, it is a natural handicap for a country to have hundreds of islands; however it is a natural advantage to the Philippines Communist Party, which has been able to strategically establish 26 major guerrilla areas along the archipelago. Another advantage is that it provides protection from the danger of the Marcos reactionary government's prolonged counterrevolutionary offensives which are carried out with a very big force in a region.[37]

With the capture of Buscayno in 1976 and Sison in 1977, leadership passed to cadres whose Maoism was undermined by the revelations of political turmoil in China itself and further challenged by the PRC's strategic alliance with the United States. Today Mao is not the only teacher for the CPP-NPA, which now looks to Vo Nguyen Giap, Ho Chi Minh, and other African and Asian revolutionary leaders for ideological and tactical inspiration. For Moscow and Vietnam, however, the CPP is on a par with the CPM and CPT as far as ideological orientations are concerned. To them the Filipino Maoists are common criminals involved in banditry and highway robbery.[38] In 1974 the Moscow-oriented PKP accepted a memorandum of cooperation with the Marcos government.

What distinguished the CPP under its current leadership from fraternal parties in other ASEAN countries is the way it combines the armed struggle with political action. Many leading CPP cadres were once part of the urban milieu and are aware of the requirement for a united front through which other opponents of the regime and system can be brought into association with the struggle. While the NPA continues to build its guerrilla zone in the countryside, a simultaneous effort seeks to build a united front under the banner of the National Democratic Front (NDF), which has both overt and clandestine activities. The NDF is an umbrella organization under which various CPP-controlled groups are aligned, but which seeks to attract other, non-CPP anti-Marcos groupings, bringing the political fray to the urban middle class. As the CPP front identifies itself as "the broad alliance of nationalists and democrats seeking the overthrow of the present system and the establishment of a revolutionary government,"[39] it tries to define a common struggle linking noncommunist opponents of Marcos who were joined in the United Democratic Opposition (UNIDO)—labor leaders, students, and Catholic clergy and laity influenced by liberation theology. This is to hasten, if possible, the political polarization of the Philippines. Benigno Aquino, the most visible non-Marxist exile enemy of the regime, has indicated the acceptability, or perhaps even inevitability, of the democratic opposition's cooperation with the NDF, if not the CPP. At the 1982 Cebu convention for the founding of the Filipino Democratic Party, the basically Christian Democratic opponents of Marcos passed a resolution endorsing coalition with the NPA.[40]

During the years when the CPP-NPA was building its strength, the greatest violence in the Philippines was unleashed by the forces of the Moro National Liberation Front (MNLF). The war against the Moslem insurgents currently ties down a substantial Philippines military and police force that might otherwise be deployed against the NPA. In this sense the NPA obviously benefits from the existence of the MNLF. One of the recurring nightmares of Manila's security managers is the prospect of an NPA-NLF alliance. Although every so often this is stated as an accomplished fact, and despite known overtures to the MNLF by the CPP, no coordinated or joint program of action is known to have been developed. In part this is because of the narrow focus of the MNLF struggle. Stauffer has pointed out that the MNLF is not a progressive force because it seemingly lacks in any vision that could reach interests other than those defined as Islamic.[41] He suggests that in fact, in terms of the inexorable forces of change in the Philippines, including Mindanao, the NPA and the MNLF might be long-term rivals: "The relentless push of the capitalist world economy will probably create more new candidates for the NPA than it does for the MNLF. This is simply because its appeal is not hobbled by the exclusiveness of a religion test nor by protecting existing exploitative class relations."[42]

It is difficult to gauge the strength of CPP-mobilized opposition, in part because of the government's tendency to label all dissidence as communist.

Younger priests and students have allegedly been a major source of new recruitment to the CPP. The party also seeks to exploit the economic decline in the Philippines, where as much as one-third of the labor force may be unemployed. The government's concern about the connections between the democratic left and the totalitarian left—if such a distinction can be made—seems clear in President Marcos's latest warnings. Claiming that his opponents were "parroting the slogans of rebels," Marcos, in his 1982 Constitution Day speech, commanded them to "Stop your present conversations with those who propose violence in order to attain political power."[43] He threatened a return to emergency rule and the use of "extraordinary powers" if opposition politicians should make an alliance with rebel groups seeking to overthrow the government by force. A return to martial-law, however, might only hasten the process of alienation. Harry Eckstein's observation is pertinent here: "Repression may only make the enemies of the regime more competent in the arts of conspiracy; certainly it tends to make them more experienced in the skills of organization and sub-rosa communications."[44]

The more dismal forecasts for the Philippines' political future suggest an inevitable further polarization, with moderates forced either to submit to the rules of the game as dictated by the incumbent regime or to join the violent left. The isolated incidents of urban terrorism that have occurred may presage a new stage in the struggle. If in fact the regime's response to demands for access and change is intransigence and greater repression, then the CPP seem ideologically poised to manipulate growing discontent to its advantage. Unfettered by the ethnic, ideological, or material toils of Maoism, the party can at least doctrinally make the urban-rural connection in a united front that poses a political challenge to the regime that is much more serious than any threat from the armed struggle.

Conclusion

A process of rethinking ideological models of struggle has been forced on the originally Maoist Communist parties of ASEAN Southeast Asia. Their long-held strategies of armed struggle, rural encirclement, and peasant-based class warfare are in question. A mix of motives has stimulated CP leaderships to reexamine their premises: changed relations between regional communist states, ideological turmoil in China, regeneration of party hierarchies, lessened influence of ethnic-Chinese cadres, successful government counterinsurgency strategies, and so on. The CPM appears tentatively to be accepting communalism as an organizing basis of Malaysian politics in an effort to become relevant. The CPT seems to be on the verge of a major shift of emphasis from the rural struggle to an urban confrontation. The process of adaptation is most advanced in the Philippines, where the CPP-NPA-NDF nexus is prepared to take advantage of "power deflation" at the center.[45]

The ASEAN CP's attempts to adjust to new factors occur at the same time as—and partly as a consequence of—the emergence of a youthful, urban-based radical left in ASEAN countries, whose informing political paradigms are not Maoist but more akin to those of the establishment left of Europe and North and South America. As the ASEAN states move toward modernization, with its attendant dislocations of uneven industrialization, inequality of income, inflation, pollution, inadequate housing, corruption, and unemployment, a potentially militant mass society is coming into being that will not be mobilized on the basis of old Maoist symbols and appeals, but is understood by the urban left. It is the possibility of alliance between that urban left and the CPs that may become the internal threat of the 1980s, particularly if economies weaken, accentuating already present social, economic, and political tensions. In that event, the most likely form of violence will not be people's war, but urban terrorism.

Notes

1. R. Alsanov and B. Bolotin, "Defeat of Maoism in East and Southeast Asia," *Far Eastern Affairs* (Institute of the Far East, USSR Academy of Sciences) 1 (1981):114.
2. *Straits Times*, 22 August 1981.
3. *Straits Times*, 25 September 1981.
4. *The Star* (Kuala Lumpur), 18 December 1981.
5. *The Nation* (Bangkok), 26 January 1982.
6. Hanoi International Service, as reported in *Foreign Broadcast Information Service—Asia and Pacific*, 4 March 1981, p. K-1. (Hereafter cited as *FBIS*.)
7. Ibid.
8. "Long Live the Communist Party of Malaya," text of the CPM central committee's statement on the occasion of the CPM's fiftieth anniversary. Broadcast by the VOMR, 28-29 April 1980, as reported in the *Journal of Contemporary Asia*, 10, no. 3 (1980):344-355.
9. "Long Live the Communist Party of Malaya."
10. Michael Stenson, "The Ethnic and Urban Bases of Communist Revolt in Malaya," in *Peasant Rebellion and Communist Revolution in Asia*, ed. John Wilson Lewis (Stanford, Calif.: Stanford University Press, 1974), p. 126.
11. "Long Live the Communist Party of Malaya."
12. Text as broadcast by the VOMR on 20 June 1981, reported in BBC, *Short Wave Broadcasts* (hereinafter cited as *SWB*), 7 July 1981, FE/6768/B/3.
13. Musa's TV statement is extensively reported in the *New Straits Times* and *The Star*, 8 January 1981.

14. "Announcement of the Central Committee of the Communist Party of Malaya on the Counter-Revolutionary Incident of Musa Ahmad's Betrayal of the Party," 10 January 1981; as reported in *FBIS*, 21 January 1981, p. O-1.

15. "Joint Statement by Comrades Abdullah C.D. and Rashid Maidin, members of the CPM Central Committee, on the Counter-revolutionary Incident of Musa Ahmad's Betrayal of the Party," 12 January 1981; broadcast by the VOMR, 24 January 1981; as reported in *FBIS*, 28 January 1981, p. O-1.

16. "Make Ready Your Strength to the Utmost of Your Power," Message of the Central Committee of the Islamic Brotherhood Party on Mohammed's birthday, reported in *FBIS*, 27 January 1981, p. O-1.

17. Sharon Siddique, "Some Aspects of Malay-Muslim Ethnicity in Peninsular Malaysia," *Contemporary Southeast Asia* 3, no. 1 (June 1981): 83; see also M.L. Lyon, "The Dakwah Movement in Malaysia," *RIMA* 13, no. 2 (1979):34-35.

18. Manifesto of the MNRPM, as reported in *SWB*, 18 June 1981, FE/6752/B/1.

19. *Straits Times*, 30 October 1981.

20. As reported in *SWB*, 6 August 1981, FE/6794/B/1.

21. "Our Message," inaugural broadcast of the VOMD, 4 July 1981, as reported in *SWB*, 14 July 1981, FE/6774/B/5.

22. Parliamentary reply of Deputy Home Affairs Minister Encik Abdul Rahim Thamby Chik, *New Straits Times*, 15 October 1981.

23. "The People All Over the Country Unite More Closely and Resolutely Overthrow the Traitorous Reactionary Regime," Statement in commemoration of the thirty-fifth anniversary of the founding of the Communist Party of Thailand (1942-1977), 30 November 1977, as given in Andred Turton, Jonathon Fast, and Malcolm Caldwell, eds., *Thailand, Roots of Conflict* (London: Spokesman, 1978), app. 3, p. 177.

24. "A Brief Introduction to the History of the Communist Party of Thailand (1942-1977)," official statement of the CPT, December 1977, text as given in Turton, Fast, and Caldwell, *Thailand*, app. 1, p. 164.

25. For the early states of the insurgency, see Donald E. Weatherbee, *The United Front in Thailand* (Columbia: University of South Carolina Press, 1970). For a recent review of the insurgency, see R. Sean Randolph and W. Scott Thompson, *Thai Insurgency: Contemporary Developments*, The Washington Papers, vol. 9, no. 81 (Beverly Hills and London: Sage Publications, 1981).

26. *Bangkok Post*, 27 October 1981.

27. ISOC spokesman, as reported in *SWB*, 29 May 1981, FE/6738/B/5.

28. As reported in Singapore Broadcasting Corporation's *Monitoring Digest* (hereafter cited as *MD*), 81/1979, p. 13.

29. An account of Vietnamese-CPT intraparty relations based on Thai documents is given in Santi Mingmongkol, "Thai Resistance Caught in the Crossfire," *Southeast Asia Chronicle*, 79 (August 1981):13-17.

30. Yuangrat (Pattanapongse) Wedel, "The Thai Radicals and the Communist Party: The Interaction of Ideology and Nationalism in the Forest, 1975-1980," Paper presented to the Institute of Southeast Asian Studies (Singapore), August 1981; cf. Yuangrat Wedel, "Modern Thai Radical Thought: The Siamization of Marxism and Its Theoretical Problems," Ph.D. diss. Univerity of Michigan, 1979.

31. These can be found in ISOC releases appearing in the Bangkok press in 1980 and 1981. Wedel, "The Thai Radicals and the Communist Party," is based on interviews with twenty-five returnees.

32. Interview with Sri Intapanti, *Nation Review*, 13 January 1982.

33. *Bangkok Post*, 6 November 1981.

34. *Nation* (Bangkok), 27 December 1981.

35. "The Philippines New People's Army Is Progressing and Growing," *Voice of the People of Burma*, as reported in *FBIS*, 9 January 1981, P-9.

36. Sheila Ocampo, "The Communists' Growth Strategy," *Far Eastern Economic Review*, 21 August 1981, p. 22.

37. "The Philippines New People's Army is Progressing and Growing."

38. Aslanov and Bolotin, "Defeat of Maoism," p. 117.

39. "The Policies of the Radicals" (interview with Horacio Morales), *Far Eastern Economic Review*, 21 August 1981, p. 20.

40. *Visayan Herald* (Cebu City), 8 February 1982.

41. Robert B. Stauffer, "The Politics of Becoming: The Mindanao Conflict in a World-System Perspective," *The Diliman Review* 29, no. 2 (March-April 1981):21.

42. Ibid., p. 26.

43. *Straits Times*, 18 January 1982.

44. Harry Eckstein, "On the Etiology of Internal War," *History and Theory* 4, no. 2 (1965):154.

45. The concept of "power deflation" is developed by Chalmers Johnson, *Revolutionary Change* (Boston: Little, Brown, 1966).

14 Australians' Perceptions of Threats to Their Security

Robert J. O'Neill

Australian Public Attitudes toward International Dangers

It may surprise informed analysts from the United States or from countries located close to the USSR to learn that for generations the Australian people have been acutely conscious of threats to their security. Such a perception conflicts with the lotus-land image of Australia that is widely accepted abroad. The pleasure-bent hordes of Australians who supposedly do little more than adorn the nation's surf beaches; explore the vast interior in four-wheel-drive vehicles; and live well off their sheep, wheat, minerals, and modest manufacturing industries, scarcely seem the sort of people to be concerned about invasions, much less the balance of power between NATO and the Warsaw Pact.

A little firsthand acquaintance undermines this view of Australians. Ever since continuous European settlement of the continent began in 1788, those who have lived there have entertained fears for their own security. The principal causes of these fears have been the remoteness of Australians from the countries of their social and cultural origins, essentially Western Europe; an awareness of the attraction that Australia's natural riches must hold for less well endowed nations; and the relative sparseness of settlement over Australia's approximately 3 million square miles.

Fears of French aggression were rife in the late eighteenth and early nineteenth centuries, as Napolean's empire reached its zenith. After the outbreak of the Crimean War, these gave way to fears of Russian naval raids—the most popular scenario for which involved a squadron of hostile cruisers holding one of the rich coastal cities for ransom until the banks had disgorged their substantial holdings of newly won gold and other forms of wealth. An array of well-constructed coastal fortifications was built to protect the seaward approaches to these major cities; and other key strategic points were fortified, such as Thursday Island in the Torres Strait between Australia and its colony, Papua. Coastal artillery became one of the major components of the six colonial, or state, defense forces before they were joined into one by federation in 1901.

Fears of Russia subsided somewhat in the late nineteenth century, to be replaced—particularly after the battle of Tsushima—by concern about the Japanese threat. Germany did not figure as strongly as Japan as a danger to

Australia in the public mind, although fears of an extension of Bismarckian imperialism from German New Guinea over Papua led to the latter's annexation by Queensland in 1884. Acute anxieties for Britain's position in Europe and the world during World War I led Australians generally, though with some dissent, to put their defense resources at the disposal of the motherland and to accept Japan's cooperation as Britain's ally. This mood did not long outlive the armistice of 1918: fears of Japanese imperialism impelled Prime Minister Hughes to launch a diplomatic offensive at Versailles that resulted in the extension of a considerable Australian mandate over former German territories of the South Pacific.

These fears of Japan were well justified, as the events of 1941-1942 proved, and did not disappear from Australian public thinking after 1945. Next to the Soviets, the Australians were probably the United States' most difficult partner in the negotiations leading to the Japanese peace treaty in the years 1945-1951. Australia's agreement to a rearmed Japan was obtained only by the extension of the formal security guarantees embodied in the ANZUS treaty.

With the communist victory in China in 1949 and Chinese entry into the Korean War one year later, Australian popular threat perceptions altered visibly. For the next twenty years, except for a brief period in the 1960s, the imagined invading hordes marched down through Southeast Asia under the banner of the red star rather than that of the rising sun. In the late 1940s Australians began to be concerned about the security of their own immediate region, particularly Southeast Asia. It was apparent that decolonization was underway, commencing in Indonesia. Although few imagined that Malaya, Vietnam, Laos, and Cambodia would win independence as quickly as they did, Australians appreciated that at some point in the not too distant future the Europeans would depart, leaving Australia as a relatively isolated outpost of a civilization that was alien to its neighborhood. Furthermore, this neighborhood was inhabited by people who numbered twenty times the population of Australia, who were crowded into confined areas, and who for the most part enjoyed a much lower standard of living than Australians did. The prospect of communist revolutions succeeding in several Southeast Asian states in the 1950s and 1960s alarmed most Australians, and they voted for governments that were pledged to oppose these threats.

This concern gave rise to Australia's regional strategy of forward defense, whereby small combat units were stationed in Malaya to assist the British in keeping communism at bay. More pretentious Australian aims of controlling allied planning for the defense of the region came to nought; Britain, France, and the United States could not take seriously such aspirations on the part of a power that at the height of the Cold War in the 1950s could deploy ground forces no larger than two infantry battalions for combat duties overseas.

Chinese participation in the Korean War had set the hounds in Australia (and elsewhere) off on the wrong scent. This very localized action, with the fighting confined to within two hundred miles of the Chinese border, was seen as a forerunner of massive armies of conquest marching down through Vietnam, across Cambodia and Thailand, down the Malayan peninsula, and on through Indonesia. Australian and British intelligence staffs prepared serious estimates of how long this epic journey would take, arguing among themselves over whether it would require eight months or ten. Eventually some perceptive analysts asked how the Chinese were going to accomplish this immense feat of mobility, given the state of their army in the 1950s, and why the Chinese would be likely to undertake so risky a venture in the wake of Japan's failure to carry it through under more favorable circumstances.

The scenario was thereby exploded in the minds of many official strategic advisors, but it survived in the rhetoric of Australian political leaders. When conflict between North and South Vietnam escalated at the beginning of the 1960s, it was interpreted to the Australian people as Chinese inspired. Even in the mid-1960s the Vietnam conflict was described by the prime minister as a Chinese thrust between the Indian and Pacific oceans. Misperception piled on misperception, and many Australians entered the 1970s still regarding China as a major direct threat to their security.

The 1960s were marked by another strongly perceived threat to Australia: Sukarno's Indonesia was seen as a malevolent local agent of communism, dedicated to swallowing up Malaysia after Dutch New Guinea. More extreme scenarios were painted in which Indonesia would go on to occupy Papua New Guinea, where it could sit like a huge boa constrictor, contemplating its next meal across the Torres Strait. Fears of Indonesia did not disappear in Australian public thinking after Sukarno's downfall. Although relations between the Suharto government and the various Australian governments since 1965 have been friendly, and Indonesia's military capabilities are not regarded as sufficient to threaten Australian interests significantly, there has been a coincidence of views between far right and far left groups that nonetheless Indonesia does represent a potential danger to Australia. The Indonesian invasion of East Timor did much to resuscitate these fears and to complicate the task of the Australian government in advocating the closest of neighborly relations.

Throughout this account of the development of Australian popular perceptions of dangers, the USSR has not figured strongly. This is not to say that Australians are not worried by the extension of Soviet power and the growth of Soviet military force that have continued steadily since 1945. The USSR, however, has not loomed on Australia's horizon in the direct way of Japan, China, and Indonesia. The Soviets tend to be regarded as a problem that is largely beyond Australia's capacity to handle. Most Australians would argue that fending off the Soviets is now the chief purpose of the ANZUS alliance. It is up to the Western alliance, Australians believe, to keep the Soviets and their allies in check. As a member of this alliance, Australia can provide support for the common objective; but, as most Australians would readily admit, this support is likely to be of only marginal significance. In the early 1950s it was fine for Australia to commit forces to the Middle East as part of a concerted British Commonwealth force to block any Soviet drive for the Suez Canal. As the superpowers grew increasingly strong and the military capabilities of the second-tier powers, particularly Britain, declined somewhat, however, such Australian commitments to joint Commonwealth undertakings became relatively pointless. There are surviving Australian force deployments abroad, such as those made in accordance with the Five Power Defense Arrangements; but these are not regarded as the wave of the future. Rather, Australian commitments of forces abroad are seen as probably limited to deployments with U.S. forces in the Indian and Pacific oceans and multinational peacekeeping forces.

At the onset of the 1980s Australians are not consciously aware of imminent direct or major threats to their security. Doubts about the future intentions of Japan, China, and Indonesia have lingered in the minds of many; but most believe that all three powers lack both the intention and the capability to threaten Australia seriously. Furthermore, most Australians appreciate that it will be a long time, a decade or more, before Japan, China, or Indonesia can develop such capabilities even if any of them would wish to do so. In that time, Australians hope, resolute government action will sound the tocsins if necessary and commence the strengthening of Australia's defenses to the point at which a major attack on Australia would require more resources than could be justified by success. Since the Soviet invasion of Afghanistan, Australian mistrust of the USSR has deepened; but the Soviets are regarded as the problem of the alliance as a whole. The Soviets have not yet become troublesome or threatening enough in the minds of most Australians to justify new Australian force commitments abroad.

The Australian Government's Perception of Threats

Current attitudes and the historical forces that have shaped Australians' perceptions of danger are relevant to what any Australian government is likely to accept as serious planning contingencies. The government's perspective is nonetheless recognizably different from that of public opinion because it is shaped by different forces. In particular, the government receives information to which the public has no access for security reasons. It also is in close contact with allied governments, and—in order both to make the alliance effective and to achieve smooth working relationships generally—the government must give weight to joint interests that are not always readily apparent to the general public. Hence the government's perceptions of the Soviet threat in particular are likely to differ from those of public opinion, with the consequence that the government is vulnerable politically to charges of overreaction or even of misrepresentation of international events for internal political purposes. Any student of the Australian press over the past thirty years will be aware of a continuing stream of articles, headlines, editorials, and cartoons depicting prime ministers and ministerial colleagues as scaremongers or as too subservient to the United States.

This is not to suggest that all such comment is totally ill founded or that contrary views are not also prominent in the Australian press. As a normal fact of political life, however, all Australian governments must treat public perceptions of the Soviet threat and of the conduct of the ANZUS relationship as sensitive matters.

This having been said, the present Australian government's views on the Soviet threat are clear: the USSR is the major danger to world peace because of its overt outward thrusting and its covert support of subversion in both the Third World and the West. This threat must be taken particularly seriously in the 1980s for three reasons: (1) the intensity of the Soviets' drive to strengthen their armed forces; (2) the clearly demonstrated way in which the Soviets are prepared to use force in their national interests, both directly, as in the case of Afghanistan, and indirectly, as in the case of their support for African and Asian client states; and (3) the dangers of Soviet preemptive war raised by the longer-term prospect of poor Soviet economic performance and increasing difficulties in Eastern Europe. The Australian government has subscribed substantially to the window-of-opportunity theory and believes that the only way the West can deal with the Soviets is to negotiate from strength.

Nonetheless, the Australian government considers the likelihood of nuclear war between the superpowers remote, likely to be caused only by irrationality or miscalculation. It puts its weight behind proposals for strengthening the Western deterrent by hosting facilities such as the North West Cape communications station for improved command and control of the U.S. second-strike capability, and the monitoring station at Pine Gap, which plays an important part in the verification of strategic-arms limitations agreements. When the U.S. capacity to react to Soviet pressures around the Persian Gulf required strengthening in 1980, the Australian government offered naval facilities in Western Australia and B-52 landing rights in Darwin. If the need to host more facilities should arise, there is little question that the government would accommodate them.

Although the capacities of the Australian Defense Force for conventional operations cannot be compared with those of the USSR in a global sense, in regional terms they represent a factor that the Soviets must think about. These capabilities are particularly important in situations short of actual warfare: it is unlikely that any Soviet surface warship can pass through the waters of Southeast Asia, the Southwest Pacific, or the eastern Indian Ocean without detection by the Australian Defense Force. If the Soviets were to establish any major base within the operational reach of the Australian Defense Force, they would have to devote serious thought both to its protection in time of war and to the security of lines of communication with it. They know this: deterrence is a function not confined to nuclear forces.

Of more direct relevance to the shaping of the Australian Defense Force is the government's acceptance of a need to meet regional threats and to cooperate actively with neighbors to maintain the current highly favorable regional environment. By *regional threats,* the government means destabilization of relations between important states or groups of states, such as ASEAN and Indochina, or direct menacing of Australia and its regional interests. Contingencies such as closure of straits, sea bed boundary infringements, attacks on shipping or drilling rigs, commando raids, or lodgments of larger forces on the mainland or on Australian islands are all real future possibilities despite their present improbability. Action must be taken to deter their occurrence; should the deterrent fail, capabilities must exist for successful defense.

These considerations are all the more important for Australia because of clearly stated U.S. policies that its allies must be primarily responsible for their own security against regional threats. Although some U.S. spokesmen recently have thrown a little cold water on President Nixon's Guam Doctrine of 1969, U.S. allies have to pay heed to the limited capabilities of U.S. forces to perform both a global deterrent role against an increasingly powerful USSR and to meet regional crises. The Australian government recognizes that the United States, with the best will in the world, may be unable to come to Australia's assistance if a regional crisis should coincide with a period of high global tensions. Consequently, the prime task of the Australian Defense Force has to be the preservation of regional security. It must be able to discharge that responsibility with substantial self-reliance in terms of both combat forces and logistic support.

The Australian Labor Party's Views

Before leaving the subject of governmental threat perceptions, it is salutary to note some differences between the views of the present Australian government and those of its principal political rival, the Australian Labor Party (ALP). The latter is the alternate government; although history suggests that the Australian people normally prefer their affairs to be conducted by moderately conservative politicians, there have been times—and doubtless will be again—when the Liberal and Country parties exhaust their credibility. In these moments, which have been associated with wars on the past two occasions when Labor won office—the looming threat of Japan in 1941 and the frustrations of Vietnam in 1972—Australians are heartily glad to have an alternative government. They may wish it had been better informed while in opposition and they may be concerned that there are few men of outstanding talent in the Cabinet; nonetheless, Australians are prepared to take the ALP on trust when the Liberals have faltered badly.

In essence the Labor party is a little more detached from the tensions of the East-West contest than are the Liberal and Country parties. Labor seeks in the way of socialist parties elsewhere in the West, to play a more independent role through being less automatically committed to supporting U.S. policies. This is not to say that a Labor government would be in any way pro-Soviet, although some of its trade-union supporters and left-wing members of Parliament might be on occasion and for limited purposes. The Labor party has condemned Soviet policy in Afghanistan and has exhorted the Soviets not to intervene in Poland. Nonetheless, it is a party with a strong tradition of criticism of U.S. policies, particularly with respect to aspects of rearmament, support for conservative authoritarian governments in the Third World, and intervention in regional crises.

Although the Labor party agrees with the Liberal and Country parties that the ANZUS alliance is of fundamental importance to Australia's security, it is more inclined to limit Australia's obligations under the treaty. For example, it is current labor policy to renegotiate the agreement by which the joint Australian-United States naval communication facility at North West Cape is operated. Mr. Hayden, the leader of the opposition, after his inspection tour of major joint facilities last year, declared himself satisfied with all except North West Cape. This station, he claimed, infringes on Australia's sovereignty unacceptably because it can retransmit messages from the United States to U.S. warships and submarines without specific Australian approval of the possible actions ordered by such messages. Hayden suggests that Australia could be seen, particularly by a hostile power, as party to an act that carries serious consequences, whether the Australian government approves of it or not. Thus Australia could face retaliatory action without having had any voice in the matter.

One can raise several objections to this line of criticism of the North West Cape agreement—not least, the physical manner of retransmission by the station, which does not permit Australian interposition into the traffic circuits in order to read their contents. The important aspect of the whole affair, however, is that these objections exist and are supported by the Labor party. Should the party return to office, the U.S. government would have to work out a new modus vivendi with Australia. There would probably be other points of friction, particularly with respect to the type of commitment Australia might make to forces of the alliance in time of crisis and to the extent of the geographic area for which Australia might assume some protective responsibility. Smooth relations within the ANZUS alliance therefore ought not to be taken for granted, particularly in the case of a hawkish administration in Washington coinciding with a Labor government in Canberra.

Some Personal Views

The principal threat that Australia must consider are, in order of magnitude from greatest to least: destabilization of the East-West balance; conflicts between states of Southeast Asia or the Southwest Pacific, particularly Vietnam versus ASEAN members; and subnational violence from abroad that seeks to use Australia either as a stage or as a means to achieving ends elsewhere. With respect to probabilities, the order appears to be different. The prospect of regional friction is more likely than that of external subnational violence being used against Australia. Both are considerably more likely than a major breakdown in the strategic balance between East and West. This is not to say that a major war between Vietnam and Thailand is the most likely contingency for Australia to consider, but rather that continued tensions between the two are a virtual certainty. Hence Thailand and, to a lesser extent, other ASEAN states, particularly Malaysia and Singapore, need to strengthen their defenses. To offset continued Soviet support for Vietnam, they will need assistance from their friends in turn. Currently Australia's strategic environment is benign, and the best way to keep it so is to help those friends and neighbors that are closer to sources of threat, both overt and covert. With respect to subnational threats by terrorists or guerrillas, attention should be paid to dangers to national leaders and vulnerable, valuable national interests. Offshore oil rigs, minerals-exporting facilities, power stations, communications facilities, and transport systems are among the more obvious targets to be protected. Intelligence, surveillance, and ready-reaction forces—both police and military—are the main components of security against this type of threat; and Australia is making substantial progress in providing them and putting them together.

The East-West balance, for all its unevenness, does not seem likely to become critically unstable in the next few years. Although the Soviets have made impressive gains in many forms of strategic power in the past two decades, they do not appear to be within early reach of a degree of superiority that would enable them to use strategic weapons against the West with any prospect of success. Of course, if the trends that were established in the 1970s continue unchecked through the 1980s, the USSR might reach the necessary degree of superiority. The danger signals have been noted, however, and corrective action is underway. It is too early to say that it will be maintained for long enough or pursued with the necessary insight and effectiveness by the West, but it is proceeding in a favorable direction.

The formidable powers of the SS-20 as a theater weapon must be either nullified by negotiated removal or balanced by U.S. deployments of Pershing and cruise missiles in Europe. The vulnerability of the U.S. land-based ICBM force must be reduced. The range and striking power of the Poseidon submarine-launched ballistic missile will be improved by the Trident system. Most particularly, corrective action is necessary with respect to conventional forces. Army and marine divisions, logistic support, mobility and fire support—both ground-based and by tactical aircraft—are required for containment of Soviet limited-warfare operations. More surface and subsurface naval vessels are needed to offset increased Soviet naval power. More fighter and strike aircraft are required to defend vital airspace and strike at attacking forces.

Although the main burden of strengthening the defenses of the West inevitably falls on the United States, there are two ways in which other allies can help to share the burden: by serving as hosts for U.S. facilities and weapons that help preserve the balance, and by strengthening their conventional forces. All due care must be exercised, both by U.S. authorities and by allied governments, with respect to the first of these means. In the long run it will not help matters if weapons or facilities are forced on a host country despite resistive public opinion. Consultation, public discussion, and willingness to compromise in pursuit of more fundamental objectives are vital elements for all partners in the alliance.

The obstacles to development of stronger conventional forces by the allies are more of an internal nature: costs, scarcity of suitable male and female recruits, and political opposition in the name of disarmament and arms control. In the cases of Britain and France, the cost of maintaining nuclear forces is an added complication that is unlikely to disappear for some years at least, although a Social Democratic or Labor successor to the Thatcher government in 1984 may scrap the proposed Trident-based system.

The internal obstacles to the development of stronger allied conventional forces remain formidable, but most governments are committed to enlarged programs. The position is not hopeless, but neither is it full of promise. Constant recollection of the power of Soviet and allied conventional forces will be necessary to stimulate countervailing developments by Western nations.

Conclusion: Australia's Contribution

Australia is not among the laggards in contributing to the maintenance of a stable balance. The joint facilities that Australia hosts serve to strengthen the U.S. second-strike capability and to monitor arms-control agreements. In the event of a major crisis, Australia would be able to provide more direct support to U.S. forces in the Pacific and Indian oceans. Although problems may arise between a future Labor government and U.S. authorities, they should be able to be overcome by sensible compromise without substantially damaging the alliance or weakening the Western deterrent capability.

In terms of conventional forces, Australia is maintaining and improving a moderate but regionally powerful surface fleet, which will include an aircraft carrier and ten FFG-7s or closely related destroyers. It is acquiring seventy-five F/A-18 air defense and strike aircraft and a second squadron of P3C Orions. These probably will be backed by long-range over-the-horizon radar, early-warning and control aircraft, tanker aircraft, and an expanded basing system in northern Australia. The army's reserve has been increased by 50 percent in the past year. An operational deployment force of a brigade is in readiness; and major orders of supporting weapons, communications equipment, armored personnel carriers, and transport vehicles either have been placed or will be placed soon. Joint and combined exercises are held with increasing frequency. The regional defense-cooperation program is being expanded through provisions of more training, equipment, and support for the forces of regional partners. Much more remains to be done, and Australia will require stimulus to keep to currently stated goals. Australia cannot always be an easy alliance partner, any more than can any other sovereign Western state; but it can be accepted that any power that threatens either the security of Australia's region or the stability of the East-West balance in some way that is obviously relevant to Australia's interests will meet effective and determined opposition.

15 Wanted: A U.S. Policy for Asia in the 1980s

Bernard K. Gordon

Even before the Polish crisis highlighted the differences between the United States and its allies in Europe, the disarray in the West was already evident. In NATO, one reflection of the problem was in the popular opposition to the neutron bomb. Other signs of the same trouble were in the European reluctance to deploy cruise missiles and in the sharp differences with Washington about theater nuclear weapons. Each of these reflected a widening disaffection from U.S. policy, which was seen as at best insensitive to Europe's concerns, and by some as even more of a threat to European peace than Soviet behavior.

In Asia, although the problem is not yet as urgent, evidence of incipient disarray has begun to surface. There is a nagging fear in Asian capitals that U.S. policy is without direction and that its impulses are wrongly grounded and sometimes dangerous. This has not reached the proportions in Asia that are now so disturbing in Europe, but the signs of trouble are clear and undeniable. Although there may be time and latitude to resolve the differences, there are at least three main issues with respect to which warning signals are readily apparent.

Perhaps the most obvious has to do with China. The view is widespread among East Asian leaders that the United States overrates the benefits of its strategic consensus with Peking and underrates China's propensity for regional troublemaking. A number of subsidiary issues and differences stem from this main one; some of these will be discussed later.

A second concern pertains to Vietnam and to the question of how to assess Hanoi's role in the region. On this matter there are sharply different perspectives, most notably among the five ASEAN states. Evaluations of the USSR's intentions and capabilities in the region are involved here, as is the extent to which it may be possible to wean Hanoi from its tight Soviet dependence. Although some of the intra-ASEAN differences on these points would exist independent of any U.S. view, the U.S. posture has done nothing to help and may even have contributed to widening the gap.

Japan represents a third area on which assessments of the wisdom of U.S. policy differ widely. The Reagan administration has gone further than any other in publicly pressing the Japanese to increase both their defense

---

Portions of this chapter originally appeared in Bernard K. Gordon, "Asian Angst," *Foreign Policy* 47 (Summer 1982). Used with permission of *Foreign Policy*. Copyright 1982 by the Carnegie Endowment for International Peace.

expenditures and their defense responsibilities in the Pacific. Many Japanese welcome these pressures, but many others—in and out of Japan—see them as evidence of misguided U.S. policy. Here too the issue gives rise to a number of corollary questions, among them issues of burden sharing, relations with the USSR, and issues affecting Korea.

The common strand in each of these issues is a conviction that the United States, enmeshed in the difficulties of Europe, the Persian Gulf, and sometimes Latin America, has yet to focus sufficiently on Asia. It is widely believed that the United States has not established any coherent posture for the region, and the policies it does advance are often regarded as insensitive or irrelevant to deeply held Asian concerns. One example is the Pacific Basin concept, which—despite the undisguised coolness with which it has been received almost everywhere—continues to attract the interest of otherwise well-intentioned people in Washington. Another is the notion of an enlarged ANZUS—sometimes referred to as JANZUS to signify the possible addition of Japan to that white man's alliance.[1] Both notions are seen as largely irrelevant to Asia's needs. If Washington presses too hard in these or related directions, the prospect—as in Europe—is for greater disarray and disaffection from the United States.

Although this suggests that as a long-term consequence there are similar threats to Western cohesion in Europe and in Asia, the explanations for the phenomena are not the same. In Asia there is no analog for the fear that appears to have gripped some of the European states in the face of the Polish crisis. The characterization, for example, of Germany (and by implication all of Europe), as guided by a "demoralized leadership whose best vision of [the] future is as a Finlandized, industrial vassal" is simply not applicable in any sense to East Asian governments.[2] Although each is acutely aware of the problems they face, especially in assuring that economic development keeps pace with rising expectations, the mood in the Pacific is decidedly upbeat. Economic growth rates are the highest in the world, and prospects for the future are almost uniformly bright throughout the region.[3]

Although economic success is not the only factor involved, it certainly contributes to the low sense of security threat that now characterizes every Pacific-region capital. It is that relatively low assessment of threat that most sharply distinguishes the view from Washington as compared with that from almost any capital in the region. Whether the issue is China, Vietnam, the capacity of internal insurgency movements, or even the role of the USSR—whose military buildup in the Pacific has not been ignored—the perspective in the region is one of much more equanimity than most Americans have on questions of Pacific security. Accordingly, Asian leaders see little reason to be alarmed in today's environment and are hardly inclined to contemplate innovative or strong new steps to bolster security in the region.

The keystone on which that relaxed posture is based, however, is the implicit assumption that the United States will remain actively engaged in the defense of the region—and therein lies the rub. The problem is that the United States has no settled and widely supported doctrine for its presence in the region; it has been seeking to implement one since President Nixon and Henry Kissinger outlined the shape of a new approach at Guam in 1969. However well conceived was that format, it was undertaken in an era quite different from today. In 1969 there was still optimism about the eventual political outcome in Vietnam; there was a different global strategic balance than now exists; and in Washington there was an understanding of the global economy (and of U.S. economic and political conditions) that has changed dramatically since the announcement of the Guam Doctrine.

The approach outlined at Guam called on friendly governments to do more in support of their own security, while assuring them that the United States would remain a Pacific power. In the wake of the debacle in Vietnam, however, and with the decline in the foreign-policy vigor of the Nixon administration that followed Watergate (to say nothing of the domestic and international economic constraints that had such a clear impact on the United States after 1971), the Guam Doctrine was never fully elaborated and implemented. Indeed, there was a time—in the first months and perhaps even the first year or two following the collapse of Saigon in 1975—when it was feared that the United States might somehow leave the region altogether. The election of Jimmy Carter in 1976, following a campaign in which he stressed the pullout of ground forces from Korea, did nothing to allay those concerns. In Japan, for example, a common view until 1977 or even 1978 was that the United States was turning away from Asia.

As the Carter administration ultimately reversed that Korean gesture and began to emphasize strengthening U.S. naval forces in the Pacific, however, those fears began to decline. The Reagan election in 1980, with its greater-than-ever emphasis on defense expansion (and its special attention to Pacific naval forces), put those particular fears almost entirely to rest. As a result, Asian assessments reverted to a much older perception of the United States. They adapted to that portion of the Guam Doctrine that was comfortable and familiar, but they gave little attention to its other and more innovative elements. In other words, the affected Asian-Pacific governments—without entering into the dialogue with the United States implied by the Guam Doctrine and without doing much to implement its injunction that Asian governments would have to take on more of the burden of their own security—accepted only half of what was outlined at Guam. This was the portion that emphasized that the United States is an Asian power and that it is in the region to stay.

This recidivism has been easy and certainly understandable for the United States that what Asia wants is a benevolent but powerful presence, a residual guarantor of security. Figuratively, it looms safely just over the horizon, with large and mobile military forces ready to be called on should the need arise. Although this is its most important role, it is not the only one. The United States that Asia wants is also a vital and active economic presence, with the Americans at home seen as a large and open market and, through Japanese eyes, as a large farm as well. To the extent that it is economically active in Asia itself, the desired U.S. presence is as a counterweight—to the Germans; the British; the French; and, most important, the Japanese. The United States is also, for a few, an infinitely more attractive and equally safe Switzerland, in which to bank surplus assets—just in case. For fewer still it is a center for training and technology, a source of ideas, and a place for intellectual cross-fertilization from which it would be a shame to be cut off.

In that sense most Asian-Pacific states retain a preference for major elements of the structure of east Asia's international politics in the 1960s and earlier—and especially the U.S. role in that structure. Although none would endorse every element of U.S. policy in the region in that period, it was nevertheless an era in which the Americans provided for ultimate security (and much else) and sought little if anything tangible in return.

The clock will not be pushed back, however, nor can any such pleasant one-way street long be sustained. This is not to say that the United States seeks to disengage from the Pacific; it does not. Americans of all persuasions recognize that East Asia and the Pacific region are vital to U.S. security—no less so than are Europe and the Atlantic sphere. Indeed, the message is beginning to be understood that in business and economic terms, more U.S. commerce flows across the Pacific these days than across the Atlantic.

What the United States seeks is a reordering of Pacific-region relations based on the circumstances that now exist. The nations of the region today are in situations profoundly different—and generally far better—than those of a generation ago. New political patterns must reflect that change; and U.S. foreign policy, which to be effective must gain and hold the support of the U.S. people, must also be seen as consistent with those new realities.

That task has hardly been achieved. Instead, U.S. foreign policy in recent years has sought on its own to adapt to a number of changes and to bring about change where that has appeared desirable. It is precisely those efforts, however, combined with the often different perceptions and assumptions held by the Asian-Pacific states, that have brought us to the present disarray in the region and the concomitant prospects for a further decline in Western cohesion.

U.S. China Policy and Asian Relations

The case of China policy illustrates this well. No one in the region is at all critical of the superb initiative—undertaken precisely ten years ago by

Kissinger and Nixon—that led to the Shanghai Communique. Those 1971-1972 accords stemmed as much from Chinese needs as from the U.S. conviction that it was long past time to correct the anomaly of nonrecognition. Since then, however, U.S. policy toward China has been much less carefully managed; and the intent of the original Shanghai communique has often been lost.

The main feature of Kissinger's agreement with China in 1971-1972 was that he agreed to nothing. In the Shanghai Communique the United States said only: "The United States acknowledges that Chinese on both sides of the Strait agree that there is but one China and Taiwan is part of China. We do not challenge this position." Those words merely restate the obvious fact that Chinese people, both on Taiwan and in China, regard Taiwan as a Chinese province. That was never at issue; what was at issue was the status of Taiwan, which of course was not resolved at Shanghai. It was precisely the tacit agreement to let Taiwan's status remain unresolved that provided the basis for the Nixon-Kissinger success at Shanghai.

In President Carter's normalization agreement with the Chinese on 15 December 1978, however, he went much further. There he stipulated that the United States "acknowledges the Chinese position that there is but one China and Taiwan is part of China [and] recognizes the People's Republic of China as the sole legal government of China." That statement is far different from what was agreed on in Shanghai. Not only did Carter's normalization specify (as was not done in Shanghai) which government is legitimate in China, but it goes a long way toward legitimizing Beijing's rule over Taiwan. Victor Li, formerly professor of Chinese law at Stanford and now president of the East-West Center, is the leading authority on these subjects; he has written that as a result of the Carter normalization, "The United States has increased the degree of its acquiescence in the Chinese position."[4] Li and many others have been critical of that change in U.S. policy under Carter, which among other things makes the United States hostage to China on every issue affecting Washington's dealings with Taiwan.

The Reagan administration has been caught in this dilemma, as its troubled and confused handling of arms sales—to both Taiwan and Beijing—illustrates. On the one hand, it has hankered after the Nixon-Kissinger posture, in which the United States was not specifically limited in its dealings with Taiwan. In this mode, U.S. policy has been inclined to sell Taiwan almost anything it wants; this has evidently been the preference of the president himself. At the same time, the administration has not been able to ignore altogether either the change brought about by Carter or the barely concealed warnings from China that sales of sophisticated weapons to Taiwan would endanger Sino-American relations. In the end, as the decision *not* to sell Taiwan the most advanced version of the F-5 fighter aircraft demonstrates, Washington—although it failed to satisfy China—bowed to Beijing nevertheless.

This is the feature about U.S.-China policy that most worries others in the region. Whether the issue has been Vietnam and Cambodia, arms sales to China, or Washington's latitude in dealing with Taiwan, the view has grown in Asia that U.S. policy defers far too much to Chinese preferences. Often this appears to be at the expense of those whose record of friendly relations with the United States is much longer and better grounded in a structure of compatible interests and values.

For example, there is growing discomfort with U.S. support for China's well-known insistence on bleeding Vietnam until it leaves Kampuchea. None in ASEAN favors the Vietnamese occupation, but there is little conviction that much effectively can be done about it. What is aimed for is a process of negotiations that would result in the Vietnamese loosening their hold over the Khmer; but to the extent that China continues to support the Pol Pot forces in Kampuchea, the prospects for achieving that are slim. To the extent that Washington supports China's position—which is precisely how U.S. policy on this matter is perceived—the United States is regarded as following a foolish and potentially dangerous policy. After negotiations at the United Nations in mid-1981, at which ASEAN developed a position on the issue not favored by China, an ASEAN foreign minister complained bitterly that the United States had betrayed ASEAN by not supporting that position.

Arms sales to China provide another illustration. Here the United States loudly proclaims that if it does decide to sell military equipment to the Chinese, there will be stringent qualitative limits. Nothing remotely resembling strategic weapons will be sold. It is suggested, for example, that what China needs is to modernize its conventional army strength; for this purpose the United States may be prepared to sell and otherwise provide weapons suited for small units, transport equipment, and communications gear. From the perspective of smaller Asian states, however, it is just such conventional military equipment in Chinese hands that is feared. They note, for example, that Washington does not seriously consider providing China with the most modern or sophisticated weapons, despite the U.S. goal of countering the USSR in part by increasing China's military strength. Thus they are tempted to conclude that the United States, in its effort to build closer military ties with China, is prepared to help provide the PLA with equipment that is not threatening to the United States but can become a serious problem for smaller and closer nations.

Asian Assessments of the Soviet Threat

Asians believe that a too narrow U.S. preoccupation with the USSR principally motivates these and other efforts. Although the USSR is not admired or trusted in the region, its presence in the Pacific is generally judged differently by Asians than by Americans. In particular, Soviet prospects for success in East Asia are not rated highly; this largely accounts for the widespread view among Asian-Pacific states that Americans exaggerate the Soviet threat to the region.

In military terms, not even the Soviet presence at Cam Ranh Bay has sparked much concern. The Japanese, who traditionally monitor Soviet Pacific-region military activities most closely, have recently taken to discounting the significance of these activities. They note, for example, that while the United States has been warning of the growing Soviet threat in Asia, China has leveled off and even begun to reduce its military expenditures, and has not found it necessary to strengthen its strategically inferior forces on the Soviet border. Indeed, some Japanese even tend to argue that Americans overstate the Soviet threat mainly as a prod to bring about a rise in Japan's defense budget.[5]

Another consideration that contributes to the discounting of Moscow is that Soviet capabilities in intelligence and support for subversion are not rated highly in the region. The mid-1981 success of the Malaysians in uncovering yet another Soviet infiltration effort reinforces that estimate. Probably the largest reason, however, is the growing conviction in Asia that the USSR is weak at the core. To leaders in the Asian-Pacific region, where successful economic planning has been widespread, the failures of the Soviet economy are especially apparent. Its well-known problems of internal distribution and its deep structural flaws are well understood in the region, and largely for this reason the USSR is regarded today as holding out no attractive subversive potential. Instead, there is a widening belief among leadership groups in Asia and elsewhere that the USSR represents an altogether failed model.

For reasons similarly based in local considerations, Moscow's military foothold in Vietnam is not expected to endure. The explanation lies in the Asian experience with nationalism, with its roots in colonialism and foreign dominance. From that perspective, Asian leaders simply refuse to believe that Hanoi will long continue its dependence on the USSR. Their belief, despite some evidence that the Vietnamese have largely made their own decisions, is that Hanoi leans so heavily to the Soviet side principally because China and the United States have given it no other choice. Even those not enamored of the Vietnamese argue that, when those pressures are eased, Hanoi on its own will loosen its Soviet dependence and assure that Cam Ranh does not become a Soviet base.

In any case, the presence of the USSR at those facilities has been widely discounted in the region. Moscow's use of Cam Ranh Bay and Danang is seen more as an effort to project a Soviet political presence than as a military step of consequence. To the extent it is conceded to bear on the effectiveness of U.S. facilities in the Philippines, it is regarded less as an issue of regional security than as a reflection of Soviet-American global competition. Reflecting precisely that spurious parity about which Secretary of State Haig has so bitterly complained in Europe, in the view of some Asians, U.S. bases in the Philippines have somehow entitled the USSR to its presence in Vietnam. In this perspective, if the United States has bases at Clark and Subic, then who can complain about the (implicitly) equivalent Soviet use of Cam Ranh and Danang?

This is not intended to suggest that the Soviet presence is welcomed anywhere in the region. The point is that the USSR is *not* as widely regarded there as it is in the United States as a specifically Asian threat. To the extent that it is, most local assessments place China higher on the list of worries.

There are, however, some exceptions, principally in South Korea and to some extent in Australia. Few Koreans would argue that there is not a Soviet threat, and recent experience merely underlines the recollections of history. In today's environment the USSR is seen principally as a main agent behind a potential North Korean offensive, rather than as a likely direct threat. Yet only Moscow is considered capable of sustaining a significant northern war effort, and Koreans do not quibble when the United States emphasizes the USSR as the principal problem for Asian security. In Australia, too, a number of leading people share the general U.S. assessment of the USSR, including its threat to the global strategic balance. That view has if anything been reinforced by recent Soviet efforts to promote ties with the small island nations of the South Pacific—activities that have drawn considerable public interest and probably some suspicion.

Even this degree of consensus has to be qualified, however. In Australia there is perhaps just as much support for the view that U.S. policy has polarized affairs in the region in recent years. A minority, but an articulate and important one, goes further, insisting that the main threat to Australian security these days stems from the alliance with the United States and from the presence in Australia of U.S. military communications and intelligence installations. This view holds that in the event of a crisis, even in other regions of the world, Australian territory would be vulnerable to Soviet attack and would be high on the list of Soviet targets because of those U.S. installations. Even in Korea there are influential voices who caution that U.S policy must not become too sharply anti-Soviet, lest it cause a response whose first impact would be felt again in Korea.

U.S. Foreign Policy in the Pacific

Can an effective U.S. foreign policy be developed from such disparities? Some liabilities first must be dealt with. One is that the sheer weight of the United States has been so disproportionately large in Asia during the postwar era—even more so than in Europe—that Americans may find it difficult to accept that Washington has no monopoly on wisdom. Because others have developed analytic and intelligence skills of the highest order, neither the particular policies nor the more general postures the United States proposes will necessarily be best. That may take some getting used to.

Another liability is the controversial place in U.S. politics that foreign policy in Asia has occupied. In ways that never characterized relations with Europe or Latin America, the U.S. role in the Pacific has often been enmeshed in domestic politics, sometimes with damaging consequences. At the turn of the century the issue was the taking of the Philippines—and then what to do with them. After the war the divisive question was "Who lost China?" That was soon followed by the impatient frustrations of a so-called limited war in Korea. Finally came the ten-year trauma in Vietnam. In each case, U.S. emotions regarding foreign policy toward this one part of the world have run higher than toward any other.

Vietnam stands out as especially important in this respect. This is in part because the memories are so fresh and so many of the scars not yet healed. No less important is the fact that Americans, accustomed to so many victories in war, are ill prepared for defeats. Even now many ask why the United States, which in the past has been so generous after wars, remains so stiff-necked and even vindictive toward Hanoi today. Much of the answer, which applies as well to the Vietnamese who sought reparations after the war, is that for Americans, postwar largesse is reserved for those who were conquered. For those who win, victory itself is the brass ring at the end of the ride. U.S. policy in Southeast Asia will have to grapple with that viewpoint.

These are only some illustrations of the emotional and intellectual baggage that Americans bring to considerations of their foreign policy in the Pacific, and not all of it is helpful. Ignorance is another element of this heritage, for the region is still less well known and understood by Americans than are the other major areas of the world in which the United States plays a heavy role. Myths constitute still another portion, as in the U.S. view (probably growing) that Japan avoids higher defense responsibilities largely out of material selfishness and a desire for a free ride. A third portion stems from the forces of habit, and one of those—a tendency to apply military solutions to political problems—will be particularly difficult to overcome. It has characterized much of the U.S. approach to postwar Asia, often has worked, and for that reason will be tempting again.

Although it is too much to ask that these liabilities will disappear, four changes in U.S. policy in the Pacific are called for that can help transcend them. The first is a shift in posture—what Henry Kissinger, referring to the problem in Europe, has called the need for a conceptual change. The others have to do with our relations with China, next with Indochina and ASEAN, and finally with Japan.

The essential *conceptual change* is for the United States to adopt a much more relaxed posture in the Pacific than it has for a generation. The main factor allowing for that is Asian nationalism, by far the most important force in the region today. As mentioned earlier, the Asian-Pacific nations are in situations profoundly different and far better than in the early postwar years, when Americans found themselves in the dominant role in every respect. There has been a sea change, and its most striking aspect is in the nature and success of the several nationalisms of the Pacific. They are not characterized by the fears and feudalism of a Khomeini or by the vindictive and messianic hatreds of a Khadaffi. Instead, what makes Asia's nationalisms both powerful and attractive is that they are forward-looking and, increasingly, led by figures committed to and capable of achieving economic development and the liberalization of their societies.

Obviously not all the states in the region are equally well off in that respect; there are readily forseeable problems in the Philippines and possibly Korea, and observers of Indonesia and even Malaysia caution that political recidivism could recur. Prospects for peaceful change in the region are nevertheless good, and from the vantage point of U.S. foreign-policy interests—which require mainly that there be no single hegemony in the Pacific—the outlook is very bright.

That assessment stands when we recall what Americans have long hoped for in the Pacific and what they have achieved. The United States began its Asian involvements early in the century to assure equality of access in the region—politically, and not solely or merely for trade. Its later confrontation with Japan—whose aim clearly was East Asian dominance—stemmed inevitably from that U.S. strategic commitment to avoid any single control in the Pacific. In the postwar era, when the United States moved to its reverse-course occupation policy in Japan (a shift designed to accelerate Japanese industrial recovery) and soon afterward defended South Korea through three years of war, the adversary was different but the goal was the same. Even the Vietnam War (although that effort was based on an early misreading of what would follow a Ho Chi Minh victory) grew from the same roots: a U.S. conviction that security in East Asia and the national interest of the United States called for a Pacific region of many actors and the dominance of none.

Now that has been achieved. The powerful forces of Asian nationalism, buttressed by the often remarkable prosperity of the region, guarantee long-standing U.S. goals in the Pacific. An East Asian structure of multiple nations, with no one of them realistically capable or likely to achieve hegemony, is now assured. That reality underlies the opportunity for a more relaxed U.S. posture. Several implications flow from this. In defense, for example, it will become increasingly questionable to press for a higher defense posture than is sought by those for whose security the United States shares a concern. Moreover, an overzealous U.S. willingness to increase the military capability of some regional actors whose political goals are not seen as altogether friendly by many others will probably bring only new tensions and insecurities.

The case of U.S. arms sales to China is the clearest illustration. As suggested earlier, East Asian states who already question China's long-term aims do not welcome U.S. boosting of China's conventional military capacity. They will not welcome it more if the help is labeled as U.S. compensation to an irritable China. Yet this is precisely what is in the offing now. The United States, unwilling to cast off Taiwan completely, yet mindful that China will be angered over any weapons sales there, shows every sign of attempting to soothe that upset by authorizing compensatory weapons and military-equipment sales to the PLA.

Such an approach is bound to raise doubts in Southeast Asia about the wisdom of U.S. policy. At the minimum it is a complicating factor in the U.S. relationship with friendly states in the region: explanations must be made, assurances given, and perhaps undertakings extended (probably on some other issue) to satisfy complaints on this one. The benefits, moreover—other than the dubious likelihood of satisfying the Chinese in connection with Taiwan—have to be seriously questioned. The United States does have an interest in dissuading the USSR from attempted aggression in China, and a militarily weak China conceivably could tempt that. Few would seriously argue, however, that any imaginable level of U.S. arms sales to China would prevent a Soviet attack.

The issues involved are, of course, those of the so-called China card. Generally the criticism of that approach is that a U.S. policy that leans too far in China's direction needlessly adds to Soviet apprehensions. The point here, in addition to that Soviet consideration, is that other East Asian states regard a China-card policy as dangerous and upsetting. Among Asian leaders who fear that the United States has already gone too far in shaping parallel policy lines with Beijing, the conviction has begun to set in that it is China, and not the United States, that has gained the most. Not surprisingly, many now conclude that despite U.S. intentions, what exists today is an American card in Chinese hands.

Vietnam Policy

Some of these same considerations are involved in the Vietnam issue, which in turn includes the question of the Soviet presence there and the widening gap within ASEAN on how to proceed on Kampuchea. From the perspective of the United States, the compelling factor is—or should be—the need to reduce the Soviet military presence in Vietnam as soon as possible. Moscow's

Hanoi connection is an achievement of the first order, since it provides the use of naval and air facilities only 800 miles from the U.S. bases in the Philippines. (The U.S. naval installations at Subic Bay are the largest anywhere outside the United States.) Hanoi regularly extends assurances that it will not allow the establishment of any Soviet base, but the history of Soviet dealings with smaller nations, including some far less dependent on Soviet generosity than Vietnam is today, casts doubts on Vietnam's ability to make those assurances stick.

For this reason more than any other, this Soviet presence should impel the United States finally to end the war with Vietnam—something that intellectually it has not yet done. U.S. policy endorses China's well-known willingness to bleed Vietnam, for years if necessary, and strongly encourages everyone else to continue isolating Hanoi. Japan, for example, has frozen economic assistance pending an acceptable settlement of the Kampuchea issue. The ASEAN countries—backed by the United States and China—have lobbied hard for a full withdrawal of Vietnamese troops from Kampuchea. for its direct part, the United States maintains a near-total embargo on trade with the Indochina countries and has sought to prevent multilateral assistance from reaching them.

Obviously, Vietnam's invasion and occupation of Kampuchea makes those policies easy to oppose; but this opposition has now passed the point of diminishing returns. The reasons go beyond those usually mentioned—in particular, the circumstances that led to Vietnam's invasion in the first place, and the foul nature of the Pol Pot regime that Hanoi ousted, although neither is a small factor. Nevertheless, there are at least two other major considerations that warrant a change now in U.S. policy toward Vietnam. One is that China's aims in supporting a separate Kampuchea are strongly suspect and derive from interests that are of little consequence to the United States. The essence of China's goal is an Indochina that is not unified; to support that aim, Beijing also supported Pol Pot through the worst of his barbarities. China now cloaks itself in the rhetoric of small states' rights to be free from the aggression of larger neighbors, but that should fool nobody.

The second factor is that the longer Vietnam's political and economic isolation continues—and its dependence on the USSR grows—the more difficult it will be to eject the Soviet military presence from the South China Sea. Even now evidence suggests that the USSR again seeks (as it did in an earlier period) to make use of the Kampuchean port facilities at Sihanoukville. The Soviets also reportedly seek to maintain a separate economic and diplomatic status in Kampuchea. Both efforts are probably Moscow's hedge, should it find that relations with Vietnam become too burdensome. In either case, the Soviet presence is not helpful to U.S. and Western interests; and the continued conflict over Kampuchea facilitates the leverage of the USSR, both in Indochina and in Southeast Asia generally.

There is at least one other main reason, at least as seen by some ASEAN leaders, to bring an end to the Kampuchea conflict: the stalemate allows China to heighten its role in the region. Beijing's chilling offer of assistance to Thailand in fending off the Vietnamese—even with troops if asked—represents precisely that potential for China's intervention in local affairs that Southeast Asians most fear and want to avoid. ASEAN until recently has kept those concerns quiet, largely in deference to Thailand's role as the front-line state facing Vietnamese troops on the Thai-Kampuchea border. Several members are unwilling to continue that posture much longer, however, and want to settle the Kampuchean issue soon. They are inclined to negotiate with Vietnam, and they envisage a trade: acceptance of Hanoi's leading role in Kampuchea in return for ironclad assurances that its territory will again be a genuine buffer protecting Thai security.

The stalemate is classic in its proportions and will be classically difficult to break; among other problems, the Vietnamese leadership is extremely arrogant. Any suggestion of accommodation to Hanoi is likely to be pounced on instead as evidence of capitulation. Yet recent reports from occasional Western observers in Vietnam underline the spartan scarcity and general backwardness that was evident to this observer in 1980, and make it clear that economic conditions have worsened since then. Genuine disaster has been avoided, probably because of Moscow's fairly large-scale support; but relations with the Soviets—never really good—have reportedly deteriorated further. No doubt Vietnam's calls for added Soviet help are seen by the USSR as even more burdensome in light of Moscow's growing problems in other areas, in particular its hard-currency difficulties.

Against this background Vietnam has for some time wanted to loosen its Soviet connection, and that interest should be explored. The Vietnamese increasingly make known their desire to break out—as in the recent invitation to American Vietnam veterans to tour the country, and in a lengthy visit just before that of a group of Australian scholars. These are signals sent to convey Vietnam's hope of loosening its dependence on the USSR and to expand its Western ties. For the United States the question is neither one of establishing diplomatic relations, nor the false option of economic aid, nor even whatever is meant by normalization. The issue instead is how to end this stalemate, with its dangerous potential for Sino-Soviet involvement and its corrosive effect on ASEAN's cohesion.

One way is to loosen—gradually, in steps that must be matched by clearly reciprocal action by Hanoi—the economic isolation of Vietnam. Another is to begin the movement for a conference (under auspices *mutually* acceptable to ASEAN and Vietnam) designed to negotiate phased Vietnamese troop reductions from sectors of Kampuchea. At such a conference, neither the United States, China, nor the USSR need be a participant—nor is the best format the United Nations, where discussions resisted by Vietnam have been going on. Far better would be a meeting under Japanese or perhaps Swedish auspices; both countries have generally good relations all around, and the Swedes have maintained a degree of assistance to Hanoi. Finally, the United States can loosen its own trade embargo affecting Vietnam and Kampuchea, but again, only in conjunction with clear understandings about the reciprocity required from Hanoi.

Vietnam wants the embargo lifted; in both Cambodia and South Vietnam in earlier years, U.S. equipment was installed that is still basic to the economic infrastructure or to industrial development (for example, electric-power generating equipment in Phnom Penh, and manufacturing and processing machinery in Ho Chi Minh City). These days, some of these facilities are not operating because essential parts are often unobtainable under the present U.S. embargo. Even aside from the political leverage this may provide the West, it has to be asked why U.S. suppliers, who installed the equipment there in the first place, should be prevented from selling non-military spare parts to willing buyers now. What U.S. national interest will be served if ultimately the Vietnamese scrap their U.S.-supplied capital equipment and replace it altogether from France, Japan, or even the USSR?

U.S. Policy toward Japan

The final Asian sector in which U.S. policy needs early change pertains to Japan and its role in Pacific security. For years the Japanese defense effort has proceeded largely on an ad hoc basis, keyed more to issues of U.S.-Japanese economic relations than to the needs of the Asian security environment. Nevertheless, the effort has grown to the point where Japan's defense spending now ranks sixth or seventh in the world, and even moderate Japanese voices believe more should be spent. Among those who participate in Japan's current defense debate, increases of at least 50 percent and often up to twice as much are called for as defense spending targets.

These developments have themselves raised newer questions: in Japan, for example, it is widely assumed that U.S. insistence is a main cause of the pressures for higher defense spending, and the Soviets find justification in this for adding still further to *their* military presence in the Pacific. Moreover, close friends raise questions about where Japan's efforts fit into U.S. and Western security planning. Coherence is in fact lacking, but a major obstacle to its development is that the nature of Japan's relationship to the region is itself undefined.

This is especially true where defense and security issues are involved, and a large reason for that lies in the nature of the unique U.S.-Japanese relationship. Even today the approach that both countries take to Pacific-region defense strongly reflects their special connection dating back to the occupation period. Consequently, before an effective U.S. policy pertaining to Japan's role in Asia can be shaped, at least three features of that special relationship will need to be recognized and somehow overcome.

First, in each phase of the postwar era, they have dealt with broad defense issues largely on a bilateral basis, and that practice continues today. In the occupation years and through the early peace-treaty period, the United States was simply responsible on its own for Japan's defense. Later, under U.S. pressure (though aided by some domestic support), the Japanese took on responsibility not only for internal security, but for coastal security as well. In the past fifteen or so years, while Japan has built a very significant military capability, its role has nevertheless continued to be conceived of primarily as part of its bilateral U.S. relationship.

Second, a major feature of the bilateral connection has been its strong emphasis on dollar costs and defense burden sharing. There have long been U.S. complaints about the so-called free ride; as far back as the Nixon years, at least some U.S. officials sought to pressure Japan for higher defense spending. At one time the focus of attention was on the costs of U.S. bases in Japan. After negotiations in the mid-1970s that probably left a sour taste for many Japanese, Tokyo increased its contribution. Then, when the imbalance in trade and payments grew extraordinarily large in Japan's favor, Tokyo sought to compensate by purchasing more U.S.-supplied military equipment and advanced aircraft. Most recently, as U.S. economic conditions, Pentagon budget limits, and new demands in the Persian Gulf and the Indian Ocean forced the United States to stretch Pacific forces even thinner, Japan was entreated to help fill the gap. One result is the Japanese prime minister's commitment to extend Japan's naval responsibility to 1,000 miles south.[6]

The third and probably most difficult aspect of the bilateral emphasis in U.S.-Japanese defense planning derives from the centrality of their relationship. Everyone recognizes that no connection is more important to either of them, but everyone also recognizes that its entire fabric is constantly being pulled at. Up to now, strong efforts in both countries have succeeded in accommodating often emotionally charged differences. Nevertheless, the sense exists among both elites that the other country sometimes makes unfair demands and is, at a minimum, insensitive to one's serious problems at home. Ironically, because both Japan and the United States have been so committed to preventing differences from getting beyond control, their concerns have reinforced the focus on defense burden sharing as a way to smooth over differences. That is another way of saying that incremental and ad hoc defense measures—rather than creative long-term regional planning—have been dominant. The result has been to defer issues, which in some cases may be the best course but in others merely makes old issues harder to solve, and sometimes gives rise to new problems.

For example, the thousand-mile commitment will raise new questions about Japan's defense doctrine, and ultimately rekindle the old argument about what weapons Japan should (or can) possess. The figure itself is of course an arbitrary one that can just as easily be extended, but even at 1,000 miles it will aid those who for years have urged that Japan must have an autonomous defense posture and capability. At a minimum it will erode the case of those Japanese who have argued for tight limits on aircraft range and refueling; strengthen the argument for larger and more capable naval vessels; and further complicate the distinction between defensive and offensive weapons. For some, the responsibility for defense so far removed from Japan's shores will also call forth a need for strategic weapons; and their case will not be inherently flawed.

The question is whether this is principally the way to increase Japan's contribution to Asian security. Even aside from some Southeast Asian sensitivities to a much larger Japanese defense role, there are other issues of importance. Lacking a long tradition of civilian control of the military, many Japanese, for example, associate a strong military with military-dominated government and do not believe that their society can build a significantly larger military capacity without jeopardizing the civil liberties and democratic government of the postwar period. They also believe that once Japan embarks on a large-scale defense buildup, the momentum for a more clearly independent foreign-policy role will accelerate. It is for this reason—and not to save money—that they prefer the close U.S.-Japanese alliance, with its continued heavy reliance on the United States for ultimate security.

It is a valid question for Americans as well. The prospect does exist that as Japan is repeatedly asked to do more for its defense—and as the United States continues to hold out veiled threats of trade protection—the arguments in Japan for a generally more independent international posture will grow. Should that happen, the structure of international politics in the Pacific will have begun to change fundamentally. From a Soviet perspective, for example, a Japan with a modest defense capacity, closely tied politically to the United States, is one thing; a significant defense buildup in Japan, which by its nature will make Japan less dependent on the United States, is quite another. An East Asia that has those features and that sees increased reasons for the Soviets to expand further their own Pacific forces, is not a more secure place than today.

Some Policy Considerations

Are there better ways to deal with Pacific defense problems than even *beginning* to tinker with this Pandora's box and its dangerous unknowns? Not long ago, Robert Barnett, a former deputy assistant secretary of state for East Asia and the Pacific, proposed one way in which Japan could usefully contribute to security needs in the region. He suggested the establishment of an ASEAN coastal-defense force, with ships built and supplied by Japan. It was a worthwhile suggestion at the time, and it warrants exploration and possibly extension now. Since Barnett wrote, the requirements for naval defense in the region have not lessened; the capacities of the United States to assure security in the South China Sea (and in the Pacific generally) have not much improved; the pressures within and on Japan to boost defense spending have, if anything, intensified.

Of course there are problems with the suggestion: ASEAN is not a defense alliance, and naysayers will point quickly to NATO's failed effort many years ago to establish a multinational naval force. Europe is not ASEAN, however; nowhere else in the world has a group of nations been able so quickly and effectively to develop a consensus on foreign-policy issues or to achieve such practical cooperation on security problems. For years ASEAN members have engaged in important bilateral cooperation on defense and security, and without fanfare they have overlapped some of those bilateral arrangements. The result is that in certain fields, modest but effective regional-security cooperation now exists within ASEAN.

This provides a basis from which to explore further steps. One approach is to develop a much improved naval capacity among the ASEAN nations, with significant Japanese assistance along the lines Barnett suggested. Another—briefly proposed some years ago by Singapore Prime Minister Lee Kwan Yew—called for a Pacific-region naval task force composed of units drawn from Australia, Japan, and the United States. No doubt that was premature at the time, and even now it may be considered radical. Given today's circumstances, however, it is worth exploring, if for no other reason than the growth of Soviet naval power in the Pacific—a problem that needs to be met better than it is today. Another alternative—no less radical but in the long term perhaps more politically acceptable—would combine the two approaches. Its aim would be to improve significantly the naval and related air capacities of the ASEAN states, but as an integral part of assistance from Japan, Australia, and the United States.

Here attention should be drawn to the very important role that can be played by the U.S. bases in the Philippines, where difficulties exist that demand U.S. attention in any case. A far better resolution of those problems—which stem from the profoundly unequal relationship between the two countries—might be found in a broad regional context, rather than by simply attempting to continue the present uneasy bilateral connection.

The U.S.-Philippine relationship is periodically troubled, and the long-term reliability of the bases must be questioned; like it or not, their presence can be readily exploited as an affront to Filipino nationalism, especially in

Manila. It is true that good and sincere efforts have been made to reduce the altogether American coloration of the bases. Similarly, the personnel and management practices that the United States has instituted there recently are sophisticated and sensitive. Ultimately, however, these too must be recognized as a cosmetic effort that cannot overcome the long-term and powerful forces of Asian identity and nationalism in the Philippines. Despite the assurances of Manila's leaders that the base problem can be managed, the U.S. presence continues to represent an ideal focal point for unrest and for promoting further tension in U.S.-Philippine relations.

Yet the bases also represent an outstanding opportunity for the United States both to transcend its difficulties with Manila and, simultaneously, to take a long step toward improving security in the region. What is called for is a U.S. proposal, in conjunction with the Philippines, to transform the present status of the bases into an ASEAN installation—with its maintenance costs borne principally by Japan, the United States, and Australia, and with the use-rights of those three assured at least through the end of the century.[7] Such a transferral has several aims and assets. It would, for example:

Provide ASEAN members with a single focal point to strengthen their naval and related air forces, including facilities for advanced training and maintenance.

Promote intra-ASEAN cooperation in regional security, and facilitate any desired cooperation with the three others.

Improve the legitimacy and acceptability of the bases, not only to Filipinos but also among all ASEAN members, and thereby help assure that the bases remain reliable elements in protecting the interests of Asian-Pacific nations.

Reduce the direct costs for Pacific security now borne almost alone by the United States.

The last consideration cannot be ignored. Asia's circumstances today no longer require the United States to be sole defender of Asian security, and the American people cannot be expected to support a foreign policy that pretends otherwise. Although the bases in the Philippines are clearly important to Pacific-region defense and thereby to U.S. interests, they are no less essential to Japan and all others in the region who are part of the broadly Western world. That fact needs to be reflected in their policies, for as I suggested on another occasion:

Greater legitimacy for the Philippine bases, among both Japan and the ASEAN states, would help to reduce their present image as a solely U.S. responsibility, in which therefore the United States must continue alone to bear all the costs. To accept such an image is to be resigned to the present division of labor, in which Japan's "contribution" to Asian security is measured in terms of development loans ultimately payable to the Bank of Japan, while that of the United States is in military assistance grants and a growing defense budget.[8]

Unfortunately, this division of labor is still largely in place today. Although the Reagan administration, like its predecessors, wants Japan to do more, its even greater emphasis on increased U.S. defense spending suggests a willingness to continue in a largely unilateral U.S. role. Indeed, the administration's sometimes strident emphasis on defense during its first year has led to the ultimate irony that the United States, the protector of security, has come to be regarded even by its friends as occasionally a source of security problems.

The Reagan administration can avoid that and make a historic contribution to U.S. foreign policy if it soon begins the true post-Vietnam shift in U.S. posture in the Pacific. In doing so, it will be resuming the process begun by President Nixon at Guam in 1969, for that was where the United States signaled that it would no longer do the job alone or be expected to. In this era the United States can bring new momentum to that process through some of the policy changes suggested here—but only, of course, in the closest consultation with those many other states in the region that share the main values of the United States.

Sadly, however, there is no clear format for that. One of the major obstacles in the way of an effective U.S. and Western policy in the Pacific is the lack of any mechanism for useful multilateral discussions on security. Neither ANZUS nor the recent practice of U.S. attendance at annual ASEAN meetings nor any of the other bilateral forums in which Americans meet with their counterparts in the region genuinely meets the need.

For that reason there is a first requirement for the Reagan administration in the Pacific. It is to take the lead in calling for a wide-ranging conference on Asian security—a combined governmental-private Pacific forum—to begin dealing together with the foreign-policy concerns of the many nations in the Pacific that now look separately to the United States. Such a Pacific forum would have as its concerns the whole of the region, reaching from Japan's Wakkanai in the north to New Zealand's Waikiwi in the south.

Notes

1. See, for example, William F. Tow, "ANZUS and American Security," in *Survival*, November-December, 1981 (London: International Institute for Strategic Studies), pp. 261-271, esp. p. 268.

2. Editorial, *The Wall Street Journal*, 4 January 1982.

3. For one of many commentaries making this point, see E.S. Browning, "East Asia in Search of a Second Economic Miracle," *Foreign Affairs* (Fall 1981):123-147. Among the noncommunist East Asian nations, only the Philippines is a clear soft spot, with some difficulties in attracting foreign investment reinforced by the uncertainties of political succession. Even there, annual growth rates normally exceed 6 percent—a figure that in other developing regions is one to be admired and seldom achieved.

4. Victor H. Li, "The Legal Status and Political Future of Taiwan after Normalization," in *The Future of US-China Relations*, ed. J.B. Starr (New York: New York University Press, 1981), p. 227. As Li points out, in the original Shanghai documents the Americans used the word *acknowledge* to apply to the view of Chinese people about Taiwan; the Chinese used the word *renshi*, which carries the same connotation as *acknowledge*. In the Carter normalization agreements, however, the word *acknowledge* was extended to "the Chinese position." On this occasion the Chinese used the word *chengren*, which, as Li explains, "carries a clear connotation of acceptance or agreement."

5. As one authoritative source puts it, in China "the position of national defense within the Four Modernizations has declined." *Asian Security, 1981* (Tokyo: Research Institute for Peace and Security, 1981), p. 95. As this and other studies show, the proportion of the Chinese budget allocated to defense has been declining steadily since at least 1977.

6. There is some vagueness about whether this is measured from the main islands or from Japan's southernmost territory (the difference is not small).

7. The following cost-sharing formula could be proposed: the ASEAN members at 5 percent each for a total of 25 percent; Australia at 10 percent; Japan at 25 percent; and the United States at 40 percent.

8. Bernard K. Gordon, "Japan, the U.S., and Southeast Asia," *Foreign Affairs* (April 1978):595. Excerpted by permission of *Foreign Affairs*. Copyright 1978 by the Council on Foreign Relations, Inc.

Participants at the Waikoloa Conference

Zainal Abidin B. Abdul Wahid, Professor of History, Universiti Kebangsaan, Malaysia

Byung-joon Ahn, Professor of Political Science, Visiting Scholar, University of California, Berkeley

Tristan E. Beplat, International Finance Consultant, Princeton, New Jersey

Herbert C. Cornuelle, President, H.C. Cornuelle, Inc.-Trustee, Campbell Estate, Honolulu, Hawaii

Jacquelyn K. Davis, Senior Staff Member, Institute for Foreign Policy Analysis, Inc., Cambridge, Massachusetts

Shinkichi Eto, Professor of International Relations, University of Tokyo

Philip C. Gevas, President and Chief Executive Officer, Aphton Corporation

Bernard K. Gordon, Professor of Political Science, University of New Hampshire

Philip C. Habib, Former Undersecretary of State, Belmont, California

Robert B. Hewett, Corporation Secretary and Special Assistant to the President, East-West Center, Honolulu

Lau Teik Soon, Professor of Political Science, National University of Singapore

Malcolm MacNaughton, Chairman, Executive Committee, Castle & Cooke, Inc.; Chairman, Pacific Forum Policy Council

Charles E. Morrison, Research Fellow, East-West Center, Honolulu

Alejandro B. Melchor, Jr., Executive Director, Asian Development Bank, Philippines

Carlos F. Nivera, Executive Director and Executive Editor, *ASIAPACIFIC Monthly*, Philippines

Robert J. O'Neill, Head, Strategic and Defence Studies Centre, Australian National University, Canberra

Seiichiro Onishi, Executive Director, Research Institute for Peace and Security, Tokyo

Thomas O. Paine, President and Chief Operating Officer, Northrop Corporation; Chairman, Pacific Forum Board of Trustees

Guy J. Pauker, The Rand Corporation and The Resource Systems Institute, East-West Center

Robert L. Pfaltzgraff, Jr., President, Institute for Foreign Policy Analysis, Inc., Cambridge, Massachusetts

Prasong Soonsiri, Secretary-General, Thai National Security Council, Thailand

Sang-Woo Rhee, Professor of Political Science, Sogang University, Republic of Korea

Sarasin Viraphol, Policy and Planning Division, Thai Ministry of Foreign Affairs, Thailand

Robert A. Scalapino, Robson Research Professor of Government and Director, Institute of East Asian Studies, University of California, Berkeley

Thomas P. Shoesmith, Deputy Assistant Secretary of State, East Asian and Pacific Affairs, Washington, D.C.

Gaston J. Sigur, Director, Institute for Sino-Soviet Studies, The George Washington University

Edward Janner Sinaga, Special Assistant to the Minister; Coordinator for Political and Security Affairs, Indonesia

Richard L. Sneider, Former U.S. Ambassador to Korea

Somsakdi Xuto, Professor, National Institute for Development Administration (NIDA), Thailand

Participants at Waikoloa Conference

General Richard C. Stilwell, Deputy Undersecretary of Defense for Policy, Washington, D.C.

The Honorable Dr. Thanat Khoman, Deputy Prime Minister, Thailand

Stephen Uhalley, Jr., Director, Center for Asian and Pacific Studies, University of Hawaii

L.R. Vasey, Rear Admiral USN (Ret.), President, Pacific Forum

Jusuf Wanandi, Member, Board of Directors, Centre for Strategic and International Studies (CSIS), Jakarta, Indonesia

Donald E. Weatherbee, Visiting Fellow, Institute of Southeast Asian Studies, Singapore; Professor of Contemporary Foreign Policy, University of South Carolina

Maurice F. Weisner, Admiral USN (Ret.); Former CincPac

Takeshi Yasukawa, Former Japanese Ambassador to United States

About the Contributors

Zainal Abidin B. Abdul Wahid is a professor of history at the Universiti Kebangsaan, Malaysia. He is a former assistant secretary in the Ministry of External Affairs, Federation of Malaya. He is the author or editor of five books on Malaysian and Asian history and has published over twenty articles on Asian history, politics, and foreign policy.

Jacquelyn K. Davis is a special assistant to the president and senior staff member of the Institute for Foreign Policy Analysis, Inc., Cambridge, Massachusetts. She was previously a research associate at the Foreign Policy Research Institute and has conducted numerous studies on U.S. foreign policy and national-security affairs.

Shinkichi Eto is a professor of international relations at the University of Tokyo and has written extensively on Asian politics, especially on Japan and China. He has been a visiting professor in the Department of History, University of Hawaii, and in the Department of East Asian Studies, Princeton.

Bernard K. Gordon is a professor of political science at the University of New Hampshire. He has written four books and over fifty articles on a wide range of foreign-policy issues concerning the Asian-Pacific region and has held professorial positions at American University, The Johns Hopkins University, George Washington University, the University of Singapore, and Vanderbilt University.

M. Hadisoesastro is director of studies at the Centre for Strategic and International Studies, Jakarta. His publications include scholarly articles on trade, energy, and the Pacific Community Concept.

Lau Teik Soon is a professor and head of the Department of Political Science, National University of Singapore. He has published numerous articles concerning ASEAN political and security issues.

Carlos F. Nivera is the executive director and executive editor of *ASIA-PACIFIC Monthly*. He has extensive current affiliation and past experience with both national and international press organizations.

Robert J. O'Neill is the director of the International Institute of Strategic Studies, London. At the time of this conference he was head of the Strategic and Defence Studies Centre and a Professorial Fellow in International

Relations, Research School of Pacific Studies, Australian National University. He has written widely on wars and warfare, foreign policy, and peacetime defense strategy.

Sang-Woo Rhee is a professor of political science at Sogang University, Seoul. He has published books and articles on Korean security issues, Asian defense and security affairs, and international relations.

Sarasin Viraphol works in the Policy and Planning Division of the Thai Ministry of Foreign Affairs. He has taught on the Political Science Faculty, Chulalongkorn University, Bangkok, and has served as political officer in the Royal Thai Embassy, Beijing. He is the author of numerous articles, particularly on Sino-Thai relations.

Robert A. Scalapino is Robson Research Professor of Government, director of the Institute of East Asian Studies, and a professor of political science at the University of California at Berkeley; he also serves as the editor of *Asian Survey*. He has undertaken extensive travel and research in Asia, the Middle East, and Africa, and has published fourteen books and over two hundred articles. He is a member of the Council on Foreign Relations and the Pacific Forum Research Council.

Somsakdi Xuto is a professor at the National Institute of Development Administration (NIDA), Bangkok. He is past minister in the Thai prime minister's office and a government spokesman. At Chulalongkorn University he has served as director of the Institute of Asian Studies, and as chairman of the Department of International Relations in the Faculty of Political Science. He is the author of over twenty books and articles on economics, policies, and foreign affairs in Southeast Asia.

Thanat Khoman is Deputy Prime Minister of Thailand and a member of the Parliament for Bangkok. He has held numerous key government positions, including advisor to the prime minister of Thailand, minister of foreign affairs, deputy minister of national development, and Thai ambassador to the United Nations. He has written a number of publications on foreign affairs and international relations in Southeast Asia. He is a founding member of the Pacific Forum and vice-chairman of its Policy Council.

Lloyd R. Vasey, Rear Admiral, USN (Ret.), is president and executive director of the Pacific Forum. He founded and organized the forum in 1975, following thirty-seven years of naval service. He has served as Chief of Plans and Policies for CINCPAC (U.S. joint military forces in the Pacific) and as official U.S. delegate to international-treaty meetings with Japan, the Republic of Korea, the Republic of China, the Philippines, SEATO, and ANZUS. Other service included secretary to the U.S. Joint Chiefs of Staff, deputy director of the U.S. National Military Command Center, and naval aide in the White House. He lectures on political and strategic developments in the Pacific region.

Jusuf Wanandi is a member of the board of directors of the Centre for Strategic and International Studies (CSIS) in Jakarta. He also serves as deputy treasurer of the Central Board of the Functional Group (Golkar), and as a member of the Peoples Consultative Assembly (MPR). He has published numerous articles and books concerning Asian-Pacific security and policy issues.

Donald E. Weatherbee is Donald S. Russell Professor of Contemporary Foreign Policy at the University of South Carolina. During the time of this conference he was a visiting fellow at the Institute of Southeast Asian Studies, Singapore. He has taught at the U.S. Army War College, Gajah Mada University in Indonesia, and the Free University of Berlin. He is the author of numerous publications on the politics and international relations of Southeast Asia.

About the Editor

Charles E. Morrison is concurrently a fellow at the East-West Center in Honolulu and at the Japan Center for International Exchange in Tokyo. He is a former legislative assistant to Senator William V. Roth, Jr., of Delaware. Dr. Morrison received the Ph.D. from The Johns Hopkins School of Advanced International Studies and is coauthor of *Strategies of Survival*, which deals with the foreign policy dilemmas of several East and Southeast Asian countries.